THE PRINCIPLE OF PROPORTIONALITY IN THE LAWS OF EUROPE

The Principle of Proportionality in the Laws of Europe

Edited by
EVELYN ELLIS,
MA, PH.D., Barrister,
Professor of Public Law in the University of Birmingham

•HART•
PUBLISHING
OXFORD – PORTLAND OREGON
1999

Hart Publishing
Oxford and Portland, Oregon

Published in North America (US and Canada) by
Hart Publishing
c/o International Specialized Book Services
5804 NE Hassalo Street
Portland, Oregon
97213-3644
USA

Distributed in Netherlands, Belgium and Luxembourg by
Intersentia, Churchillaan 108
B2900 Schoten
Antwerpen
Belgium

Distributed in Australia and New Zealand by
Federation Press
John St
Leichhardt
NSW 2000

Hart Publishing Ltd is a specialist legal publisher based in Oxford, England.
To order further copies of this book or to request a list of other
publications please write to:

Hart Publishing Ltd, 19 Whitehouse Road, Oxford, OX1 4PA
Telephone: +44 (0)1865 434459 or Fax: +44 (0)1865 794882
e-mail: hartpub@janep.demon.co.uk

British Library Cataloguing in Publication Data
Data Available
ISBN 1 84113–007–9 (cloth)

Typeset by Hope Services (Abingdon) Ltd.
Printed in Great Britain on acid-free paper
by Biddles Ltd.,
Guildford and King's Lynn

Foreword

EVELYN ELLIS

This work is the product of a one-day conference held on 20 March 1998, at the Institute of European Law, University of Birmingham, at which the majority of the papers included here were delivered.

The subject matter of the conference, the doctrine of proportionality, provided fertile ground for both written and oral contributions. Given its origins in continental European law, proportionality prompts one to think about the process by which legal systems cross-fertilise one another. The possibilities for the transplantation of legal ideas are clearly great within a Europe linked by the European Convention on Human Rights (ECHR) and an ever-developing economic and political union; indeed the enactment in the UK of legislation giving effect to the ECHR provides an express example of this process and its likely future impact is discussed in Professor David Feldman's paper. Whilst reservations may properly be entertained about the wholesale lifting of concepts from one jurisdiction and their removal to a wholly foreign jurisdiction, there can be little doubt that there is much common ground when it comes to the application of the doctrine of proportionality within Europe. The standards by which judges in countries which all share a broadly similar economic, political and cultural heritage measure the acceptability of the acts of their legislators, governors and administrators cannot surely vary very greatly. The prospects for a rational and constructive debate in this area are therefore good.

At least on first hearing, the notion of proportionality has an attractively common-sense ring to it. Lacking the extravagances of irrationality or behaviour which is so unreasonable that no reasonable person could ever be expected to indulge in it, it appears to offer a sensible civilian yardstick for the application of judicial review—the prospect, some might say, of capable Germanic engineering applied to a temperamental old piece of machinery. Yet the reality of the situation is, of course, somewhat different. As the contributions of Advocate General Francis Jacobs, Mr Jeremy McBride, Professor Walter van Gerven and Professor Takis Tridimas, in particular, demonstrate, the precise content of the principle of proportionality is far from settled; not only does it appear to apply differently in different contexts, but it seems to mean different things to different courts and it also develops over time.

In addition, the doctrine of proportionality brings one face to face with perplexing issues which are the inevitable consequence of closer ties within Europe. Most significant amongst these issues are the respective jurisdictions of the

European Court of Justice (ECJ) and the national courts of the Member States of the European Union. Many of the contributors to this work examine the extent to which the general principles of European Community law, including proportionality, restrain action within the Member States. Lord Hoffmann's paper challenges the proposition that the introduction of a specific doctrine of proportionality into UK law would produce significant change in the practice of judicial review, a challenge which is enthusiastically taken up in the contributions of Professor Paul Craig and Mr Nicholas Green.

Most people would agree that one of the most difficult questions in relation to the doctrine of proportionality is the extent to which it contributes to a breaking down of the traditional barrier between the legality of an action and its substantive merits; in other words, the question is one of the proper constitutional role of judicial review. This matter is also adverted to by many of the contributors to this work, but in particular by Professor Takis Tridimas and Professor Evelyn Ellis.

Table of Contents

Table of Cases ix
Table of National Legislation xxi
Table of EC Secondary Legislation xxiii
Table of Treaties xxv
List of Contributors xxvii

RECENT DEVELOPMENTS IN THE PRINCIPLE OF PROPORTIONALITY IN EUROPEAN COMMUNITY LAW 1
Francis G. Jacobs

PROPORTIONALITY AND THE EUROPEAN CONVENTION ON HUMAN RIGHTS 23
Jeremy McBride

THE EFFECT OF PROPORTIONALITY ON THE ACTIONS OF MEMBER STATES OF THE EUROPEAN COMMUNITY: NATIONAL VIEWPOINTS FROM CONTINENTAL EUROPE 37
Walter van Gerven

PROPORTIONALITY IN EUROPEAN COMMUNITY LAW: SEARCHING FOR THE APPROPRIATE STANDARD OF SCRUTINY 65
Takis Tridimas

UNREASONABLENESS AND PROPORTIONALITY IN UK LAW 85
Paul Craig

THE INFLUENCE OF THE EUROPEAN PRINCIPLE OF PROPORTIONALITY UPON UK LAW 107
The Rt. Hon. Lord Hoffmann

PROPORTIONALITY AND THE HUMAN RIGHTS ACT 1998 117
David Feldman

PROPORTIONALITY AND THE SUPREMACY OF PARLIAMENT IN THE UK 145
Nicholas Green

THE CONCEPT OF PROPORTIONALITY IN EUROPEAN COMMUNITY SEX DISCRIMINATION LAW 165
Evelyn Ellis

Index 183

Table of Cases

Abdulaziz, Cabales and Balkandali v United Kingdom (ECHR) (1985) 7 EHRR 741 24
Advanced Nuclear Fuels v Commission (C-308/90) [1993] ECR I-309 77
Affish BV v Rijksdienst voor de keuring van Vee en Vlees (C-183/95) (July 17, 1997) 77
Ahmed and others v United Kingdom (ECHR) (September 2, 1998) 25
Alpine Investments BV v Minister van Financien (C-384/93) [1995] ECR I-1141 .... 12, 78
Andronicou v Cyprus (ECHR) (October 9, 1997) 28
Anklagemyndigheden v Hansen (C-326/88) [1990] ECR I-2911 16
Arbeiterwohlfahrt der Stadt Berlin eV v Botel (C-360/90) [1992] ECR I-3589 175
Associated Provincial Picture Houses Ltd v Wednesbury Corporation [1948] 1 KB 223 .... 20, 56, 59, 63, 85, 88, 89, 90, 91, 94–105, 122, 126, 127, 128, 129, 134, 149, 150, 151, 152, 155, 164, 165, 170
Atalanta Amsterdam BV v Produktschap voor Vee en Vlees (C-240/78) [1979] ECR 2137 3
Austria v Italy (ECHR) (1961) 4 YBECHR 112 28

Balkan-Import-Export (C-5/73) [1973] ECR 1091 .... 76, 77
Bela-Muhle Josef Bergmann KG v Grons-Farm GmbH & Co KG (C-114/76) [1977] ECR 1211 .... 3, 77
Belgium v Commission (Tubermeuse case) (C-142/87) [1990] ECR I-959 66
Benjamin (Conseil d'Etat, France) (May 28, 1971) Leb. 409 49
Bickel and Franz (C-274/96) 10
Bilka-Kaufhaus GmbH v Weber von Hartz (C-170/84) [1986] ECR 1607; [1986] 2 CMLR 701 .... 166, 167, 170, 173
Binder v Hauptzollamt Stuttgart-West (C-205/94) [1996] ECR I-2871 .... 8, 73, 74
Biovilac v European Economic Community (C-59/83) [1984] ECR 4057 71
Bock v Commission (C-62/70) [1971] ECR 897 73
Borrell and others (C-104/91) [1992] ECR I-3003 67
Bosphorus v Minister for Transport, Energy and Communications, Ireland and Attorney General (C-84/95) [1996] ECR I-3953 .... 14, 15
Bowman v United Kingdom (ECHR) (February 19, 1998) 25
Bozetti v Invernizzi (C-179/84) [1985] ECR 2301 71
Brannigan and McBride v United Kingdom (ECHR) Series A, No. 258-B (1993) 131

Brind and McLaughlin v United Kingdom (E Comm HR) App. Nos. 18714/91 and 18759/91; (1992) 77-A DR 42 123
Bugdaycay v Secretary of State for the Home Department (HL) [1987] AC 514 ....92, 129, 133

Campbell and Fell v United Kingdom (ECHR) Series A, No. 233; (1985) 7 EHRR 165 ....28, 124
Campus Oil Ltd v Minister for Energy and Industry (C-72/83) [1984] ECR 2727 84
Canadian Union of Public Employees Local 963 v New Brunswick Liquor Corporation (Sup Ct, Canada) [1979] 2 SCR 227 137
Casado Coca v Spain (ECHR) (1994) 18 EHRR 1 26
Central-Import Munster v Hauptzollamt Munster (C-291/86) [1988] ECR 3679 73
Chahal v United Kingdom (ECHR) (1997) 23 EHRR 413; (1997) 1 BHRC 405 134
Choquet (C-16/79) [1978] ECR 2293 11
Commission v Atlantic Container Line and others (C-149/95P(R)) [1995] ECR I-2165 66
Commission v Belgium (C-229/89) [1991] ECR I-2205 177
Commission v Denmark (C-302/86) [1989] ECR 4607 38
Commission v France (C-265/95) Times, December 11, 1998 89
Commission v Germany (C-116/82) [1986] ECR 2519 82
Commission v Germany (C-28/84) [1985] ECR 3097 82
Commission v Germany (beer case) (C-178/84) [1987] ECR 1227 ....67, 78
Commission v Greece (FYROM case) (C-120/94) [1996] ECR 1513 ....66, 77
Commission v Italy (Italian vinegar case) (C-193/80) [1981] ECR 3019 78
Commission v United Kingdom (UHT milk case) (C-124/81) [1983] ECR 203 78
Commission v United Kingdom (C-165/82) [1983] ECR 3431 ....169, 180
Corsica Ferries Italia v Corpo dei Piloti del Porto di Genova (C-18/93) [1994] ECR I-1783 11
Cremieux v France (ECHR) (1993) 16 EHRR 357 27
Criminal proceedings against Bonchara, nee Wurmser (C-25/88) [1989] ECR 1105 79
Criminal proceedings against Anton Adriaan Fietje (C-27/80) [1980] ECR 3839 79
Criminal proceedings against Bernard Keck and Daniel Mithonard (C-267/91, C-268/91) [1993] ECR I-6097 41
Criminal proceedings against Rene Kieffer and Romain Thill (C-114/96) [1997] ECR I-3629 5
Criminal proceedings against Lothar Messner (C-265/88) [1989] ECR 4209; [1991] 2 CMLR 545 ....12, 40

Criminal proceedings against Aime Richardt (C-367/89) [1991] ECR I-4621 ....66, 78
Criminal proceedings against Timothy Frederick Robinson (C-220/81) [1982] ECR 2349 79
Criminal proceedings against Sofia Skanavi and Konstantin Chryssanthakopoulos (C-193/94) [1996] ECR I-929; [1996] All ER (EC) 435; [1997] RTR 344 10
Criminal proceedings against X (C-74/95, C-129/95) [1996] ECR I-6609 166
Crispoltoni v Fattoria autonoma Tabacchi & Donatab Srl (C-133/93, C-300/93, C-362/93) [1994] ECR I-4863 ....71, 72
Crispoltoni v Fattoria autonoma Tabacchi di Citta di Castello (C-368/89) [1991] ECR I-3695 71

De Haes and Gijsels v Belgium (ECHR) (February 24, 1997) 26
De Peijper (Adriaan) Managing Director of Centraform BV (C-104/75) [1976] ECR 613; [1976] 2 CMLR 613 79
De Vriendt v Rijksdienst voor Pensioenen (C-377/96 to C-384/96) 170
Decock (Council of State, Belgium) Judgment no 20,116 (February 19, 1980) 26
Defrenne v Sabena (C-149/77) [1978] ECR 1365; [1978] 3 CMLR 312 166
Denkavit Nederland v Hoofdproduktschap voor Akkerbouwprodukten (C-15/83) [1984] ECR 2171 68
Depelchin (Council of State, Belgium) Judgment no 17,101 (June 26, 1975) 52
Deschamps v Ofival (C-181/88, C-182/88, C-218/88) [1989] ECR I-4381 82
Di Pede v Italy (ECHR) (September 26, 1996) 27
Doherty v Ministry of Defence (CA, Northern Ireland) [1991] NIJB (No. 1) 68 133
Doetinchem (Hoge Raad, Netherlands) (February 25, 1949) [1949] NJ 558 ....56, 57, 59, 63
Dudgeon v United Kingdom (ECHR) Series A, No 45; (1982) 4 EHRR 149 ....31, 108
Durbeck v Hauptzollamt Frankfurt am Main-Flughafen (C-112/80) [1981] ECR 1095 66

Ebony Maritime and Boden Navigation v Prefetto della Provincia di Brindisi and others (C-177/95) [1997] ECR I-1111 15
ED & FR Exp ED & F Man (Sugar) Ltd v IBAP (C-181/84) [1985] ECR 2889 3
Effem v Hauptzollamt Luneburg (C-95/75) [1976] ECR 361 74
Einfuhr- und Vorratsstelle v Henck (C-26/70) [1970] ECR 1183 69
Einfuhr- und Vorratsstelle v Koster (C-25/70) [1970] ECR 1161 69
Ensslin, Baader and Raspe v Germany (1978) 14 DR 64 28

Faust v Commission (C-52/81) [1982] ECR 3745 73
Fayed v United Kingdom (ECHR) (1977) 18 EHRR 393 123
Federation Charbonniere Belgique v High Authority (C-8/55) [1954–56] ECR 292 69
Findlay v Secretary of State for the Home Department (HL) [1985] AC 318; [1984] 3 WLR 1159; [1984] 3 All ER 801 91
Francovich v Italy (C-9/90) [1991] ECR I-5357 148
Franzen (C-189/95) (October 23, 1997) 67
Freers v Deutsche Bundespost (C-278/93) [1996] ECR I-1165 176
Freistaat Bayern v Eurim-Pharm (C-347/89) [1991] ECR I-1747 78
Fritz Werner Industrie-Ausrustungen GmbH v Germany (C-83/94) [1995] ECR I-3231 13
Fromancais SA v FORMA (C-66/82) [1983] ECR 395 .....37, 38, 68, 146

Garage Molenheide BVBA and others v Belgium (C-286/94, C-340/95, C-401/95, C-47/96) [1997] ECR I-7281 .....16, 42
Gasus Dosier- und Fordertechnik GmbH v The Netherlands (ECHR) (1995) 20 EHRR 403 32
Germany v Council of the European Union (bananas case) (C-280/93) [1994] ECR I-4973 .....15, 72
Germany v Council of the European Union (C-426/93) [1995] ECR I-3723 83
Germany v European Parliament and Council of the European Union (C-233/94) [1997] ECR I-2405 .....5, 38, 83
Glasenapp (ECHR) (1987) 9 EHRR 25 28
Goodwin v United Kingdom (ECHR) (1996) 22 EHRR 123 26
Grigoriades v Greece (ECHR) (November 25, 1997) 26
Groupement Producteurs, Importateurs et Agents Generaux d'Eaux Minerales Etrangeres, VZW v Peeters NV (Piageme II) (C-385/94) [1995] ECR I-2955 79

Hall & Co Ltd v Shoreham-by-Sea UDC [1964] 1 WLR 240 95
Hammersmith and Fulham LBC v Secretary of State for the Environment (HL) [1991] 1 AC 521 .....96, 137
Handels- og Kontorfunktionaerernes Forbund i Danmark v Dansk Arbejdsgiverforening, acting on behalf of Danfoss (C-109/88) [1989] ECR 3199 173
Handyside v United Kingdom (ECHR) Series A, No 24; (1979-80) 1 EHRR 737 .....30, 33, 108, 125, 126
Hauer v Land Rheinland-Pfalz (C-44/79) [1979] ECR 3727 .....15, 39, 60
Hauptzollamt Hamburg-Jonas v Werner Faust OHG (C-24/90) [1991] ECR I-4905 .....5, 74, 75
Hauptzollamt Hamburg-Jonas v Wunsche Handels- GmbH & Co KG (Wunsche I) (C-25/90) [1991] ECR I-4939 .....5, 74, 75

Hauptzollamt Hamburg-Jonas v Wunsche Handels- GmbH & Co KG (Wunsche II) (C-26/90) [1991] ECR I-4961 ....5, 66, 74
Hentrich v France (EHCR) (1994) 18 EHRR 440..26
Hertel v Switzerland (ECHR) (August 25, 1998) 25
Hupeden v Hauptzollamt Hamburg-Jonas (C-295/94) [1996] ECR I-3375 ....5, 6, 75, 76, 77

Informationsverein Lentia v Austria (ECHR) (1994) 17 EHRR 93 27
Internationale Handelsgessellschaft v Einfuhr- und Vorratsstelle Getreide (C-11/70) [1970] ECR 1125..1, 3, 66, 69
Ireland v United Kingdom (ECHR) Series A, No. 25 (1978).........................131
Italy v Commission (C-13/63) [1963] ECR 338 82
Italy v Commission (Alfa Romeo case) (C-305/89) [1991] ECR I-1603 66

Jacubowski v Germany (ECHR) (1995) 19 EHRR 64 24
Johnson v Chief Constable of the RUC (C-222/84) [1986] ECR 651 168
Judgment No. 47/88 (Court of Arbitration, Belgium) [1988] AA 223; [1987-8] RW 1311..54
Judgment No. 23/89 (Court of Arbitration, Belgium) BS November 8, 1989, 18,386; [1989] TRV 527 54
Judgment No. 1/94 (Biorim) (Court of Arbitration, Belgium) [1994] AA 1.....55
Judgment No. 21/96 (Court of Arbitration, Belgium) [1996] AA 203 55
Judgment of October 5, 1990 (Court of Cassation, Belgium) [1990-1] RW 330
Judgment of May 9, 1996 (Council of State, Netherlands) [1996] JB 158........57

Kalanke v Freie und Hansestadt Bremen (C-450/93) [1995] ECR I-3051; [1996] All ER (EC) 66 168
Kapadiya v New India Assurance Co Ltd (EAT/25/97) (Unreported) 126
Karlheinz Schmidt v Germany (ECHR) (July 18, 1994) 33
Kirsammer-Hack v Sidal (C-189/91) [1993] ECR I-6185 ....169, 180
Kokkinakis v Greece (ECHR) Series A, No. 260-A (1993)............................124
Kowalska v Freie und Hansestadt Hamburg (C-33/89) [1990] ECR I-2591 174
Kraus v Land Baden-Wurttemberg (C-19/92) [1993] ECR I-1663 67
Kruger GmbH & Co KG v Hauptzollamt Hamburg-Jonas (C-334/95) [1997] ECR I-4517 63
Kuratorium fur Dialyse und Nierentransplantation eV v Lewark (C-457/93) [1996] ECR I-243 176

Laker Airways v Department of Trade (CA) [1977] QB 643 140
Laperre v Bestuurscommissie (C-8/94) [1996] ECR I-273 178
Lehideux and Isorni v France (ECHR) (September 23, 1998) 26
Leifer (C-83/94) [1995] ECR I-3231 ....78, 84

Lewark (C-457/93) [1996] ECR I-243 80
Lingens v Austria (ECHR) (1986) 8 EHRR 407 ..... 30, 34
Lithgow v United Kingdom (ECHR) (1982) 4 EHRR 149 31
Lonrho Plc, Re (HL) [1990] 2 AC 154 128
Lubella v Hauptzollamt Cottbus (C-64/95) [1996] ECR I-5105 73

M v Home Office (HL) [1994] 1 AC 377; [1993] 3 WLR 433; [1993] 3 All ER 537 147
McCann v United Kingdom (ECHR) (1996) 21 EHRR 97 29
McLeod v United Kingdom (ECHR) (September 23, 1998) 27
Marschall v Nordrhein Westfalen (C-409/95) [1997] All ER (EC) 865 168
Megner and Scheffel v Innungskrankenkasse Venderplatz (C-444/93) [1995] ECR I-4741 ..... 178, 179
Mehemi v France (ECHR) (September 26, 1997) 27
Mercury Communications Ltd v Director General of Telecommunications (HL) [1996] 1 WLR 48; [1996] 1 All ER 575 158
Mignini SpA v AIMA (C-256/90) [1992] ECR I-2651 77
Miro (C-128/84) [1985] ECR 3731 152
Modinos v Cyprus (ECHR) (1993) 16 EHRR 485 31
Molenbroek v Bestuur van de Sociale Verzekeringsbank (C-226/91) [1992] ECR I-5943 177
Muller and others v Switzerland (ECHR) (1991) 13 EHRR 212 ..... 30, 31
Murray v United Kingdom (ECHR) (1995) 19 EHRR 193 27

Netherlands v High Authority (C-6/54) [1954-56] ECR 103 71
Nimz v Freie und Hansestadt Hamburg (C-184/89) [1991] ECR I-297 ..... 174, 175
Nold v Commission (C-4/73) [1974] ECR 491 65
Nolte v Landesversicherungsanstalt Hannover (C-317/93) [1995] ECR I-4625 ..... 178, 179
Norris v Ireland (ECHR) (1991) 13 EHRR 186 31
Nottinghamshire CC v Secretary of State for the Environment (HL) [1986] AC 240 137

Oberhausener Kraftfutterwerk Wilhelm Hopermann GmbH v Bundesanstalt fur landwirtschaftliche Marktordnung (C-358/88) [1990] ECR I-1687 68
Oberschlick v Austria (No. 2) (ECHR) (July 1, 1997) 26
Observer and Guardian v United Kingdom (ECHR) Series A, No. 216 (1991) 123
Ojutiku v Manpower Services Commission (CA) [1982] ICR 661 ..... 170, 171, 179
Olsson v Sweden (ECHR) (1989) 11 EHRR 259 93

Open Door Counselling Ltd & Dublin Well Woman Centre v Ireland (ECHR) Series A, No. 246-A; (1993) 15 EHRR (1) 244 ....43, 44
O'Reilly v Mackman (HL) [1983] 2 AC 237 158
Osman v United Kingdom (ECHR) (October 28, 1998) 28
Otto-Preminger Institut v Austria (ECHR) (1995) 19 EHRR 34 ....26, 31, 34

Pastoors and Trans-Cap v Belgium (C-29/95) [1997] ECR I-285 9
Pepper (Inspector of Taxes) v Hart (HL) [1993] AC 593 ....157, 162
Petrovic v Austria (ECHR) (March 27, 1998) 34
Pietsch v Hauptzollamt Hamburg-Waltershof (C-296/94) [1996] ECR I-3409 ....5, 6, 75, 76
Purcell v Ireland (E Comm HR) App. No. 15404/89; (1991) 70 DR 262 123

R. v Barnsley MBC Ex p Hook (CA) [1976] 1 WLR 1052 ....91, 92
R. v Blackledge and others (1996) 8 Admin LR 361 160
R. v Boundary Commission for England Ex p Foot [1983] QB 600 95
R. v Cambridge Health Authority Ex p B (CA) [1995] 2 All ER 129 86
R. v Chief Constable of Kent Ex p Absalom (QBD) (Unreported, May 6, 1993) 90
R. v Chief Constable of Sussex Ex p International Trader's Ferry Ltd (HL) (November 11, 1998) 89, 96
R. v Chief Constable of Sussex Ex p International Trader's Ferry Ltd (CA) [1997] 3 WLR 132; [1997] 2 All ER 65 reversing [1995] 3 WLR 802; [1995] 4 All ER 364 ....66, 67, 86, 127, 140
R. v Coventry City Council Ex p Phoenix Aviation (QBD) [1995] 3 All ER 37 67
R. v Criminal Injuries Compensation Board Ex p Cook (CA) [1996] 1 WLR 1037; [1996] 2 All ER 144 128
R. v Criminal Injuries Compensation Board Ex p P (CA) [1995] 1 All ER 870 ....130, 137
R. v Crown Court of St Albans Ex p Cinnamond [1981] QB 480 95
R. v Customs and Excise Ex p Lunn Poly (DC) (April 2, 1998) 163
R. v Customs and Excise Ex p National Dried Fruit Trade Association (C-77/86) [1988] ECR 757 ....73, 74
R. v Goldstein (HL) [1983] 1 WLR 151 ....61, 108
R. v Highbury Magistrates' Court Ex p Uchendu (1994) 158 JP 409 92
R. v Hillingdon LBC Ex p Royco Homes Ltd [1974] QB 720 95
R. v HM Coroner for Greater Belfast Ex p Ministry of Defence (CA, Northern Ireland) (1994, transcript 2439-41) 133
R. v International Stock Exchange of the United Kingdom and the Republic of Ireland Ex p Else (1982) Ltd (CA) [1993] QB 534; [1993] 2 WLR 70; [1993] 1 All ER 420; [1993] BCLC 834; [1993] BCC 11 ....89, 90
R. v Lancashire CC Ex p Huddlestone [1986] 2 All ER 941 158

R. v Manchester Metropolitan University Ex p Nolan (Unreported, July 14, 1995)....................92
R. v Medicines Control Agency Ex p Pharma Nord Ltd (QBD) Times, July 29, 1997 126
R. v Minister for Agriculture, Fisheries and Food Ex p Bell Lines [1984] 2 CMLR 502....................89, 150, 151
R. v Minister for Agriculture, Fisheries and Food & Secretary of State for Health Ex p Fedesa and others (C-331/88) [1990] ECR I-4023 ....3, 4, 20, 38, 68, 70, 72, 77, 110
R. v Minister for Agriculture, Fisheries and Food Ex p First City Trading Ltd (QBD) [1997] 1 CMLR 250....................84, 87, 89, 90, 100, 153, 154
R. v Minister for Agriculture, Fisheries and Food Ex p Hamble (Offshore) Fisheries Ltd (QBD) [1995] 2 All ER 714....................91, 153
R. v Minister for Agriculture, Fisheries and Food Ex p Roberts (QBD) [1990] 1 CMLR 555....................89, 151
R. v Minister for the Civil Service Ex p Council of Civil Service Unions (GCHQ case) (HL) [1985] AC 374....................88, 94, 109, 112, 121, 131, 132
R. v Ministry of Defence Ex p Smith (CA) [1996] QB 517; [1996] 2 WLR 305; [1996] 1 All ER 257....................92, 126, 129
R. v Parliamentary Commissioner for Administration Ex p Balchin (QBD) [1997] COD 146....................95
R. v Pieck (C-157/79) [1980] ECR 2171....................40
R. v Radio Authority Ex p Bell [1998] QB 294 ....126, 136
R. v Reigate Justices Ex p Curl [1991] COD 66....................158
R. v Royal Pharmaceutical Society of Great Britain Ex p Association of Pharmaceutical Importers (C-266/87, C-267/87) [1989] ECR 1295 78
R. v Secretary of State for Employment Ex p Equal Opportunities Commission (HL) [1995] 1 AC 1; [1994] 2 WLR 409; [1994] 1 All ER 910 ....171, 172, 179
R. v Secretary of State for the Environment Ex p. Hammersmith and Fulham LBC (HL) [1991] 1 AC 521....................96, 137
R. v Secretary of State for the Environment Ex p. London Lesbian & Gay Centre, Independent, September 6, 1991....................158
R. v Secretary of State for the Environment Ex p. NALGO (1992) 5 Admin LR 785....................69, 92
R. v Secretary of State for the Home Department Ex p Adams (QBD) [1995] All ER (EC) 177....................89, 90, 132
R. v Secretary of State for the Home Department Ex p Brind (HL) [1991] 1 AC 696; [1991] 2 WLR 588; [1991] 1 All ER 720....................69, 88, 89, 92, 96, 98, 102, 110, 112, 121, 122, 127, 130, 132, 139, 140, 152
R. v Secretary of State for the Home Department Ex p Bugdaycay (HL) [1987] AC 514....................92, 129, 133

R. v Secretary of State for the Home Department Ex p Chahal (CA) [1995] 1 WLR 526; [1995] 1 All ER 658 .....132, 134
R. v Secretary of State for the Home Department Ex p Cheblak (CA) [1991] 1 WLR 890; [1991] 2 All ER 319 .....84, 132
R. v Secretary of State for the Home Department Ex p Gallagher Times, February 16, 1994 132
R. v Secretary of State for the Home Department Ex p Hargreaves (CA) [1997] 1 WLR 906; [1997] 1 All ER 397 .....90, 91, 128, 153
R. v Secretary of State for the Home Department Ex p Hosenball (CA) [1977] 1 WLR 766 132
R. v Secretary of State for the Home Department Ex p Leech (No. 2) (CA) [1994] QB 198; [1993] 3 WLR 1125; [1993] 4 All ER 539 .....92, 142
R. v Secretary of State for the Home Department Ex p McQuillan [1995] 4 All ER 400 .....92, 93, 132, 133
R. v Secretary of State for the Home Department Ex p Mann Singh Shingara (C-65/95, C-111/95) [1997] All ER (EC) 577 67
R. v Secretary of State for the Home Department Ex p Stitt, Times, February 3, 1987 132
R. v Secretary of State for Social Security Ex p Bomore Medical Supplies Ltd (CA) [1986] 1 CMLR 228 151
R. v Secretary of State for Social Security Ex p Schering Chemicals Ltd (QBD) [1987] 1 CMLR 277 150
R. v Secretary of State for Transport Ex p Factortame (No. 2) (HL) [1991] 1 AC 603; [1990] 3 WLR 818; [1991] 1 All ER 70; [1990] 3 CMLR 375; [1991] 1 Lloyd's Rep 10 .....145, 147, 148, 149
R. v Secretary of State for Transport Ex p Factortame (No. 2) [1996] ECR I-3905 159
R. v Secretary of State for Transport Ex p Factortame (No. 3) (C-46/93, C-48/93) [1996] ECR I-1029 .....149, 155, 156, 157, 160
R. v Secretary of State for Transport Ex p Factortame (No. 3) (CA) [1998] 3 CMLR 192 affirming [1988] Eur LR 475 (QBD) 147, 159, 161
R. v Warwick Crown Court Ex p Smalley [1987] 1 WLR 237 92
Reiseburo Broede v Gerd Sanker (C-3/95) [1996] ECR I-6511 13
Rewe-Zentrale AG v Bundesmonopolverwaltung fur Brantwein (Cassis de Dijon) (C-120/78) [1979] ECR 649 70
Rewe-Zentrale v Landwirtschaftskammer Rheinland (C-37/83) [1984] ECR 1229 82
Rinner-Kuhn v FWW Spezial-Gebaudereinigung GmbH (C-171/88) [1989] ECR 2743 174
Roquette Freres v Council of Ministers (C-138/79) [1980] ECR 3333 .....72, 77
Roquette Freres v ONIC (C-47/86) [1987] ECR 2889 68

SAM Schiffart GmbH and Heinz Stapf v Germany (C-248/95, C-249/95) [1997] I-4475 .... 39, 71
Schrader v Hauptzollamt Gronau (C-265/87) [1989] ECR 2237 6
Schroeder v Germany (C-40/72) [1973] ECR 125 72
Schumacher v Hauptzollamt Frankfurt am Main-Ost (C-215/87) [1989] ECR 617 78
Scollo v Italy (ECHR) (1996) 22 EHRR 514 32
Secretary of State for Social Security v Thomas (C-328/91) [1993] ECR I-1247 .... 170, 176
Sermide v Cassa Conguaglio Zucchero (C-106/83) [1984] ECR 4209 77
Sheffield and Horsham v United Kingdom (ECHR) (July 30, 1998) 25
Sidoropoulos and others v Greece (ECHR) (July 10, 1998) 25
Silver v United Kingdom (ECHR) (1983) 5 EHRR 347 93
Singh v Rowntree Mackintosh Ltd (EAT) [1979] ICR 554 170
Societe pour l'exportation des sucres (C-56/86) [1987] ECR 1423 68
Society for the Protection of Unborn Children (Ireland) Ltd v Grogan (C-159/90) [1991] ECR I-4685 .... 37, 43, 68, 146
Spadea and Scalabrino v Italy (ECHR) (1996) 21 EHRR 482 .... 32, 34
Spain v Commission (C-169/95) [1997] ECR I-135 66
Ste civ St Marie de l'Assomption (Conseil d'Etat, France) (October 20, 1972) Leb. 657 50
Steel v Union of Post Office Workers (EAT) [1978] ICR 181 170
Stoke-on-Trent City Council and Norwich City Council v B&Q Plc [1991] 1 AC 49; [1991] Ch. 48; [1990] 3 CMLR 31 .... 79, 103, 151
Stoke-on-Trent City Council and Norwich City Council v B&Q Plc (C-306/88, C-304/90, C-169/91) [1992] ECR I-6457; [1993] 1 CMLR 426 .... 40, 113, 145, 151
Stolting v Hauptzollamt Hamburg-Jonas (C-138/78) [1979] ECR 713 71
Stubbings v United Kingdom (ECHR) (1997) 23 EHRR 213 .... 27, 34
Sunday Times v United Kingdom (ECHR); Series A, No 30; (1979-80) 2 EHRR 245 .... 30, 93, 108, 124

Tesco Stores Ltd v Secretary of State for the Environment (HL) [1995] 1 WLR 759; [1995] 2 All ER 636 .... 113, 114, 137
Teuling v Bedrijfsvereniging voor de Chemische Industrie (C-30/85) [1987] ECR 2497 .... 176, 177
Tinnelly & Sons Ltd and others and McElduff and others v United Kingdom (ECHR) Case No. 62/1997/846/1052-1053 (July 10, 1998) 28, 134, 135
Torfaen BC v B&Q Plc (C-145/88) [1989] ECR 3851 .... 19, 113
Transactiones Maritimas and others v Commission (C-12/95P) [1995] ECR I-467 66
Transocean Marine Paint v Commission (C-17/74) [1974] ECR 1063 2

Trustees of the Dennis Rye Pension Fund v Sheffield City Council (CA) (1998) 10 Admin LR 112 158

UKAPE v ACAS [1981] AC 424 95
UNECTEF v Heylens (C-222/86) [1987] ECR 4097 67
United Kingdom v Council of the European Union (Organisation of Working Time Directive case) (C-84/94) [1996] ECR 1-5755 ....4, 81, 83, 84

Van der Linde and Tracotex v Minister Van Landbouw (C-351/93 to C-353/93) [1995] ECR I-85 73
Van Duyn v Home Office (C-41/74) [1974] ECR 1337 69
Van Cant v Rijksdienst voor Pensioenen (C-154/92) [1993] ECR I-3811 170
Velosa Barreto v Portugal (ECHR) (November 21, 1995) 32
Verband Sozialer Wettbewerb v Clinique Laboratories and Estee Lauder (C-315/92) [1994] ECR I-317 78
Vereinigte Familiapress Zeitungsverlags- und vertriebs GmbH v Verlag (C-368/95) [1997] ECR I-3689 ....41, 42, 62
Vereinigung Demokratischer Soldaten Osterreichs and Gubi v Austria (ECHR) (1995) 20 EHRR 56 25
Ville Nouvelle Est (Conseil d'Etat francais) (May 28, 1971) Leb. 409 ....49, 51
Vlassopoulo v Ministeriam fur Justiz, Bunder- und Europaangelegenheiten Baden-Wurtemburg (C-340/89) [1991] ECR I-2357 67
Vogt v Germany (ECHR) (1996) 21 EHRR 205 29

Wachauf v Bundesamt fur Ernahrung und Forstwirtschaft (C-5/88) [1989] ECR 2609 15
Weber v Switzerland (ECHR) Series A, No. 177 (1990) 123
Werner (C-70/94) [1995] ECR I-3189 13
Wingrove v United Kingdom (ECHR) (1997) EHRR 1 ....26, 31
Winterwerp v The Netherlands (ECHR) (1979) 2 EHRR 387 27
Wollast v European Economic Community (C-18/63) [1964] ECR 97 69
Wuidart and others v Latierie cooperative eupenoise (C-267/88 to C-285/88) [1990] ECR I-435 72
Wunsche v Germany (C-345/82) [1984] ECR 1995 73

X, Y and Z v United Kingdom (ECHR) 1997-II R&J 619; (1997) 24 EHRR 143 128

Zardi v Consorzio agrario provincale di Ferrara (C-8/89) [1990] I-2515 72
Zuckerfabrik Bedburg v OBEA (C-291/84) [1987] ECR 49 68

Table of National Legislation

Germany

Code of Criminal Procedure s. 12 para. 4....................46
Law of Administrative Procedure 1976 para. 113....................47

The Netherlands

Algeme Wet Bestuursrecht 1992
Art. 1:1....................55
Art. 3:1....................55
Art. 3:4....................55, 56, 62
Art. 8:72....................58
Ambtenarenwet 1929
Art. 58, para. 3....................55
Wet Arob 1976....................55, 57

United Kingdom

Criminal Justice Act 1991....................91
Employment Protection (Consolidation) Act 1978....................172
European Communities Act 1972....................145, 149
Fair Employment (Northern Ireland) Act 1976
s. 42....................135, 136
Human Rights Act 1998....................58, 99, 105, 117–44
s. 2(1)....................119, 120, 121
s. 3....................119
s. 3(1)....................129
s. 3(2)(c)....................129
s. 4....................119, 139
s. 6....................93, 119
s. 6(1)....................129
s. 6(6)....................140
s. 6(1)....................141
s. 10....................140
Sched. 1....................119, 120, 123, 140
Sched. 2....................119, 120
Sched. 3....................119, 120
Prevention of Terrorism (Temporary Provisions) Act 1989....................92

Merchant Shipping Act 1988 ....159, 162
s. 14 159
s. 14(4) 159, 160, 161
Race Relations Act 1976
s.1(1)(b)(ii) 170
Rules of the Supreme Court
Ord. 24 r. 8..158
Ord. 53 ....157, 158
Sex Discrimination Act 1975 ....169, 170
s.1(1)(b)(ii) 167
Shops Act 1950 19

Table of Secondary Legislation

Commission Regulation 3429/80 adopting protective measures applicable to imports of preserved mushrooms 5, 74
Commission Regulation 796/81 adopting protective measures applicable to imports of preserved mushrooms....................5
Commission Regulation 1755/81 adopting protective measures applicable to imports of preserved mushrooms....................5
Commission Regulation 2742/82 on minimum import prices for dried grapes 73
Commission Regulation 2163/92 adopting protective measures applicable to imports of preserved mushrooms 5, 6
Council Directive 75/117 172
Council Directive 76/207 on the equal treatment of men and women....................172, 180
Art. 2(2)....................168, 169
Art. 2(3)....................168
Art. 3(3)....................168
Council Directive 79/7....................176
Art. 7(1)(a)....................169
Council Directive 80/1263/EEC on the introduction of a Community driving licence (First Directive)
Art. 8(1) 11
Council Directive 85/337/EEC on environmental impact statements 50
Council Directive 91/439/EEC on driving licences 11
Council Directive 93/104/EC concerning certain aspects of the organisation of working time....................4, 83
Council Directive 97/80
Art. 2....................167
Council Directive on VAT (Sixth Directive)
Art. 18(4)....................17
Council Regulation 1035/72 on the common organisation of the market in fruit and vegetables 72
Council Regulation 2707/72 on the common organisation of the market in products processed from fruit and vegetables....................72
Council Regulation 516/77
Art. 2(2) 6
Art. 13(2) 6
Art. 14....................6
Council Regulation 521/77 72

Council Regulation 1796/81 ....6, 7
Council Regulation 3820/85 on the harmonisation of certain social legislation related to transport 9
Council Regulation 3821/85 on recording equipment in road transport 9
Council Regulation 426/86 72
Council Regulation 990/93
Art. 1(1)(c) 15
Art. 1(1)(d) 15
Art. 8 14
Art. 9 15
Art. 10 ....15, 16
Council Regulation 2186/93 on Community co-ordination in drawing up business registers for statistical purposes 83
Council Regulation 3290/94 on the adjustments and transitional arrangements required in the agricultural sector in order to implement the agreements concluded during the Uruguay Round of multilateral trade negotiations 72
Council Regulation on the export of dual-use goods
Art. 11 13
Council Regulation on skimmed-milk powder 3

Table of Treaties

European Convention on Human Rights 1950.........ix, 23–35, 117–21, 149, 164
Art. 2......138
Art. 3......134, 138
Art. 5......27
Art. 6......138
Art. 6(1)......135, 136
Art. 9......43
Art. 10......26, 42, 93, 108, 125, 138
Art. 10(1)......43, 130
Art. 10(2)......43, 130
Art. 11......43, 93
Art. 12......138
Art. 13......119, 134, 141
Art. 14......24, 34
Art. 15......121, 131
Art. 36......34
Art. 50......28
Protocol 1, Art. 1......32, 33
Protocol 1, Art. 2......138
Protocol 11......23, 30, 34

Resolution of 20 December 1985 of the Council and the Representatives of the Governments of the Member States on effective means of prosecuting nonresident drivers and recovering fines......9

Treaty of Amsterdam 1997......168
Protocol on the application of the principles of subsidiarity and proportionality......21, 81

Treaty of Rome 1957 (EEC)
Art. 3b......2
Art. 3b(2)......81
Art. 3b(3)......62, 65, 80, 81, 83
Art. 36......2
Art. 5......146
Art. 6......9, 10, 11
Art. 8a......10
Art. 30......19, 40, 70, 150, 151

Art. 33(1) 71
Art. 34 .... 89, 151
Art. 36 .... 89, 150, 151, 152
Art. 39 1
Art. 40 .... 3, 71
Art. 40(3) 1
Art. 43 .... 3, 71
Art. 48(3) 2
Art. 52 .... 10, 11, 12, 159
Art. 59 43
Art. 92 163
Art. 93 163
Art. 115(2) 2
Art. 115(3) 2
Art. 118a 4, 82, 83, 84
Art. 119 .... 167, 168, 172, 175, 176
Art. 130t 82
Art. 169 169
Art. 173 2
Art. 177 .... 2, 5, 8, 19, 78, 169, 173, 178, 179
Art. 213 83
Art. 221 159

Treaty on European Union (Maastricht) 1993 2
Agreement on Social Policy 168

United Nations Security Council Resolution 820 (1993) para. 24 14

List of Contributors

FRANCIS G. JACOBS is an Advocate General of the European Court of Justice.

JEREMY MCBRIDE is a Senior Lecturer in the Faculty of Law, University of Birmingham.

WALTER VAN GERVEN is Professor of Law at the Catholic University of Leuven, Belgium.

TAKIS TRIDIMAS is Professor of European Law at the University of Southampton.

PAUL CRAIG is Professor of English Law at St John's College, University of Oxford.

THE RIGHT HONOURABLE LORD HOFFMANN is a Lord of Appeal in Ordinary.

DAVID FELDMAN is Barber Professor of Jurisprudence at the University of Birmingham.

NICHOLAS GREEN QC is a Barrister of Brick Court Chambers, London.

EVELYN ELLIS is Professor of Public Law at the University of Birmingham.

Recent Developments in the Principle of Proportionality in European Community Law

FRANCIS G. JACOBS

Although the principle of proportionality featured from time to time in the Court's early case law, the emergence of proportionality as a "general principle of law" can perhaps be traced to the *Internationale Handelsgesellschaft*[1] case in 1970—where it was closely related to the principle of respect for fundamental rights. Both Advocate General Dutheillet de Lamothe and the Court were perhaps responding to the concern in German legal circles that those principles, of fundamental importance in German public law, should be given full effect in Community law. That case concerned a challenge to Community provisions on the common organisation of the agricultural markets as infringing the principle of proportionality, and it had been argued that that principle could be derived from Article 40(3) of the EEC Treaty which stated that "the common organisation . . . may include all measures *required* to attain the objectives set out in Article 39" (emphasis added): thus, only the measures *necessary* for the attainment of those objectives may be used.

That view was implausible on at least three counts. First, the provision embodies a somewhat cursory reference to what is deemed to be a fundamental principle. Secondly, it does not do full justice to at least the German conception of proportionality, which requires, as well as necessity, satisfaction on two other counts. According to German law three tests must be applied[2]:

(1) the measure must be appropriate for attaining the objective;
(2) it must be necessary, in the sense that no other measure is available which is less restrictive of freedom;
(3) the measure must not be disproportionate to its aim (proportionality in the narrower sense).

Thirdly, and in any event, the appearance of the requirement of necessity in Article 40(3) of the Treaty—and even other scattered references in the Treaty to

[1] Case 11/70 *Internationale Handelsgesellschaft* v. *Einfuhr- und Vorratsstelle Getreide* [1970] ECR 1125.

[2] See, e.g., Jürgen Schwarze, *European Administrative Law* (London, Sweet & Maxwell, 1992) at 687.

similar effect[3]—could scarcely be sufficient to support a principle of general application. (The position is different since the entry into force of the Treaty on European Union which introduced a general provision in the third paragraph of Article 3b that "[a]ny action by the Community shall not go beyond what is necessary to achieve the objectives of this Treaty"; but the introduction of that provision, in that elementary form, at that stage in the development of the Community legal order can hardly be regarded as more than a perfunctory acknowledgment of the existing case law).

The Court therefore, perhaps rightly, preferred to treat proportionality as a "general principle of law". (Similarly the principle of respect for fundamental rights emerged in that case as a general principle of law.) Such general principles were to prove a fertile source of grounds for controlling Community action, a particularly valuable source given the absence of detailed guidance in the Treaty—particularly Articles 173 and 177—of the grounds of review. The notion of "general principles of law" was itself derived from French administrative law—although that law did not, it is generally thought, recognise proportionality as such a general principle.[4]

As already mentioned, the Court has derived various general principles of law from the legal systems of one or more Member States: the principle of proportionality itself substantially from German law; the principle of respect for legitimate expectations perhaps from French and German law; the right to a hearing (*audi alteram partem*) from several systems including notably English law.[5]

The notion of "general principle" has the advantage that the Court does not feel constrained to apply the principle in any preordained way. As the cases considered below demonstrate, the Court does not always articulate the principle in the full manner advocated by German theorists; on the other hand the principle is sometimes applied more effectively than, for example, the notion of reasonableness in English administrative law.

The use made by the Court of the principle in its earlier case law is admirably analysed by Gráinne de Búrca in an article in the *Yearbook of European Law*.[6] In the present paper I will examine recent developments in the principle in the light of the more recent case law.

In considering recent cases on proportionality, we can distinguish cases where Community measures are challenged and those where the lawfulness of national measures is in issue. (Proportionality may also of course be in issue in proceed-

[3] E.g. "justified" in Arts. 36 and 48(3). Art. 115(2) refers to "necessary" measures, and Art. 115(3) to measures "which cause the least disturbance of the functioning of the common market".

[4] See the authors cited by Schwarze, n. 2 above, at 680, n. 3; and on the French view of proportionality see N. Emiliou, *The Principle of Proportionality in European Law: A Comparative Study* (London, Kluwer Law International, 1996), 88 ff.

[5] See the Opinion of Warner AG in Case 17/74 *Transocean Marine Paint* v. *Commission* [1974] ECR 1063.

[6] G. de Búrca, "The Principle of Proportionality and its Application in EC Law" (1993) 13 *YEL* 105.

ings against individuals, notably against employers in cases on sex discrimination and equal pay. These are discussed elsewhere in this book[7]).

CHALLENGE TO COMMUNITY MEASURES

Where Community measures are concerned, the agricultural sector provides the best illustration of the current application of the principle, since it is in that sector that the Community legislature is most active. The sector also illustrates very clearly the flexibility of proportionality as a tool of judicial review. It allows for a more or less exacting standard of judicial review depending on the character and context of the measure under review.

In the earlier cases, as in *Internationale Handelsgesellschaft* itself, the Court was not infrequently confronted with the issue of the forfeiture of securities which were required of traders to ensure compliance with their Community obligations. In such cases the Court developed a relatively strict standard of review, and has occasionally declared provisions of Commission regulations invalid.[8]

A striking illustration from the earlier period of the application of the principle was the decision in 1977 to declare null and void a measure not of the Commission but of the Council, the Council Regulation on skimmed-milk powder,[9] embodying a substantial agricultural policy measure. In order to reduce the milk surplus, the Regulation in effect required manufacturers of animal feed to incorporate skimmed milk powder in their products. The Court found that that imposed a disproportionate burden on the manufacturers. Here a direct calculation was possible: the compulsory purchase of skimmed-milk powder was imposed on manufacturers of animal feeding-stuffs at a price equal to about three times its value as feed.

However in reviewing more general legislative measures involving an element of policy the Court has been perhaps less exacting. A standard formula is to the effect that in matters concerning the CAP the Community legislature has a discretionary power which corresponds to the political responsibilities given to it by Articles 40 and 43 of the Treaty; consequently, the legality of a measure adopted in that sphere can be affected only if the measure is "manifestly inappropriate" having regard to the objective which the competent institution is seeking to pursue.[10] That formula enables the Court to subject the measures in

[7] See E. Ellis, "The Concept of Proportionality in European Community Sex Discrimination Law" this vol.

[8] See, e.g., Case 240/78 *Atalanta Amsterdam BV* v. *Produktschap Voor Vee en Vlees* [1979] ECR 2137 and Case 181/84 *The Queen Ex.p. E.D. & F. Man (Sugar) Ltd* v. *IBAP* [1985] ECR 2889.

[9] Case 114/76 *Bela-Mühle Josef Bergmann KG* v. *Grows-Farm GmbH & Co. KG* [1977] ECR 1211.

[10] See, e.g., Case C–331/88 *R.* v. *Minister for Agriculture, Fisheries and Food & the Secretary of State for Health, Ex.p. Fedesa and Others* [1990] ECR I–4023, para. 14.

question to a relatively tolerant level of scrutiny—as for example in the hormones case of 1990.[11]

The Court adopted a similar approach in the challenge by the United Kingdom to the "working time directive" (Council Directive 934/104/EC concerning certain aspects of the organisation of working time),[12] adopted on the basis of Article 118a of the Treaty. The United Kingdom pointed out that the Council may adopt on the basis of Article 118a of the Treaty only "minimum requirements for gradual implementation, having regard to the conditions and technical rules obtaining in each of the Member States", and that those requirements must avoid "imposing administrative, financial and legal constraints in a way which would hold back the creation and development of small and medium-sized undertakings". The Court rejected each of the United Kingdom's submissions to the effect that the requirements imposed by the Directive were not minimum requirements within the meaning of Article 118a.

On the principle of proportionality, it recalled that, in order to establish whether a provision of Community law complies with that principle, it must be ascertained whether the means which it employs are suitable for the purpose of achieving the desired objective and whether they do not go beyond what is necessary to achieve it. The Court continued:

> As to judicial review of those conditions, however, the Council must be allowed a wide discretion in an area which, as here, involves the legislature in making social policy choices and requires it to carry out complex assessments. Judicial review of the exercise of that discretion must therefore be limited to examining whether it has been vitiated by manifest error or misuse of powers, or whether the institution concerned has manifestly exceeded the limits of its discretion.[13]

As regards the first condition—whether the means are suitable for the purpose—it was sufficient to find that, as followed from the earlier part of the judgment:

> the measures on the organization of working time which form the subject-matter of the directive, save for that contained in the second sentence of Article 5, contribute directly to the improvement of health and safety protection for workers within the meaning of Article 118a, and cannot therefore be regarded as unsuited to the purpose of achieving the objective pursued.[14]

The second condition was also fulfilled. Contrary to the view taken by the applicant, the Council did not commit any manifest error in concluding that the contested measures were necessary to achieve the objective of protecting the health and safety of workers. Examining five arguments on that issue in turn, the Court concluded that:

[11] Case C–331/88 R. v. *Minister for Agriculture, Fisheries and Food & the Secretary of State for Health, Ex.p. Fedesa and Others* [1990] ECR I–4023, at paras. 15 to 17.

[12] Case C–84/94 *United Kingdom* v. *Council* [1996] ECR I–5755.

[13] *Ibid.*, at 5811.

[14] *Ibid.*, at 5811–2.

in taking the view that the objective of harmonizing national legislation on the health and safety of workers, while maintaining the improvements made, could not be achieved by measures less restrictive than those that are the subject-matter of the directive, the Council did not commit any manifest error.[15]

The Court took a very similar type of approach in a challenge to Community legislation by way of Article 177, on a reference by the Tribunal de Police, Luxembourg.[16] The reference put in issue the validity of the Council regulation setting up the "Intrastat system" for collecting statistics on trade in goods between Member States. Although the checks required by the regulation had restrictive effects on trade between Member States, the Court found on analysis that the aim pursued by the regulation was justified, that its restrictive effects were commensurate with that aim, and moreover (a separate test), that those restrictive effects were consistent with the principle of proportionality.

Another good illustration of challenge to Council legislation on the basis of proportionality is provided by *Germany* v. *Parliament and Council*,[17] a challenge to the directive on deposit-guarantee schemes. The German government challenged two distinct provisions of the directive on grounds of breach of proportionality; both challenges were rejected by the Court, deploying, in a more complex context, a similar line of analysis to that used in the "working time" and "Intrastat" cases.

In other cases, however, scrutiny will be more intensive. Good illustrations are provided by *Hüpeden*[18] and *Pietsch*.[19] In these cases the Court had to consider whether the Council and the Commission had infringed the principle of proportionality by setting a charge levied on imports of preserved mushrooms at an excessively high level. A rather full account will show how the principle is applied by the Court in a case which justifies detailed scrutiny.

In its judgment in the earlier cases of *Werner Faust*[20] and *Wünsche*,[21] the Court had held Article 1 of Commission Regulations 3429/80, 796/81 and 1755/81 adopting protective measures applicable to imports of preserved mushrooms invalid as regards the level of the "additional amount" payable under those regulations for imports in excess of the import quota, on the ground of breach of the principle of proportionality. The regulations had set the additional amounts for consecutive periods at ECU 175 per 100 kg net, ECU 175 per 100 kg net and ECU 160 per 100 kg net respectively. In order to comply with the Court's judgment the Commission adopted Regulation 2163/92, by which it reduced, with retroactive effect, to ECU 105 per 100 kg net the additional amount provided for in the three regulations for imports carried out during the

[15] *Ibid.*, at 5813.

[16] Case C–114/96 *Criminal proceedings against René Kieffer and Romain Thill* [1997] ECR I–3629.

[17] Case C–233/94 [1997] ECR I–2405.

[18] Case C–295/94 *Hüpeden* v. *Hauptzollamt Hamburg-Jonas* [1996] ECR I–3375.

[19] Case C–296/94 *Pietsch* v. *Hauptzollamt Hamburg-Waltershof* [1996] ECR I–3409.

[20] Case C–24/90 [1991] ECR I–4905.

[21] Case C–25/90 [1991] ECR I–4939 and C–26/90 [1991] ECR I–4961.

periods in question. At issue in *Pietsch* was the validity of that replacement Regulation.

At issue in *Hüpeden* was the validity of Council Regulation 1796/81, which followed the third of the partially invalid regulations. Unlike those regulations, which were based on Article 14 of Council Regulation 516/77 (protective measures), Regulation 1796/81 was based on Article 13(2) of Regulation 516/77 (measures of market management). The Regulation set the additional amount to be levied when the import quota was exceeded at ECU 160 per 100 kg net.

The issue put to the Court by a Hamburg court was essentially whether the level of the additional amounts set in Regulations 2136/92 and 1796/81 was in conformity with the principle of proportionality. The Court held that it was not. It noted that by virtue of that principle measures imposing financial charges on economic operators were lawful provided that they were appropriate and necessary for meeting the objectives legitimately pursued by the rules in question. However, when there was a choice between several appropriate measures, the least onerous measure must be used and the charges imposed must not be disproportionate to the aims pursued.[22]

In *Pietsch* the Court noted that the previous regulations were annulled because the level of the additional amount was set, without any distinction, for preserved mushrooms of all origins and grades, the effect of which was to increase the cost of imported preserved mushrooms, particularly those of lower quality, thus penalising imports of lower quality mushrooms to a greater extent. Turning to Regulation 2163/92, the Court observed that the requirement of an additional amount where the authorised quota was exceeded was appropriate and necessary to the attainment of the aims of the regulation, namely to discourage imports of preserved mushrooms into the Community beyond the quota. The Court rejected Mr Pietsch's argument that the additional amount should have been set at an amount corresponding to the difference between the production costs in the Community and the price of imported mushrooms, including customs duties. That would not achieve the aim of discouraging imports. However, while the Commission had a discretion to set the additional amount at a higher level, that level should not be so high as to amount to a prohibition on imports. By setting the amount at ECU 105 per 100 kg net, which represented two-thirds of the cost price of grade one mushrooms, the additional amount was tantamount to a prohibition. The Commission had therefore infringed the principle of proportionality.

In *Hüpeden* the Council and the Commission argued that, because Regulation 1796/81 was not adopted on the basis of Article 14 of Council Regulation 516/77, Article 2(2) of the latter regulation, which stated that measures under Article 14 could be taken only to such extent and for such length of time as was strictly necessary, did not apply. In fixing the additional amount the Commission was obliged to observe only the general principle of proportional-

[22] Case 265/87 *Schräder* v. *Hauptzollamt Gronau* [1989] ECR 2237, para. 21.

ity, which was less strict. The Court simply replied that the two institutions acknowledged that the general principle of proportionality was applicable.

The Court also rejected the Council and the Commission's argument that the long-term market management measures adopted by the Council in Regulation 1796/81 could be distinguished from the temporary protective measures adopted by the Commission, noting that the measures adopted in the former regulation were substantively identical to the protective measures previously adopted by the Commission regulations. From the point of view of its purpose, namely the protection of the Community market, and the techniques used, namely the setting of import quotas, the control of imports by means of import licences and the setting of additional amounts where quotas were exceeded, the Regulation did not differ fundamentally from the Commission Regulations.

The Council and the Commission also contended that the principle of proportionality was complied with because the additional amount was less restrictive of trade than a complete prohibition of imports, a measure which the Council could have taken in the exercise of its wide discretionary powers under the common agricultural policy. The Court rejected that argument on the ground that the regulation was not designed to exclude imports above certain quantities completely but left open the possibility of issuing import licences against payment of an additional amount. Having opted for that solution, the Council was obliged to comply with the principle of proportionality. The Court also rejected the Council's contention that the additional amount had to be set at a high level in order to ensure that the measures of market management established by the regulation at issue were effective. Although the Council had some discretion in setting the level of the additional amount, it was not entitled to set it at such a high level that it amounted to a prohibition. The aim of the regulation was not to prohibit all imports above the quantities set but to protect the Community market in mushrooms from disruption due to excessive imports from non-Member countries.

The Court also rejected the Commission's argument that the level of the additional amount was justified because it corresponded to the cost price of top-grade mushrooms, thus ensuring that imports exceeding the quantities set were principally of that type of mushroom. The level of the additional amount set by the regulation, which corresponded to the cost price of grade one mushrooms produced in the Community, represented at least 100 per cent of the production costs of those imported mushrooms. Furthermore, the additional amount was set on the basis of the cost of top-grade mushrooms produced in the Community. It followed that the level of the additional amount for lower grade mushrooms imported from non-member countries had a much more serious effect and in consequence considerably exceeded the cost of lower grade mushrooms produced in the Community.

The Court concluded that a flat-rate charge which was set at a very high level and was levied on all traders who exceeded the quantities laid down, regardless of whether they did so inadvertently or fraudulently, was excessive, because it went beyond the objective of the regulation, which was to protect the Community market, and penalised importers. Consequently, the principle of proportionality had been infringed. The relevant Council and Commission measures were accordingly declared invalid as regards the level of the additional amount set.

By way of contrast, in the *Binder* case[23] the Court rejected a challenge to Commission regulations on protective measures applicable to imports of frozen strawberries and other fruits. Here again the Court undertook detailed scrutiny of the Community measures, their effects and their justification, but concluded that Binder's three distinct pleas on the proportionality of the protective measures were unfounded.

From the above brief survey of recent cases, it is difficult to draw any general conclusions about the standard of review. That may be a difficulty inherent in any analysis, simply because the context varies greatly from one case to another, the type of issue addressed also varies, and much will depend on the nature of the evidence and the level of argument addressed to the Court. It can however perhaps be concluded at least that the principle of proportionality does provide an effective and rationally coherent basis for judicial review of Community legislative and administrative measures. It enables the Court to undertake what may in some cases be intensive and detailed scrutiny.

CHALLENGE TO NATIONAL MEASURES

More frequently, in recent years, the principle of proportionality has been invoked (often successfully) in challenging national measures. In addressing the review by the Court of national measures for compliance with the principle of proportionality, I would suggest that three fundamental issues can be identified for discussion. First, what is the appropriate level of review? In particular, how do the nature and intensity of scrutiny by the Court compare with its review of Community measures? That issue goes to the substance of review. Secondly, how far does review by the Court of national measures extend, where those measures are adopted in implementation of Community law, or where they otherwise fall in some respect within the scope of Community law? In other words, what link between the national measures and Community law is required for the principle of proportionality to be applicable? That issue, for which there is no analogy in the review of Community measures, goes to the scope of review: the scope of application of the principle. Thirdly, how far, in Article 177 proceedings, should the principle be applied by the Court itself? How far should the Court itself decide whether the measure is proportionate, and how far should the Court merely give guidance on the appropriate criteria, their application in the concrete case being left to the national court? That issue,

[23] Case C–205/94 *Binder* v. *Hauptzollamt Stuttgart-West* [1996] ECR I–2871.

for which again there is no analogy in the review of Community measures, raises some central questions about the function of the Court and its relation with the national courts.

These three issues (which I hasten to say I seek to raise, rather than to resolve) can be illustrated in the recent case law. Among recent decisions of the Court where national measures have been in issue, five types of case can be distinguished. The first is exemplified by the *Pastoors* case[24] which concerned measures designed to ensure the enforcement of criminal penalties. It illustrates the point that, in that context, a difference of treatment between residents and non-residents, which may thus constitute indirect discrimination between nationals of Member States contrary to Article 6 of the Treaty, will be prohibited under that Article if it infringes the principle of proportionality. The case concerned the Belgian legislation implementing Council Regulation 3820/85 on the harmonisation of certain social legislation related to transport and Council Regulation 3821/85 on recording equipment in road transport. Under the Regulations Member States were to adopt the necessary provisions to ensure compliance with the Regulations. A resolution of 20 December 1985 of the Council and the Representatives of the Governments of the Member States required Member States to adopt effective means of prosecuting nonresident drivers and recovering fines. Under the Belgian rules an offender who is apprehended has the option of either paying BFR 10,000 per breach forthwith, which normally extinguishes prosecution, or, in default, allowing the criminal proceedings provided for by law to take their course against him. The latter option is however subject to the further condition that, where the offender has no official or permanent residence in Belgium, he is required to lodge by way of deposit the sum of BFR 15,000 per breach to cover the amount of any fine and legal costs, in default of which his vehicle is impounded at his risk and expense.

The issue put by the national court was whether Article 6 of the Treaty precluded national legislation adopted in implementation of a Community regulation which imposed only on non-residents who opted for continuation of normal criminal proceedings against them an obligation to lodge by way of security in respect of each offence a fixed sum higher than that provided for in the case of immediate payment, in default of which their vehicle was impounded. In the proceedings before the national court a German road transport company and one of its drivers, who resided in Germany, were being prosecuted in respect of offences committed on Belgian territory. The Court noted that there was no convention between the Kingdom of Belgium and the Federal Republic of Germany to secure the enforcement of court decisions in criminal matters. There was therefore a real risk that enforcement of a judgment against a non-resident would be impossible or, at least, considerably more difficult and onerous. That situation therefore objectively justified a difference of treatment between resident and non-resident offenders, the obligation imposed on the

[24] Case C–29/95 *Pastoors and Trans-Cap* v. *Belgian State* [1997] ECR I–285.

latter to pay a sum by way of security being appropriate to prevent them from avoiding an effective penalty simply by declaring that they did not consent to the immediate levying of the fine and opting for the continuation of normal criminal proceedings. However, the penalties imposed had to be appropriate and necessary to achieve the aim pursued. The sum of BFR 15,000 by way of security was demanded separately for each infringement with which the offender was charged. However, where various infringements were simultaneously found to exist and were mentioned in the same document, they did not each form a subject-matter of distinct criminal proceedings since they all gave rise to a single set of proceedings against the offender. The Belgian legislation was therefore manifestly disproportionate and prohibited by Article 6 of the Treaty.

It will be observed that the case concerned measures giving effect to Community legislation. I do not think that the same result would have been reached if the criminal proceedings in question had no direct connection with Community law. If, in the absence of discrimination, the question arose of the proportionality of national measures, there would be no scope for the application of the principle in proceedings which had no connection with Community law. In the case of discrimination on grounds of nationality, however, it is arguable that the prohibition of discrimination extends to all national measures, and to all legal proceedings, whether or not those proceedings have any specific connection with Community law.[25]

Both principles are likely in any event to be applicable where a Community national (or citizen of the European Union) is exercising a right of free movement. This leads to consideration of the second type of case. This is one where the principle of proportionality is invoked in testing the compatibility of a national measure with a fundamental freedom of the Treaty, such as the freedom of establishment. That issue is illustrated by the *Skanavi* case.[26]

Mrs Skanavi and her husband, Mr Chryssanthakopoulos, both Greek nationals, took up residence in Germany in order to take over a German company. Mrs Skanavi was charged under the relevant German regulation for driving without a driving licence, an offence punishable by up to one year's imprisonment and a fine, or, if the offence was committed as a result of carelessness, by up to six months' imprisonment or a fine. Her husband faced the same penalties for directing or allowing his wife to drive his motor vehicle without a licence. The national court took the view that the accused had committed the offences in question as a result of carelessness, since Mrs Skanavi had neglected to exchange her Greek licence within one year of taking up her normal residence in Germany. However, it sought a ruling from the Court on the compatibility of the German rules with Articles 6, 8a and 52 of the EC Treaty.

The Court noted first of all that at the material time the Treaty on European Union, which introduced Article 8a, was not yet in force. It appeared however

[25] See Case C–274/96 *Bickel and Franz*, not yet reported.

[26] Case C–193/94 *Criminal Proceedings Against Sofia Skanavi and Konstantin Chryssanthakopoulos* [1996] ECR I–929.

that the national court could apply the principle, recognised by German law, that a more favourable rule of criminal law should take retroactive effect; this aspect of the reference was therefore admissible because it was for the national court to determine the need for the ruling and the relevance of the questions which it submitted.

The Court therefore went on to consider whether, as Community law then stood, the Treaty precluded a Member State from requiring the holder of a driving licence issued by another State to exchange his licence within one year of taking up normal residence. Referring to *Corsica Ferries*,[27] the Court pointed out that Article 6 of the Treaty, which laid down the general principle of the prohibition of discrimination on grounds of nationality, applied independently only to situations governed by Community law in respect of which the Treaty laid down no specific prohibition of discrimination. Similarly, Article 8a of the Treaty, which set out generally the right of every citizen of the Union to move and reside freely within the territory of the Member States, found specific expression in Article 52 of the Treaty. Since Article 52 was applicable here, it was not necessary to rule on the interpretation of Article 8a. As regards Article 52 the Court had already held in *Choquet*[28] that, while national rules concerning the issue and mutual recognition of driving licences exerted an influence on the exercise of rights guaranteed by the Treaty provisions on freedom of movement, it had to be accepted that, in view of the requirements of road safety, mutual recognition of driving licences could not be contemplated unless the requirements for the issue of the driving licences were harmonised to a sufficient extent. The Directive applicable at the material time was Directive 80/1263/EEC, the First Council Directive on the Introduction of a Community Driving Licence. Article 8(1) of the Directive provided that a national driving licence was to remain valid in another Member State for a maximum of one year following the taking up of residence there. At the request of the holder within that year, and against surrender of his licence, the host State was obliged to issue him with an equivalent Community model driving licence without requiring further tests. The Court noted that Council Directive 91/439/EEC of 29 July 1991 on driving licences, which would repeal Directive 80/1263 as at 1 July 1996, marked a new stage in the harmonisation in this area by providing for the mutual recognition of driving licences. On that point the Court concluded that the obstacles to freedom of movement could be totally removed only by the application of Directive 91/439 as from 1 July 1996.

The most interesting part of the judgment was however yet to come. The national court asked secondly whether the Treaty precluded a person who failed to exchange his licence from being treated as driving without a licence and hence subject to imprisonment or a fine. The Court noted that, although under Directive 80/1263 a licence had to be exchanged within one year, the licence

[27] Case C–18/93 *Corsica Ferries Italia* v. *Corpo dei Piloti del Porto di Genova* [1994] ECR I–1783.

[28] Case 16/78 [1978] ECR 2293.

remained valid in the State which issued it after that period. Consequently, the issue of a driving licence by a Member State in exchange for a licence issued by another Member State did not constitute the basis of the right to drive a motor vehicle in the territory of the host State, which was a right directly conferred by Community law, but was evidence of the existence of such a right. The obligation to exchange driving licences was essentially a way of meeting administrative requirements.

While acknowledging that, in the absence of Community rules, the Member States remained competent to impose penalties for breach of such an obligation, the Court pointed out that in laying down formalities concerning residence Member States were not entitled to impose a penalty so disproportionate to the gravity of the infringement that it became an obstacle to free movement of persons; that would be especially so if the penalty consisted of imprisonment.[29] In view of the importance of the right to drive a motor vehicle for the exercise of the right to freedom of movement, the same principle extended to breach of the obligation to exchange driving licences.

The Court added that to treat a person who failed to exchange his licence as a person driving without a licence, thereby causing criminal penalties even if only of financial nature, would be disproportionate to the gravity of the infringement in view of the ensuing consequences. A criminal conviction might have consequences for the exercise of a trade or profession by an employed or self-employed person, particularly with regard to access to certain activities or certain offices, which would constitute a further, lasting restriction of freedom of movement. Consequently, the Court ruled that Article 52 of the Treaty did not allow driving without exchanging a licence to be regarded as driving without a licence and hence punishable by imprisonment or a fine.

It should be noted, however, that even where a national measure restricts the exercise of a fundamental Treaty freedom, a test of proportionality will not necessarily be applied in its strictest form. The point is well illustrated by the *Alpine Investments* case,[30] a challenge to a ban imposed by the Netherlands on a company specialising in commodities futures which prohibited it from contacting potential clients by unsolicited telephone calls (cold calling). Alpine Investments contended that a general ban on cold calling was not necessary for the achievement of the objectives of the Dutch authorities: it would be sufficient, for example (as was the case in the UK), to require firms to tape-record telephone calls made by them. The Court considered however that the fact that one Member State imposes less strict rules than another Member State does not mean that the latter's rules are disproportionate and hence incompatible with Community law. The Court may have considered it necessary to leave national authorities some discretion in determining the level of protection for investors; otherwise, Member States would in every case need to align their legislation with that of the Member State which imposed the least onerous requirements.

[29] Case 265/88 *Criminal proceedings against Lothar Messner* [1989] ECR 4209.

[30] Case C–384/93 *Alpine Investments BV* v. *Minister van Financien* [1995] ECR I–1141.

A similar result was reached in *Reisebüro Broede*[31] where the Court held that the Treaty provisions on freedom to provide services do not preclude a national rule which reserves to qualified lawyers the professional recovery of debts by way of judicial proceedings.

A third set of cases illustrates the application of the principle of proportionality where a fundamental interest related to national or international security is at stake. The *Werner* and *Leifer* cases[32] concerned the export to third countries of dual-use goods—goods which could be used for military purposes. In *Leifer* the defendants were charged with delivery to Iraq of plant and chemicals in breach of German licensing requirements. The German authorities considered that the materials might be used for the production of chemical weapons. The German court referred a series of questions which, among other things, put in issue the compatibility with Community law of the German licensing requirements. It expressed doubt whether Germany had the competence, under Community law, to introduce a licensing procedure for trade with third countries and to introduce criminal sanctions in relation thereto.

The Court held that national rules whose effect is to restrict exports of certain products fall within the scope of the common commercial policy. The fact that the restriction concerned dual-use goods did not affect that conclusion. National measures of commercial policy were therefore permissible only if they were specifically authorised by the Community. However, the Court reached the conclusion that, under Article 11 of the Export Regulation, a Member State may, exceptionally, adopt national measures restricting the export of dual-use goods to non-member countries on the ground that this is necessary in order to prevent the risk of a serious disturbance to its foreign relations or to the peaceful coexistence of nations which may affect the public security of a Member State within the meaning of that Article. It may be no cause for surprise that the Court also held *inter alia* that it was for the national court to consider whether there was a threat to public security; and that the principle of proportionality did not preclude the national authorities from requiring the applicant to prove that the goods would be used exclusively for civil purposes, or from refusing to issue a licence if the goods could be used for military purposes.

On the criminal penalties applicable to a breach of the licensing procedure, the Court held:

> It is for the national court to determine whether the criminal penalties applicable comply with the principle of proportionality, taking account of all the elements of each case, such as the nature of the goods capable of endangering the security of the state, the circumstances in which the breach was committed and whether or not the trader who has illegally exported the goods was acting in good or bad faith.[33]

[31] Case C–3/95 *Reisebüro Broede* v. *Gerd Sandker* [1996] ECR I–6511.
[32] C-70/94 *Werner* [1995] ECR I–3189 and C–83/94 *Leifer* [1995] ECR I–3231.
[33] [1995] ECR I–3231, at 3251.

Two cases illustrate the balancing of interests in the context of UN sanctions against Yugoslavia, given effect by Member States pursuant to Community legislation. In *Bosphorus*,[34] Bosphorus Airways, a Turkish company, leased two aircraft owned by the Yugoslav national airline (JAT) under a "dry lease" (that is to say, one without cabin and flight crew). Bosphorus had complete control of the day-to-day management of the aircraft, JAT retaining rights of ownership. The leases were entered into in good faith and were not intended to circumvent the sanctions against the Federal Republic of Yugoslavia decided upon by UN resolutions and implemented in the Community by Regulation 990/93. In application of the sanctions the rent due under the lease was paid into blocked accounts. The aircraft were used by Bosphorus for flights between Turkey and several Member States and Switzerland. While at Dublin airport one of the aircraft was impounded by order of the competent Irish Minister under Article 8 of the Regulation, which provides that "[a]ll . . . aircraft in which a majority or controlling interest is held by a person or undertaking in or operating from the Federal Republic of Yugoslavia (Serbia and Montenegro) shall be impounded by the competent authorities of the Member States". The Irish High Court quashed the decision of the Minister but, on appeal by the Minister, the Supreme Court of Ireland asked the Court whether Article 8 was to be construed as applying to an aircraft owned by a Yugoslav undertaking but leased for a four-year term to a non-Yugoslav undertaking.

The Court held that there was nothing in the wording of the Article to suggest that the Regulation did not apply to an aircraft owned by an undertaking based in the Federal Republic of Yugoslavia but over which it did not have day-to-day operation and control. As to context and aims, the Regulation gave effect to UN Security Council Resolutions. Paragraph 24 of Resolution 820 (1993) provided for impoundment of all aircraft in which "a majority or controlling interest" was held by an undertaking operating in the Federal Republic. The word "interest" could not on any view exclude ownership as a determining criterion for impoundment. Moreover, that word was used in conjunction with the word "majority", which clearly implied the concept of ownership. The impounding of any aircraft owned by a person or undertaking based in or operating from the Federal Republic of Yugoslavia, even if an undertaking such as Bosphorus Airways had taken over its day-to-day operation and control, contributed to restricting the exercise by the Federal Republic and its nationals of their property rights and was thus consistent with the aim of the sanctions, namely to put pressure on that republic.

Bosphorus contended however that the impounding of the aircraft in such circumstances infringed its fundamental rights, in particular its right to peaceful enjoyment of its property and its freedom to pursue a commercial activity. The Court noted that it was settled caselaw that the fundamental rights

[34] Case C–84/95 *Bosphorus* v. *Minister for Transport, Energy and Communications, Ireland and the Attorney General* [1996] ECR I–3953.

invoked by Bosphorus were not absolute and their exercise could be subject to restrictions justified by objectives of general interest pursued by the Community.[35] Any measure imposing sanctions had by definition consequences which affected the right to property and the freedom to pursue a trade or business, thereby causing harm to persons who were in no way responsible for the situation which led to the adoption of the sanctions. Moreover the importance of the aims pursued by the Regulation were such as to justify negative consequences, even of a substantial nature, for some operators. As compared with an objective of general interest so fundamental for the international community, namely putting an end to the state of war in the region and to the massive violations of human rights and humanitarian international law in the Republic of Bosnia-Herzegovina, the impounding of the aircraft, which was owned by an undertaking based in the Federal Republic, could not be regarded as inappropriate or disproportionate.

A similar result was reached in the *Ebony Maritime* case,[36] in relation to the seizure of a tanker by the Italian authorities, under the same Regulation as was in issue in the *Bosphorus* case, Regulation 990/93. Article 1(1)(c) and (d) of the Regulation prohibited: "(c) entry into the territorial sea of the Federal Republic of Yugoslavia (Serbia and Montenegro) by all commercial traffic; (d) any activity the object or effect of which is, directly or indirectly, to promote the transactions mentioned under . . . (c)". Under Article 9 of the Regulation all vessels, freight vehicles, rolling stock, aircraft and cargoes suspected of having violated, or being in violation of the Regulation were to be detained by the competent authorities of the Member States pending investigation. Article 10 of the Regulation left it to each Member State to determine the sanctions to be imposed where the Regulation was infringed. Vessels etc. and cargoes which had violated the Regulation could be forfeited to the Member State whose competent authorities had detained them.

The *Lido II*, a tanker belonging to Loten Navigation and flying the Maltese flag, set sail from the Tunisian port of La Skhira bound for Rijeka (Croatia) with a cargo of petroleum products belonging to Ebony Maritime. After being inspected in the port of Brindisi (Italy) the vessel set sail for the port of Rijeka. When, during its journey, the vessel began to take on water, the master sent out distress signals, indicating that he was changing course towards the coastline of Montenegro with the declared intention of running the vessel aground. However, before the vessel entered Yugoslav territorial waters a helicopter from the NATO/WEU forces landed on its deck, and a Dutch military squad took over the vessel. The vessel was then towed to the port of Brindisi, where it was handed over to the Italian authorities. Those authorities ordered the vessel to be

[35] Case 44/79 *Hauer* v. *Land Rheinland-Pfalz* [1979] ECR 3727; Case 5/88 *Wachauf* v. *Bundesamt für Ernährung und Forstwirtschaft* [1989] ECR 2609 and Case C280/93 *Germany* v. *Council* [1994] ECR I–4973.

[36] Case C–177/95 *Ebony Maritime and Boden Navigation* v. *Prefetto della Provincia di Brindisi and Others* [1997] ECR I–1111.

impounded and the cargo confiscated pursuant to the Italian measures giving effect to the Community Regulation.

The main proceedings before the Consiglio di Stato concerned an appeal against a judgment dismissing an action for annulment brought by Ebony Maritime and Loten Navigation. One of the issues before the Court arose from the applicants' submission that the domestic provision adopted under the second paragraph of Article 10 ran counter to the principle *nulla poena sine culpa* in as much as it provided for confiscation of a cargo without any proof of fault on the part of the owner of the cargo and thus established a system of strict criminal liability. They contended further that it was contrary to the principle of proportionality for the owner of the cargo to be penalised in the same way as the owner of the vessel, regardless of their respective degrees of involvement in the infringement.

The Court noted, first, that while the choice of penalties remained within the discretion of the Member States, they were obliged to ensure that infringements of Community law were penalised under conditions, both procedural and substantive, which were analogous to those applicable to infringements of national law of a similar nature and importance and which made the penalty effective, proportionate and dissuasive. The Court had already accepted that a system of strict criminal liability penalising breach of a regulation was not in itself incompatible with Community law.[37] Accordingly, even if it were assumed that the Italian provisions prescribing confiscation of the cargo introduced a system of strict liability or failed to take into account the degree of involvement of the various traders concerned, it was for the national court to determine whether that penalty complied with the principles laid down in the caselaw and in particular whether it was dissuasive, effective and proportionate. In making that determination the national court was to take account in particular of the fact that the objective pursued by the Regulation, which was to end the state of war in the region concerned and massive violation of human rights and humanitarian international law in the Republic of Bosnia-Herzegovina, was of fundamental general interest for the international community.

Both cases illustrate the importance attached by the Court to the strong public interest at stake when applying the proportionality test to measures designed to deter breach of the sanctions.

All of the cases discussed so far illustrate the nature and intensity of scrutiny by the Court. The fourth type of case is concerned with the scope of the principle and shows that the relationship between the principle of proportionality and the national measures may be complex. How far, for example, does the principle apply to administrative arrangements made by national authorities to give effect to Community legislation on VAT? In *Molenheide*[38] the Court examined the impact of the proportionality principle on the tax authorities' right to retain

[37] Case C–326/88 *Anklagemyndigheden* v. *Hansen* [1990] ECR I–2911.

[38] Joined Cases C–286/94, C–340/95, C–401/95 and C–47/96 *Molenheide and Others* v. *Belgian State*, [1997] ECR I–7281.

refundable VAT where there are serious grounds for presumption of tax evasion or a disputed VAT debt.

Under Article 18(4) of the Sixth VAT Directive, Member States are entitled, where for a given tax period the amount of authorised deductions exceeds the amount of tax due, either to make a refund or to carry the excess forward to the following period according to conditions which they shall determine. Where the excess is insignificant Member States may refuse to refund or permit a carry forward. The Belgian rules gave effect to those provisions but also provided for retention or preventive attachment of the VAT repayable under certain circumstances, in particular where there was a VAT debt claimed by the tax authority disputed by the taxable person or where there were serious grounds for presumption of tax evasion. The national court sought a ruling on the legality of the Belgian provisions.

The Court held that Article 18(4) of the Directive did not in principle preclude measures such as the Belgian ones. The Court noted however that such measures were liable to have an impact on the national authorities' obligation to make an immediate refund of VAT under Article 18(4) of the Directive. Thus, in accordance with the principle of proportionality the Member States were required to employ means which, whilst enabling them effectively to attain the objective pursued by their domestic laws, were the least detrimental to the objectives and the principles laid down by the relevant Community legislation. It was for the national court to apply the principle to the circumstances of the case. However, the Court went on to provide the national court with a number of detailed guidelines. First, the applicants had stated that the retention of VAT was absolute and was effected automatically as soon as there was a dispute between the administrative authorities and the taxable person. The court seised of the matter was not required to consider whether such retention was necessary or whether the matter was urgent, those conditions being irrebuttably presumed to be satisfied. The Court held that, where a preventive attachment procedure constituted a derogation from the ordinary law applicable to preventive attachments, in that necessity and urgency were irrebuttably presumed, doubts could legitimately be entertained as to whether it was an indispensable instrument for ensuring recovery of the sums due. An irrebuttable presumption, as opposed to an ordinary presumption, could go further than was necessary in order to ensure effective recovery and would be contrary to the principle of proportionality, in that it would not enable the taxable person to adduce evidence in rebuttal for consideration by the judge hearing attachment proceedings.

Secondly, the applicants contended that there was a lack of any effective remedy before the judge hearing attachment proceedings and in the proceedings on the substance of the case. A judge could not order the lifting of the retention until such time as evidence contained in the official reports of the tax authority was refuted or the genuineness of the transactions emerged from the particulars obtained through the Community procedures for exchange of information between Member States. The judge was therefore concerned only with the formal propriety of the preventive attachment procedure, not with substantive conditions governing the attachment. For similar reasons, where there was an appeal by the tax authorities against a decision favourable to the taxable person, it was impossible to have the attachment lifted, even partially (for example, in respect of fines), since the decision did not definitively dispose of the substantive issue.

The Court noted that, in considering whether the adverse effect on the right of deduction was proportionate, the availability of effective judicial review was necessary both in the proceedings on the substance of the case and in those before the judge hearing attachment proceedings. Consequently, provisions which would prevent the judge hearing attachment proceedings from lifting in whole or in part the retention of the refundable VAT balance, even though there was evidence before him which would *prima facie* justify the conclusion that the findings of the official reports drawn up by the administrative authority were incorrect, should be regarded as going further than was necessary in order to ensure effective recovery and would adversely affect to a disproportionate extent the right of deduction. Similarly, provisions which would make it impossible for the court adjudicating on the substance of the case to lift in whole or in part the retention of the refundable VAT balance before its decision became definitive would be disproportionate.

Thirdly, the applicants observed that it was impossible for the taxable person to request a court to adopt in place of the retention a different protective measure sufficient to protect the interest of the treasury but less onerous for the taxable person, for example provision of a bond and bank guarantee. This too, if proved, would be disproportionate according to the Court.

Fourthly, the applicants observed that the retention was not limited to the principal sum due but also covered interest, procedural costs and penalties which could amount to as much as 200 per cent of the principal amount. In that regard the Court held that the exercise of effective judicial review, in particular if both the court adjudicating on the substance of the case and the judge hearing attachment proceedings were able to grant a taxable person a total or partial lifting of the retention, would suffice to eliminate any lack of proportionality in calculation of the amounts retained, in particular as far as penalties were concerned.

Fifthly, the applicants claimed that under Belgian law, in the event of release of the retained VAT balances, interest was not payable by the treasury unless the sums retained had not been duly returned by 31 March of the year following that in which the refundable balances came into being and unless the amount refundable was at least BFR 10,000, the last VAT return for the calendar year in which the VAT credit arose was signed at the place on the form indicated for that purpose and all the VAT returns had been filed within the prescribed time-limits. The Court held that it was not necessary, in order to attain the objective pursued by legislation such as that in issue in the main proceedings, namely to ensure recovery of the amounts due, for interest to be calculated from a date other than that on which the retained VAT balance would normally have been paid under the Sixth VAT Directive and that the principle of proportionality therefore precluded the application of such legislation. The same applied to the other conditions mentioned above: in particular, lateness in filing returns could be penalised in a manner unconnected with the retention procedure and without affecting the right to refund of the VAT balance.

It is clear from the ruling that, although administration largely falls outwith the provisions of the Directive, national rules fall to be tested against the proportionality principle in so far as their application undermines the basic principles and objectives of the Directive, in this case the right of deduction. Although leaving the proportionality test to be applied by the national court, the Court by the detailed guidance which it gave nevertheless demonstrated that close scrutiny of the rules was required. What the Court evidently disliked particularly about the Belgian rules was their inflexibility, that is to say, the absence of any possibility for a judge to take a fair decision on the facts. Nor was it prepared to accept the addition of other requirements, in particular filing of all returns within prescribed time-limits, which were not strictly related to the retention in question.

A final issue which arises is whether, in Article 177 proceedings, the principle of proportionality should be applied by the Court or should be left to the national courts to apply (with guidance from the Court on the appropriate criteria). The fiasco of the Sunday trading cases may have given the impression, very understandably, that the issue of proportionality should not be left to the national courts. As is well known, the first ruling of the Court, in *Torfaen*,[39] led to a chaotic situation. Throughout England magistrates' courts and others were invited to pronounce, often with substantial expert evidence, on the proportionality of the Shops Act 1950; some courts concluded that the Act was compatible with Article 30, while others reached the opposite conclusion. However the Sunday trading cases should perhaps not be regarded as symptomatic of the dangers of leaving proportionality to the national courts; perhaps indeed the correct view was that, as indeed Advocate General van Gerven argued in *Torfaen*, Article 30 had no application at all to such measures.

There are cases where it may be wise for the Court to leave the issue to the national courts. In the field of direct taxation, for example, the Court has had to assess the compatibility of national measures with the free movement of persons and with the principle of non-discrimination. The task of assessing the justification for restrictions on non-residents under a Member State's system of direct taxation may raise complex issues which it is not easy for the Court to resolve in Article 177 proceedings, and which may more satisfactorily be left to the national courts to resolve on the basis of guidance from the Court on the relevant principles. Where however the Court is in possession of the necessary facts (and has the necessary technical expertise) it may be preferable for the Court to

[39] Case 145/88 *Torfaen Borough Council* v. *B & Q Plc* [1989] ECR 3851.

make the ultimate assessment itself. Once again, it may be difficult always to draw the dividing line in the right place.

CONCLUSIONS

Some brief concluding remarks may be ventured. First, the application of the principle of proportionality in its more rigorous forms might be criticised on the ground that it goes beyond the judicial function. It might be said that it is the courts' function to adjudicate on the scope of the powers conferred on the public authorities and on the manner of their exercise. That is a role to which courts are well suited. It is also a role wholly consistent with the constitutional principle of the separation of powers. It is not, the critic may say—particularly from the perspective of an English lawyer—the function of the courts to decide whether a particular exercise of power is the most appropriate way of achieving a particular policy goal. Courts are not well suited to evaluating social, economic or political choices. That task is best performed by the executive within limits laid down by the legislature.

It is open to question, however, whether the limits traditionally accepted under English administrative law, itself historically rooted in absolute Parliamentary sovereignty, are appropriate to a Community system which explicitly requires judicial review of legislation, both Community and national, and in which the courts therefore inevitably have a broader, semi-constitutional function. Clearly the principle of proportionality could lead very far, perhaps too far. The question may be however whether the approach illustrated by the cases discussed above does not impose an unreasonable burden, or confer inappropriate powers, on Community and national judges.

Secondly, it has been shown that—as might be expected—proportionality is a flexible tool of judicial review, which is applied differently in different contexts. In that respect it resembles the *Wednesbury* test. But it is unlike *Wednesbury* in application. It is sometimes said that proportionality is not very different from *Wednesbury* unreasonableness. Those who say this, however, often take as examples cases like the *Fedesa* case on hormones of 1990 where the Court allows the Community legislature a broad margin.[40] They may overlook that such a test, more relaxed than the usual test, may be appropriate to a general legislative measure of the Community legislature. They may also overlook the fact that no real comparison with English law standards of review is possible in such a case, because in English law a general legislative measure would not be reviewable at all. The principle must be geared to the nature of the Community measure: so that a general policy measure of the Council warrants less intensive scrutiny and an implementing Commission measure may require more intensive scrutiny.

[40] Case C–331/88 [1990] ECR 4023. R. v. *Minister for Agriculture, Fisheries and Food and The Secretary of State for Health Ex.p. Fedesa and Others*.

Finally it is sometimes said, by way of criticism of the Court's approach, that it applies a double standard: a more tolerant standard when reviewing Community measures, a more demanding standard when reviewing national measures. Is this criticism justified? The cases I have discussed suggest that it may be true, but perhaps for good reasons: the scrutiny of national measures may need to be more demanding where they are likely to impair the effectiveness of Community measures. A similar disparity might be found in a federal system, with more stringent review of State measures than of federal measures. The review of general Community measures does not necessarily call for the application of an equally rigorous test.

It is possible, however, that the situation may change in the future. It is conceivable that the principles of proportionality, and indeed subsidiarity, will be applied more strictly to Community measures also.[41] Once again the principle of proportionality seems sufficiently flexible to permit of such a development.

[41] See the Protocol on the application of the principles of subsidiarity and proportionality, annexed to the EC Treaty by the Treaty of Amsterdam.

Proportionality and the European Convention on Human Rights

JEREMY McBRIDE

INTRODUCTION

The concept of proportionality is not specifically mentioned in the text of the European Convention or in any of its additional Protocols. Nevertheless it has come to be recognised as one of the central principles governing the application of the rights and freedoms contained within these instruments.[1] The significance that this concept has acquired for them does not, however, result from an approach to interpretation on the part of the Strasbourg institutions[2] which is either inappropriate or unwarranted; rather it is has been a justified and essential development for the proper application of the Convention's provisions given the general absence from them of an absolute quality in the guarantee afforded. However, it is perhaps inevitable that the specific application of such a concept will often prove to be controversial. Certainly this might be expected, given that human rights are involved, but it is also partly a consequence of the level at which the exercise of judgment is being made; the supranational character of the European Commission and Court of Human Rights[3] may induce deference and self-restraint in respect of conclusions reached at the national level as to the appropriateness of restrictions on rights and freedoms which may not always be regarded as affording sufficient protection for the latter. In any event, even if such objections to particular rulings are not necessarily justified, there is scope for concern about the way in which the proportionality concept appears to be being applied with less rigour in certain cases. This may simply be a facet of the supranational self-restraint already mentioned, but it may also reflect assumptions about the relative significance of certain rights and interests which might be open to question. Furthermore there might be grounds for wondering whether sometimes more attention could still be given to the capacity of

[1] For an earlier discussion, see M.-A. Eissen, "The Principle of Proportionality in the Case-Law of the European Court of Human rights" in R. St J. Macdonald, F. Matscher and H. Petzold (eds.), *The European System for the Protection of Human Rights* (Dordrecht, Martinus Nijhoff, 1993).

[2] In this respect the principal role has been played by the European Commission and Court of Human Rights, but the Committee of Ministers has at least tacitly endorsed the use of proportionality both in its own decision-making and in the discharge of its responsibility for supervising the implementation of all rulings.

[3] As at 1 Nov. 1998 a new European Court of Human Rights has been established by Protocol 11 to take over the role of both the Commission and Court, as well as the Committee of Ministers' decision-making power.

the Convention institutions to make an informed judgment about the acceptability of some of the interferences to which they are prepared to allow rights and freedoms to be subjected.

THE BASIS FOR APPLYING THE CONCEPT

The rights and freedoms in the Convention can be loosely divided up into three categories: those without any express qualifications (such as the prohibition of torture); those which are subjected to a number of specific limitations (such as the right to liberty and security of the person); and those which are subject to more broadly framed limitation clauses. The last of these include rights such as freedom of expression and the right to private life and, although formulated in a different way, the right to property. This last category can also be regarded as extending to all the rights subject to derogation in terms of emergency and, although there is no express qualification, the prohibition on discrimination, since an element of balancing competing interests is also found in its actual application. It is undoubtedly the need for balancing entailed when giving effect to the rights in this third category which has necessitated resort to the concept of proportionality; without it the formulation of Convention provisions would be open to restrictions depriving the rights and freedoms of all content so long as they were prescribed by law and for a legitimate purpose. Although the first task is always to judge whether a specific activity falls within the scope of the guaranteed right or freedom, the recognition that it can be constrained for certain stated objectives[4] such as public order, national security, public morality or the rights of others so long as this can be demonstrated as being necessary in a democratic society or (in the case of emergencies) the exigencies of the situation inevitably requires a weighing of the relative requirements of the right or freedom and the limiting interest; neither can be regarded as absolute. Indeed the use of terms such as "necessary" and "strictly required" would be pointless without some evaluation of how much of a contribution a particular restriction can make towards securing a given objective.[5]

In determining where the balance lies in particular cases the Strasbourg institutions have taken into account a number of factors. Thus there will be concern as to the overall effect of a particular restriction; does it actually extinguish the right or freedom or does it leave some scope for its exercise? For example in *Jacubowski* v. *Germany*[6] an injunction that restrained a former employee of a news agency from criticising the latter—which had dismissed him for alleged

[4] These may also be implied, as in the test of rationality applied to justifications for discrimination: see *Abdulaziz, Cabales and Balkandali* v. *United Kingdom* (1985) 7 EHRR 741.

[5] Such an approach is also essential once it is accepted that all differential treatment does not fall within the bounds of prohibited discrimination even though no such limitation is expressed in Art. 14 of the Convention.

[6] (1995) 19 EHRR 64.

financial mismanagement—in a circular promoting his new (rival) business was found to be acceptable because this still did not prevent him from voicing his opinions and defending himself by other means; the restriction was thus not a disproportionate means of providing protection for the news agency against the potential damage to its business interests.[7] Similarly there was no objection to restrictions on the political activities of local authority officers where their visibility meant that they were likely to be linked with a particular party line in the eyes of the public and elected councillors since the officers were still free to join a party and engage in some political activities.[8] On the other hand the injunction considered in *Hertel* v. *Switzerland*,[9] which prevented the applicant making certain statements about the dangers of microwave ovens, was found to be unacceptable because it affected the very substance of his views; it effectively prevented him making his contribution to the public debate.[10]

Another significant factor will be whether there was a sufficient basis for believing that a particular interest was in peril. Thus in the *Hertel* case there was no evidence that the sale of microwave ovens had been affected by the applicant's remarks. Similarly in *Vereinigung Demokratischer Soldaten Österreichs and Gubi* v. *Austria*[11] a prohibition on the distribution of a periodical to soldiers was seen as disproportionate where the Court was not convinced that the content of the articles in them was a serious threat to military discipline, notwithstanding that they were critical of military life.[12] Furthermore the dissolution of an association at the time of its formation was too extreme a measure to protect territorial integrity and national security where it had never had an opportunity to pose a threat to those interests and the fears about its intentions were based on mere suspicion.[13] Assessing the appropriateness of a restriction can even lead the Court to make a judgment on the proportionality of the very behaviour which is being restricted. Thus it has considered the appropriateness of remarks made by journalists about the conduct or views of judges and politicians when considering whether they had a sufficient factual basis to fall within the protection extended to the expression of value

[7] See also the view that the situations in which transsexuals had to disclose their pre-operative gender were not so frequent as to impinge on their right to respect for their private lives to a disproportionate extent: *Sheffield and Horsham* v. *United Kingdom*, judgment of the Court, 30 July 1998.

[8] *Ahmed and Others* v. *United Kingdom*, judgment of the Court, 2 Sept. 1998.

[9] Judgment of the Court, 25 Aug. 1998.

[10] On the same basis a limit of £5 on expenditure in connection with an election by someone who was not a candidate was seen as a total barrier to attempts to inform the electorate about the position of candidates on abortion: *Bowman* v. *United Kingdom*, judgment of the Court, 19 Feb. 1998. The fact that the limit could be surmounted by the applicant standing as a candidate herself was irrelevant since being elected to Parliament was not her objective.

[11] (1995) 20 EHRR 56.

[12] The need for the restriction considered in *Bowman* (n. 10 above) was undermined by the absence of comparable controls directed to either the press or on advertising by political parties and their supporters.

[13] *Sidoropoulos and Others* v. *Greece*, judgment of the Court, 10 July 1998.

judgements under Article 10.[14] Closely connected to the issue of whether a genuine concern is involved will be the question whether it can be satisfactorily addressed in some other, less restrictive, way. Thus an order requiring a journalist to disclose his source for a leak about the financial affairs of a company was considered to be unjustified in *Goodwin* v. *United Kingdom*[15] insofar as the objective was to prevent dissemination of confidential information since this legitimate concern was already being secured by an injunction restraining publication of the information that had been disclosed.[16] Similarly the availability of civil remedies as a means of rebuttal meant that in *Lehideux and Isorni* v. *France*[17] the imposition of criminal liability was a disproportionate response to a public defence of the crimes of collaboration.[18] On the other hand the refusal of a film director to cut objectionable sequences from a video meant that the refusal to give the work the certificate needed for distribution was not inappropriate.[19]

There will also be concern about the nature of any burden that is being thrown on a particular individual, particularly where a restriction is being imposed on a property interest in order to secure a wider public interest. Thus in *Hentrich* v. *France*[20] the pre-emption of property under a power to prevent tax evasion on property sales was seen as unjustified where this had been carried out with no evidence of wrongdoing on the part of the applicant and where it was effectively intended to warn others against the temptation to evade taxes. Closely related to this is the nature of the penalty that is imposed where a restriction on a right or freedom is not observed. A small fine or some form of reprimand will not be sufficient to make an otherwise acceptable restriction objectionable[21] but a loss of liberty will require considerable justification,[22] as will penalties of comparable magnitude such as exclusion from the country in

[14] Respectively *De Haes and Gijsels* v. *Belgium*, judgment of the Court, 24 Feb. 1997, and *Oberschlick* v. *Austria* (No 2), judgment of the Court, 1 July 1997; see further J. McBride, "Judges, Politicians and the Limits to Critical Comment" (1998) 23 *ELRev. HR* 76.

[15] Judgment of the Court, 27 Mar. 1996.

[16] The danger that the source might himself disseminate the information other than through the press and the possibility of unmasking a disloyal employee were also acknowledged to be relevant considerations but were still found to be incapable of outweighing the significance of protecting journalistic sources for press freedom; disclosure would impede the performance of the press's public-watchdog role.

[17] Judgment of the Court, 23 Sept. 1998.

[18] It was also significant that the defence related to events more than 40 years ago. Thus more current sensibilities might make criminal liability appropriate: see *Otto-Preminger Institut* v. *Austria* (1995) 19 EHRR 34.

[19] *Wingrove* v. *United Kingdom*, judgment of the Court, 25 Nov. 1996. Special warnings as to content were also considered an impractical alternative.

[20] (1994) 18 EHRR 440 and n. 49.

[21] E.g. *Casado Coca* v. *Spain* (1994) 18 EHRR 1 where a lawyer received a written warning from the Spanish Bar for breaching restrictions on professional advertising.

[22] See *Grigoriades* v. *Greece*, judgment of the Court, 25 Nov. 1997, where three months' imprisonment for insulting the army was regarded as excessive when there was no general dissemination of the remarks involved.

which one's wife and minor children lived.[23] Furthermore close attention will be paid to the width of powers whereby restrictions on rights and freedoms are imposed; objections are likely to be raised where they are not subjected to close supervision and there is, therefore, much scope for possible abuse. Thus in a case such as *Cremieux* v. *France*[24] search powers were condemned where these could be exercised without the need for a judicial warrant and were seen as subject to restrictions appearing too lax and full of loopholes; the police could decide upon the expediency, number, length and scale of searches and seizures and the interference with the applicant's right to respect for his private life could not be regarded as strictly proportionate to the legitimate aim of tackling tax evasion.

The specific context must, of course, always be taken into account. Thus in the conditions of extreme tension in Northern Ireland it was considered acceptable in *Murray* v. *United Kingdom*[25] for all the occupants of a house being searched to be required to assemble in one room, whereas this would undoubtedly be viewed as excessive in the more usual circumstances in which the search of premises is conducted. Equally, however, changes in circumstances may well require a re-evaluation of the acceptability of longstanding restrictions which have previously been viewed as unobjectionable. Thus in *Informationsverein Lentia* v. *Austria*[26] the state monopoly over television broadcasting could no longer be sustained as being the only way of guaranteeing pluralism; technological progress had meant that access to a wide range of broadcasting was now feasible and public interests could be served by regulation rather than exclusive control over transmission.

Although proportionality is an essential component in the application of the more broadly framed provisions of the Convention, it is also a feature of most other provisions as well. Lack of proportionality might, for example, lead a deprivation of liberty to be regarded as arbitrary and, therefore, unacceptable despite being imposed for one of the reasons expressly authorised in Article 5.[27] It is also an element in judging the acceptability both of delays in civil and criminal proceedings, with the complexity of a case being weighed against the time taken to resolve it,[28] and of interferences with an individual's access to a court.[29]

[23] As in *Mehemi* v. *France*, judgment of the Court, 26 Sept. 1997. This was notwithstanding the applicant's involvement in drug trafficking.

[24] (1993) 16 EHRR 357.

[25] (1995) 19 EHRR 193.

[26] (1994) 17 EHRR 93.

[27] Thus the need to detain someone of unsound mind in a particular case might be questioned: see *Winterwerp* v. *The Netherlands*, 2 EHRR 387 (1979). The need for the police actually to arrest someone in a given set of circumstances has not so far been successfully challenged but the absence of any risk of a breach of the peace did lead to the finding that entering a person's home was unwarranted: *McLeod* v. *United Kingdom*, judgment of the Court, 23 Sept. 1998.

[28] E.g. *Di Pede* v. *Italy*, judgment of the Court, 26 Sept. 1996.

[29] Thus in *Stubbings* v. *United Kingdom*, judgment of the Court, 22 Oct. 1996, a six-year limitation period running from a person's 18th birthday was not an excessive way of securing legal certainty and finality, even though sexual abuse during childhood was the subject of the litigation barred. On the other hand the application of an exclusionary rule protecting the police from

Even in the case of the apparently unqualified right, such as the prohibition on torture and inhuman and degrading treatment, regard has been had to the objective behind a strict security regime being pursued and not just its effects on the prisoners concerned.[30] Even the absolute necessity test in the guarantee of the right to life might be regarded as a very strict proportionality standard; the failure to intervene earlier was, for example, weighed against the potential consequences for the population of Gibraltar by not doing so where the attempted arrest of terrorists resulted in their deaths.[31] Moreover proportionality will be a factor in determining the acceptability of claims for costs to be awarded under Article 50.[32]

A VARIABLE APPROACH

Although the Convention has from its earliest days been regarded as articulating a European public order which was not, therefore, subject to the principle of reciprocity which is more generally found in the application of international obligations by States,[33] this does not mean that there is only one acceptable way of implementing its provisions. It is first and foremost for the States parties to decide how to give effect to them within the context of their own legal system. This is not just a matter of the formal means of protecting the Convention rights and freedoms—whether to incorporate or not—but also the precise scope of those rights and freedoms. This is an entirely logical position given that the specific circumstances in one country can differ markedly from those in another. Thus the espousal of communist ideology might be unlikely to have had any impact on public order in the United Kingdom at any moment from its ratification of the Convention in 1951 but the Court was prepared to regard this as a justifiable source of concern in the Federal Republic of Germany at the time of the *Glasenapp* case.[34] Although it considered that the situation had changed in

negligence actions was disproportionate where there had been a failure to inquire into the existence of competing public interest considerations pulling in the opposite direction to the granting of an immunity: *Osman* v. *United Kingdom*, judgment of the Court, 28 Oct. 1998. Similarly a conclusive certificate that the refusal of a contract was necessary for national security could not be invoked to block a claim of religious discrimination where practical arrangements existed to protect security concerns while affording the applicant a substantial degree of procedural justice: *Tinnelly & Sons Ltd. and Others* v. *United Kingdom*, judgment of the Court, 10 July 1998.

[30] Thus segregation or solitary confinement will not necessarily be unacceptable; in *Ensslin, Baader and Raspe* v. *Federal Republic of Germany* 14 DR 64 (1978) terrorist prisoners were not considered to have suffered serious adverse consequences of segregation to prevent armed attacks to secure their release.

[31] *McCann* v. *United Kingdom*, judgment of the Court, 27 Sept. 1995. *Cf.* the view that it was not inappropriate to use automatic weapons in a rescue operation in which the hostage was killed by her rescuers: *Andronicou* v. *Cyprus*, judgment of the Court, 9 Oct. 1997.

[32] Both as regards the work for which payment is being sought and the level of fees being charged: see *Campbell and Fell* v. *United Kingdom* (1985) 7 EHRR 165.

[33] *Austria* v. *Italy*, 4 *YBECHR* 112 (1961). See also A. Drzemczewski, "The Sui Generis Nature of the European Convention on Human Rights" (1980) 29 *ICLQ* 54.

[34] (1987) 9 EHRR 25.

the latter country by the time that the *Vogt* case[35] came before it, the position might still be regarded as dangerous in some of the countries of Central and Eastern Europe that have accepted the Convention system in recent years. Whether this is actually the case is, of course, a matter of debate[36] but due account of the specific circumstances should rightly lead to a variation in outcome even though the same proportionality test is being applied. However, the willingness to recognise differences in circumstances has gone well beyond that with the development of the doctrine of the margin of appreciation, whereby the Strasbourg institutions are prepared to defer to some extent to the judgment taken at the national level as to the appropriateness of imposing particular restrictions on the guaranteed rights and freedoms.[37]

The need for such a doctrine is attributed to the supranational role played by the Strasbourg institutions; there is an assumption that those nearer the decision might be better placed to assess the specific requirements of a situation. Thus the doctrine effectively amounts to a presumption of compatibility with the obligations in the Convention and its potential effect is to weaken the influence of the proportionality test. This is only a possibility since its application is acknowledged to be variable and the presumption is one that can be rebutted.[38] Nevertheless some weakening of the rigour of requiring restrictions on rights and freedoms to be proportional is inevitable since the Court has effectively tipped the scales in favour of the measure imposing them. Of course, the doctrine is also welcomed as a pragmatic response to the scope for conflict between the Court and States parties; the previous Lord Chancellor gave an express warning about the Court encroaching on the United Kingdom's freedom of action.[39] However, it also has the potential effect of increasing the burden of proof for anyone seeking to implead a State before an international tribunal and of limiting the degree of justification which must be forthcoming from the defendant State; it is the applicant who has to demonstrate both that there has been an encroachment on the right and, where the doctrine is invoked, that it is disproportionate. In the circumstances it is not surprising that the doctrine has been criticised as an abdication of responsibility and an abandonment of truly objective standards.[40] It is also questionable whether it is truly required by the supranational character of the exercise; where the limits of the margin of appreciation are reached the Court will still have to make its own judgment of the

35 By which time Germany had been reunited: judgment of the Court, 26 Sept. 1995.

36 E.g. see K. Imholz, "Word Play at Albania's Constitutional Court", 6.4 *EECR* 57 (1997).

37 On the doctrine generally see D.J. Harris, M. O'Boyle and C. Warbrick, *Law of the European Convention on Human Rights* (London, Butterworths, 1995), 12–14, and R. St J. Macdonald, "The Margin of Appreciation" in Macdonald *et al.*, n. 1 above, 83.

38 Judge Matscher thus saw the principle of proportionality as "corrective and restrictive of the margin of appreciation doctrine": "Methods of Interpretation of the Convention", in Macdonald *et al.*, n. 1 above, 63, at 79.

39 See further J. McBride, "Human Rights and The Reformation of Government" (1997) *Hold LR* 74, at 93.

40 See P. van Dijk and G. van Hoof, *The Theory and Practice of the European Convention on Human Rights* (2nd edn., Deventer, Kluwer, 1990), 585–606.

proportionality of the impugned measure. Nevertheless it remains a feature of the Convention scheme and it is doubtful whether the full-time Court created by Protocol 11, entrusted with an unqualified right of access for individuals, will feel emboldened to abandon it.[41] However, the uneven application of the doctrine and the consequences that this has for judging whether a particular restriction is or is not proportionate to the aim pursued is a serious cause for concern.

The variable approach is particularly evident in the assessment of restrictions on freedom of expression. Where speech is acknowledged to have a specifically political context then there has been a very strict approach to the margin of appreciation, whether this be criticism of litigants which might be thought to undermine the role of the judiciary as in *The Sunday Times* case[42] or in criticism of a politician which might have an adverse effect on the latter's reputation as in *Lingens* v. *Austria*.[43] In such cases there is pretty much a direct weighing of the relative merits of freedom of expression and the need for the restriction but, in the approach taken, the impression conveyed is that a very strong justification for the restriction must be forthcoming for it to prevail; the burden of justification here falls very much on the defendant State. On the other hand where the protection of morals is invoked there is a considerable readiness to accept that there is a justification for the belief that morals are being endangered, even if, as in *Handyside* v. *United Kingdom*,[44]the problem was not perceived in jurisdictions outside England, including Scotland and Northern Ireland. An equally indulgent view can be seen in the case of *Müller and Others* v. *Switzerland*[45] where the display of art considered to be obscene not only led to a criminal sanction but to the confiscation of the paintings concerned. The latter was upheld on the basis that this eliminated the opportunity for a repetition of the offence even though it was acknowledged that the unhappiness with the art exhibited was restricted to a specific city in the country.[46]

It might be possible to conclude from such cases that some assumptions are being made about the significance of the provisions concerned; that political speech is more important than other speech; that morals must be accorded whatever protection a State considers appropriate. This undoubtedly has implications for how the proportionality test is being applied but it is also questionable whether it is entirely consistent with the Convention. The pre-eminence of political speech might be sustainable given the commitment in the Convention's

[41] However, the justification for the doctrine may have been enhanced by the transformation of the Convention's supervisory mechanism into a body comprised of full-time, permanent members; the judges will no longer have the same degree of contact with conditions in individual States that part-time members had.

[42] 2 EHRR 245 (1979–80).

[43] (1986) 8 EHRR 407.

[44] 1 EHRR 737 (1979–80).

[45] (1991) 13 EHRR 212.

[46] The impact of the confiscation was also seen as being mitigated by the fact that it was possible to apply to have the order involved either discharged or varied. However, this puts the burden on the person whose freedom is being restricted and entails additional proceedings to the actual decision whose proportionality was being challenged.

preamble to an effective political democracy, notwithstanding the absence of any other indication to this effect in the instrument,[47] but there is less obvious justification for a strengthening of the weight accorded to morals in any judgment as to the proportionality of a restriction. Nor is it a matter of morals being inherently difficult for a supranational court to judge the appropriateness of; the *Müller* case can be contrasted with the decision in *Dudgeon* v. *United Kingdom*[48] where the Court would not accept that an erosion of moral standards and community opposition to the legalisation of homosexual behaviour would warrant an interference with an individual's private life. In the Court's view decriminalisation of certain homosexual acts was not to be equated with approval of them and the fear that this conclusion would be drawn by members of the public was not a sufficient justification for the retention of the offences concerned. These contrasting decisions point to an implicit assumption about the relative strength of the private life guarantee as compared with freedom of expression in the context of the protection of morals.[49] Furthermore, although it is likely that those at the national level will have a better appreciation of the moral imperatives within the country,[50] the situation addressed in the *Dudgeon* case[51] underscores the importance of scrutinising any argument for restricting a guaranteed freedom; the very formulation of the Convention provisions makes it clear that the onus of justifying a restriction is on those who advance it and the consistent application of the proportionality test is central to ensuring that that responsibility is properly discharged.

A relatively inexacting use seems to be being made of the proportionality test when it comes to disputes that arise out of interferences with property interests.

[47] However, this would be a generous construction of the text in that political democracy is cited with "understanding and observance of human rights" as being factors on which justice and peace in the world depend.

[48] (1982) 4 EHRR 149.

[49] The religious sensitivities of others also seem to trump freedom of expression with little concern for whether the price being exacted is too great: see *Otto-Preminger Institut* v. *Austria* (1995) 19 EHRR 34, and *Wingrove* v. *United Kingdom*, judgment of the Court, 25 Nov. 1996, which respectively concerned a film and a video considered by some to be blasphemous. The former decision is particularly remarkable, given that the film could only be seen in a private film club and there was no risk of seeing it under a misapprehension as to its contents. The judgment effectively deferred to outrage as to its very existence and is in marked contrast to the unwillingness to allow homosexual acts in private to be proscribed notwithstanding the apparent objection to their occurrence by the majority population in the countries from which the cases coming before the Court arose. The protection of morals will have a less compelling influence where it is information rather than ideas which is involved; see *Open Door and Dublin Well Women* v. *Ireland* (1993) 15 EHRR 244

[50] It is on this basis that it is argued that it is appropriate for a different approach to be taken when judging disputes cultural as opposed to political rights: see P. Mahoney, "Universality versus Subsidiarity in Free Speech Cases" [1997] *EHRLR* 364. However, this relies upon a stronger value for political speech which may be being accorded to it by the Court but which is not necessarily the objective behind the Convention. Nevertheless this analysis—formulated in a personal capacity by the Court's Deputy Registrar—provides a cogent rationale for its approach but it would be preferable if this were developed in a more express fashion in the judgments themselves. See also Lord Lester, "Universality versus Subsidiarity: A Reply" [1998] *EHRLR* 73.

[51] Subsequently endorsed in the face of comparable opposition in other countries in *Norris* v. *Ireland* (1991) 13 EHRR 186 and *Modinos* v. *Cyprus* (1993) 16 EHRR 485.

Thus in *Lithgow* v. *United Kingdom*[52] the Court failed to subject the approach to compensation for nationalisation to close scrutiny, declining in particular to consider whether there were any circumstances that might have had a bearing on the fairness of the approach adopted with respect to compensation. Of course, concern about this might have been assuaged by the previous openness of the government to receive representations from the entities being nationalised; the existence of this possibility might seem to bring the case within the category of those where the availability of procedural safeguards was sufficient to keep restrictions on the right side of the proportionality boundary. However, it could be contended that in reality these representations were ignored and that they were not, therefore, a sufficient safeguard to make the compensation arrangements acceptable. A similarly limited scrutiny by the Court might be discerned in a series of cases where challenges to controls over the ability of landlords to evict tenants were unsuccessful. Thus in *Spadea and Scalabrino* v. *Italy*[53] a freeze had been imposed on the enforcement of eviction orders and this was found to be justifiable because it had the aim of protecting the interests of tenants on low incomes and avoiding public disorder at a time when there was a housing shortage. In the Court's view this was seen as an emergency measure but, although that might be convincing in principle, this sort of measure had been in operation for over 40 years and there was no consideration of whether Italy had taken any other measures to redress the housing shortage; the impression given by the case was that it was leaving individual landlords to bear the whole burden of addressing the crisis.[54] The lack of proportionality might be thought to have been mitigated by the fact that rent was still recoverable, but this is not compelling given that the effect of the measures freezing rent levels was not really addressed by the Court. Similarly the acceptability of seizing all goods on a tax debtor's property regardless of ownership was seen as acceptable in *Gasus Dosier- und Fördertechnik GmbH* v. *The Netherlands*.[55] The Court discerned a safeguard for the applicant in the apparent ability to take out insurance against such an eventuality even though the person providing machinery for use by a tax debtor could not actually know the state of the latter's liability. Article 1 of Protocol 1, which allows deprivation of property by reference to public interest and control over its use in accordance with the general interest or to secure the payment of taxes, does not make any explicit reference in its text to such restrictions being necessary in a democratic society. The difference in formulation could thus be taken, contrary to the position which was suggested to be applicable to freedom of expression, to support the conclusion that the proportionality test ought to be applied in a less rigorous fashion since States were meant to be accorded a wide margin of appreciation. However, substan-

[52] (1986) 8 EHRR 329.

[53] Judgment of the Court, 28 Sept. 1995.

[54] See also *Scollo* v. *Italy*, judgment of the Court, 28 Sept. 1995, and *Velosa Barreto* v. *Portugal*, judgment of the Court, 21 Nov. 1995.

[55] 23 Feb. 1995.

tial interferences with property interests might be more readily regarded as acceptable if the Court tested with greater rigour the basis for the particular exercise of the wide discretions which it is prepared to conclude Article 1 has accorded to States.

EVIDENCE

The margin of appreciation doctrine affects the approach taken to the weighing of the evidence that is before the Court when it is applying the proportionality test but there might be grounds for concern that the information available for this purpose is incomplete[56] in some cases and that insufficient steps are being taken to remedy this deficiency. This might be thought to be less true when it comes to the specific circumstances of the case but even this can be an area in which the width of the margin of appreciation has an effect. Thus in the *Handyside*[57] case the Court's willingness to conclude that morals could be endangered by the book being seized and destroyed was not based on any hard evidence that it would have had any effect on the readers; the possibility of this occurring seems to be no more than a prejudice and one which the Court was prepared to share without testing.[58] This might be contrasted with discrimination cases where the margin of appreciation is much stricter; thus in *Karlheinz Schmidt* v. *Germany*,[59] where only men were required to serve in the municipal fire brigade or pay a tax in lieu of doing so, the Court did actually consider whether there was a sufficient pool of genuine volunteers available in the municipality so that the fact that there was could be taken to demonstrate that in reality the requirement amounted to no more than the imposition of a tax on men alone.

However, the issue of evidence goes beyond the specific circumstances of the case; the assessment of proportionality is in principle to be made by reference to a European conception of human rights.[60] This is particularly significant in the context of the democratic society yardstick; there is a need for the Court to consider whether the sort of limitation being imposed in the case before it is also being employed elsewhere. This is not because there must be uniformity of approach—the recognition of diversity has already been justified—but because the absence of such a restriction might be a counter-indication of the possibility of the public interest surviving, indeed flourishing, without such a limitation (or one of a lesser extent) being imposed even after appropriate allowance has been made for the different circumstances obtaining in the other jurisdictions. This evidence may be invoked by some applicants but it is a task that might be beyond the resources of all of them to marshall. Awareness of such evidence

[56] As opposed to there being a reluctance to probe its substance where a wide margin of appreciation is being granted to the respondent State.

[57] N. 44 above.

[58] This is not to suggest that the prejudice might not prove to be unfounded but that its validity ought to be tested.

[59] Judgment of the Court, 18 July 1994.

[60] See n. 33 above.

might also be seen as one of the benefits of a Court comprising judges from most national jurisdictions within the Council of Europe. However, this is unlikely in practice, given that a Chamber of seven comprises less than a quarter and a Grand Chamber of seventeen well under half. Even though the Chamber may represent a range of legal traditions and the Grand Chamber much more so, reliance on the judge's own knowledge about the approach taken in his or her jurisdiction may be insufficient.[61] Certainly if one looks at a case such as *Spadea and Scalabrino*,[62] the Court seemed to acknowledge the existence of housing shortages as a universal problem of modern society but there was no indication in the judgment of any sense of whether the Italian approach was the only practical solution to it, was one of several approaches or was entirely unique. The last of these possibilities would not necessarily lead to the conclusion that the restriction was disproportionate but it might prompt a closer scrutiny of the need for it. This might be contrasted with the consideration of national approaches in a case such as *Stubbings* v. *United Kingdom*,[63] where a limitation on bringing an action for sexual abuse six years after reaching adulthood was not seen as unduly restrictive given the existence of shorter periods in other jurisdictions.

The Court can be assisted in this task by its ability to receive third party interventions such as were considered in the case of *Lingens* v. *Austria*[64] where the International Press Institute provided it with a detailed analytical survey of the law and practice of ten European States and that of the United States on the issue of the extent to which the protection afforded to public figures differed from that afforded to other individuals under the law of defamation, as well as on how far a distinction was drawn there between the expression of fact and the expression of opinion. It is unlikely that such an intervention would do much more than reinforce a general attitude about the acceptability of a particular restriction but it could still substantiate scepticism and prompt closer scrutiny. It must be acknowledged, however, that such interventions will be less influential where the margin of appreciation being applied by the Court is wider, such as where a film was banned in order to uphold the religious sensibilities of the majority as in *Otto-Preminger Institut* v. *Austria*.[65] Nevertheless the submission of such interventions ought to be a feature of cases to be encouraged and the promotion of the possibility of making them from a simple rule of court to an Article of the Convention as revised by Protocol 11 is to be welcomed since, even though it is likely to remain an *ad hoc* activity, groups concerned about sustaining a European standard have a clearer basis for asserting it.[66]

[61] See further n. 41 above. A Judge may also be a national of a country other than the one nominating him or her.

[62] N. 53 above.

[63] N. 29 above. See also the importance attached to the absence of a common standard for parental leave when concluding that there was no violation of Art. 14 in *Petrovic* v. *Austria*, judgment of the Court, 27 Mar. 1998.

[64] N. 43 above.

[65] N. 49 above.

[66] This has been introduced by the new Art. 36.

CONCLUSION

The difficulty with criticising the application of a proportionality test is that one is inevitably disputing the merits of a particular restriction and disagreement with the European Court's approach can be regarded as no more than dissatisfaction with a particular outcome. Nevertheless the danger that faces the Court, particularly if it allows the margin of appreciation to weaken the test of proportionality without at least articulating more fully the rationale for the differential approaches pursued, is that its own rulings might be seen less as principled evaluations and more as its own arbitrary preference for the balance to be achieved between different rights and interests. Such a perception, regardless of whether it is justified, could have an adverse effect on the legitimacy of the Court's position in the longer term.[67] However, despite such reservations, the willingness of the Court to apply the proportionality test must also be understood as being a key element in the protection of human rights which is being afforded by the European Convention mechanism.

[67] As to which, see further J. McBride, n. 39 above.

The Effect of Proportionality on the Actions of Member States of the European Community: National Viewpoints from Continental Europe

WALTER VAN GERVEN

I have been asked to discuss, not the law of the EC, but instead the national laws of France, Germany, Belgium and the Netherlands.[1] Moreover I shall look at the law of the Member States from a national perspective and not from the perspective of the ECJ. I will nevertheless start with an overview of the meaning of proportionality, first in EC law, and then in the law of the ECHR, in order to clarify the background against which the national legal systems dealt with here, must be seen.

PROPORTIONALITY UNDER EC AND ECHR LAWS

The Meaning of Proportionality in EC Law

The case law of the ECJ acknowledges the existence of the proportionality principle but does not always attach the same meaning to it. Indeed, the Court sometimes distinguishes *three* elements in it (suitability and necessity of the measure under review and absence of disproportionate character), whereas in many other instances it refers only to *two* elements, without making it clear which of the three aforementioned elements it refers to.[2]

An illustration of the two-pronged approach is to be found in *Fromançais*[3] relating to the incompatibility with the principle of proportionality of a provision in a regulation which totally excluded the release of security if butter for which the security was paid was processed after the expiry of the period prescribed therefor. The Court held:

[1] For references to legal systems of other EU Member States, see J. Schwarze, *European Administrative Law* (London, Sweet & Maxwell, 1992), at 692–5 and 698–702.

[2] For a tentative description of those three elements, see point 27 of my Opinion in Case C–159/90 *Society for the Protection of Unborn Children Ireland Ltd* v. *Grogan* [1991] ECR I–4685. See also below for German law.

[3] Case 66/82 *Fromançais* v. *FORMA* [1983] ECR 395.

In order to establish whether a provision of Community law is consonant with the principle of proportionality it is necessary to establish, in the first place, whether the means it employs to achieve the aim correspond to the importance of the aim and, in the second place, whether they are necessary for its achievement.[4]

The Court held that withholding the security in full was a measure which was "proportionate to the aims of the regulations concerned". The expression in the quotation "correspond to the importance of the aim" may relate as well to the first element (suitability) as to the third element (disproportionate character).

An illustration of the three-pronged approach is found in *Fedesa*[5] where the Court was asked to examine the validity of a Community directive imposing an outright prohibition on the administration of certain hormone substances to animals. The Court stated in its judgment:

The principle of proportionality . . . requires that the prohibitory measures are appropriate and necessary in order to attain the objectives legitimately pursued by the legislation in question; when there is a choice between several appropriate measures recourse must be had to the least onerous, and the disadvantages caused must not be disproportionate to the aims pursued.[6]

It is worthwhile analysing the reasoning of the Court somewhat further. In view of the question, under the proportionality test, whether the outright prohibition of hormones was *appropriate* (or suitable) to achieve the aim of the directive (which was to enact a regulation assuring consumers similar supply conditions and a better product) it was argued before the Court that an outright prohibition was "impossible to apply in practice" and led "to the creation of a dangerous black market".[7] As to whether the prohibition was *necessary*, it was argued that it was not "because consumer anxieties can be allayed simply by the dissemination of information and advice".[8] Finally, as to whether the measure was proportional *sensu stricto*, it was said that "the prohibition in question entails excessive disadvantages, in particular considerable financial losses on the part of the traders concerned, in relation to the alleged benefits accruing to the general interest".[9]

As can be seen from the quotation, the Court followed the applicant's argument in distinguishing three elements in the principle of proportionality—

[4] Case 66/82 *Fromançais* v. *FORMA* [1983] ECR 395, at para. 8. See also Case C–233/94 *Germany* v. *European Parliament and Council of the European Union* [1997] ECR I–2405, para. 54 for a recent judgment relating to the validity of a Community directive. That judgment is important because it emphasises that in matters of economic complexity the ECJ must substitute its appreciation for that of the Community legislature only if the Community legislature's normative choice "appeared manifestly incorrect or if the resultant disadvantages for certain economic operators were wholly disproportionate to the advantages otherwise offered" (para. 56).

[5] Case C–331/88 [1990] ECR 4023. As regards the consistency of a *national* measure with Community law, see also Case 302/86 *Commission* v. *Denmark* [1989] ECR 4607, para. 20–21, and Slynn AG's Opinion at 4625–6.

[6] *Ibid.*, at para. 13.

[7] *Ibid.*, at para. 12.

[8] *Ibid.*

[9] *Ibid.*

without however properly defining each of these elements. Having done that, it did not find an infringement of the principle. It held, on the contrary, that the Council had made no manifest error and that the prohibition, even though it might have caused some financial loss to certain traders, could not be regarded as manifestly inappropriate. The Court came to that conclusion taking account of the discretionary power which the Community legislature has in matters concerning the common agricultural policy.

Hauer[10] remains a seminal judgment concerning the application of proportionality in the area of fundamental rights. The question submitted to the Court related to the compatibility of a Community regulation temporarily prohibiting the new planting of vines with the Community rules (as laid down in the Court's case law) concerning the protection of fundamental rights. In this regard, the ECJ said, a possible infringement of the right to property and a possible limitation upon the freedom to pursue a trade or profession were to be considered.[11]

After having analysed carefully the aims of the regulation (to limit overproduction on the wine market in anticipation of a new structural policy) and having found that a temporary prohibition on the planting of new vines was intended to put a brake on the continued increase in surpluses, the Court held that the restriction under review was "justified by the objectives of general interest pursued by the Community" and did not "infringe the substance of the right to property in the form in which it is recognized and protected in the Community legal order".[12] The Court declared the same reasoning to be valid also for the ancillary limitation on the freedom to pursue a trade or profession.[13]

It would seem that the Court, in holding that the measure did not affect the substance of the basic right and freedom, passed over the first and second element of proportionality (assuming implicitly that the measure was appropriate and necessary to achieve the aim to limit overproduction) and considered directly the third element of proportionality *sensu stricto*, that is whether the measure was disproportionately limiting the applicant's basic rights. It gave a negative answer to that question as the measure did not affect the substance of those rights.[14]

All of the foregoing judgments dealt with challenges to Community action. In other words they were concerned with the legality of provisions in regulations or directives. Since many regulations or directives emanate from the Council, or in more recent times from the European Parliament acting jointly with the Council, it is clear that not only the legality of "administrative" acts emanating

[10] Case 44/79 *Hauer* v. *Rheinland-Pfalz* [1979] ECR 3727.

[11] *Ibid.*, at para. 16.

[12] *Ibid.*, at para. 30.

[13] For a recent judgment, see Cases C–248/95 and C–249/95 *SAM Schiffart GmbH and Heinz Stapf* v. *Germany* [1997] ECR I–4475 where, with regard to the same basic right and freedom, a somewhat extended formula is used declaring impermissible "a disproportionate and intolerable interference, impairing the very substance of the rights guaranteed" (at para. 72).

[14] Thus also K. Lenaerts and P. van Ypersele, "Le principe de subsidiarité et son contexte: étude de l'article 3B du Traité CE" [1994] *Cah. dr. eur.* 3, at 59–60.

from the Commission, but also of "legislative" acts proper, is at stake. However, as discussed in the earlier chapter by Advocate General Francis Jacobs, the principle of proportionality is also used in the ECJ case law to examine the compatibility of Member State action with Community law, again regardless of whether such state action emanates from the national administration or the legislator proper.

A first illustration of such a challenge to Member State action is *Messner*[15] relating to a criminal prosecution brought in Italy against a German national who was accused of not having made, within three days of entering Italian territory, the declaration of residence prescribed by Italian legislation. Breach of that obligation was punishable by imprisonment of up to three months or a fine of up to 400,000 lire. Doubts had been expressed whether that legislation was compatible with the Community law provisions on the free movement of persons. A preliminary question was submitted to the ECJ which answered in the negative. After having found that the time-limit of three days "cannot be regarded as reasonable" because it is "excessively restrictive" and since the imposition of such a short time-limit does not appear "to be absolutely necessary",[16] the Court held:

> With regard to the penalties laid down for infringement of the legislation at issue . . . whilst national authorities are entitled to make the failure to comply with said provisions subject to penalties comparable to those attaching to minor offences committed by their own nationals, they are not justified in imposing a penalty so disproportionate to the gravity of the infringement that it becomes an obstacle to the free movement of workers.[17]

It would seem that the Court was here applying two elements of proportionality. "Excessively restrictive" and "not absolutely necessary" can be understood to refer to the element of necessity whereas "so disproportionate . . . that it becomes an obstacle to the free movement of workers" seems to contain a reference to proportionality *sensu stricto*.

An example of a case where national legislation was challenged as incompatible with the Community law provisions on free movement of goods is the Court's judgment in *Stoke-on-Trent*.[18] Confronted with the question submitted by the House of Lords as to whether the Court's previous Sunday trading judgments had to be understood in the sense that Article 30 EEC is not applicable to the English Sunday trading legislation, the Court answered in the affirmative provided that the national legislation complies with the principle of proportionality. Applying that principle of its own initiative, the ECJ held:

[15] Case C–265/88 *Criminal Proceedings against Messner* [1989] ECR 4209.
[16] *Ibid.*, at paras. 12, 10 and 11.
[17] *Ibid.*, at para. 14, referring to the Court's earlier judgment in Case 157/79 *R.* v. *Pieck* [1980] ECR 2171.
[18] Case C–169/91 *Council of the City of Stoke on Trent and Norwich City Council* v. *B&Q plc* [1992] ECR I–6635.

> Appraising the proportionality of national rules which pursue a legitimate aim under Community law involves weighing the national interest in attaining that aim against the Community interest in ensuring the free movement of goods. In that regard, in order to verify that the restrictive effects on intra-Community trade of the rules at issue do not exceed what is necessary to achieve the aim in view, it must be considered whether those effects are direct, indirect or purely speculative and whether those effects do not impede the marketing of imported products more than the marketing of national products.[19]

Interestingly enough, although the national legislation concerned was still regarded here from an angle of limiting the freedoms which individuals derive from Community law, the real issue at stake was about weighing the Community's interest in free movement of goods against the Member State's interest in enacting legislative rules pursuing (legitimate) general interests of its own. Proportionality was used therefore as a factor to determine the allocation of powers between the Community and the national legal orders. In making that assessment none of the three aforementioned elements of proportionality was clearly visible. What was considered was whether the restrictive effects of the Member State's action on intra-Community trade exceeded what was necessary to achieve the Member State's regulatory aim. If there is a certain resemblance here with one of the elements of proportionality, then it is with the third element (proportionality *sensu stricto*), in that the Member State must refrain from action, or replace it by alternative action, if the effects on intra-Community trade are more than purely speculative or are discriminatory of imported products.

Another recent, and striking, example is the judgment of 26 June 1997 in *Familiapress*[20] which relates again to national legislation being examined for its consistency with the Community law provisions on free movement of goods. In that case Austrian legislation prohibited the sale on its territory of periodicals containing games or competitions for prizes, thereby impairing access of periodicals from other Member States (where such prohibition did not exist) to the Austrian market. The ECJ (declining to apply its *Keck* case law[21]) found that the legislation fell under the prohibition of Article 30 but that an overriding requirement justifying a restriction on free movement of goods, consisting in the necessity to maintain press diversity, could be relied on.[22] In that connection the Court applied the proportionality principle according to which "the provisions of national law in question must be proportionate to the objective pursued and

[19] *Ibid.*, at para. 15.

[20] Case C–368/95 *Vereinigte Familiapress Zeitungsverlags- und vertriebs GmbH* v. *Heinrich Bauer Verlag* [1997] ECR I–3689.

[21] Cases C–267/91 and C–268/91 *Criminal proceedings against Bernard Keck and Daniel Mithouard* [1993] ECR I–6097; see paras. 11 and 12 of *Familiapress*.

[22] *Familiapress* [1997] ECR I–3689, at para. 18. In the absence of the national prohibition, small publishers, it was alleged by the Austrian government, might not be able to resist cut-throat competition from foreign periodicals: *ibid.*, at para. 14.

that objective must not be capable of being achieved by measures which are less restrictive of intra-Community trade".[23]

In order to apply that principle—which the Court said was a matter for the national court—the ECJ emphasised first that the overriding requirement of maintaining press diversity must be balanced in the present instance not only against the exercise of free movement of goods but also against the exercise of the freedom of expression, as enshrined in Article 10 of the ECHR. The Court then enumerated a number of factors to be taken into account by the national court to determine "whether [the] national prohibition is proportionate to the aim of maintaining press diversity and whether this objective might not be attained by measures less restrictive of both intra-Community trade and freedom of expression".[24] Those factors related to the position of the periodicals concerned in the Austrian market, and to the chance that the prospect of winning would bring about a shift in demand—which factors the national court must determine "on the basis of a study of the Austrian press market"[25]; in other words, it would "have to define the market for the product in question and to have regard to the market shares of individual publishers or press groups and the trend thereof".[26] Other factors to be taken into account were the circumstances which might influence the consumer's decision to buy, including "the likelihood of winning, the value of the prize or the extent to which winning depends on a test calling for a measure of ingenuity, skill or knowledge",[27] and whether less restrictive measures, such as blacking out or removing the page on which the prize competition appeared in copies intended for Austria, were made impossible by the national prohibition, in which case that prohibition "would be disproportionate".[28]

Although defining proportionality in a seemingly simple way,[29] the judgment imposes on the national courts a far-reaching balancing test, in that not only means employed to achieve a (legitimate) objective of national law are to be weighed but also the national aim so pursued against the Community law objective of free movement of goods and the freedom of expression, as enshrined in Article 10 of the ECHR. To the extent that such a complex balancing test is not wholly beyond the possibilities of a court of law, it will at least compel the court to carry out its investigation in a distant way.

[23] *Familiapress* [1997] ECR I–3689, at para. 19.
[24] *Ibid.*, at para. 27.
[25] *Ibid.*, at para. 29.
[26] *Ibid.*, at para. 30.
[27] *Ibid.*, at para. 31.
[28] *Ibid.*, at para. 33.
[29] See para. 19 of the judgment as quoted above in the text. See also, again in connection with the consistency of a national measure with Community law, the ECJ's judgment in Joined Cases C–286/94, C–340/95, C–401/95 and C–47/96 *Garage Molenheide BVBA and Others* v. *Belgium* [1997] ECR I–7281, at para. 46, where a similar (though not identical) definition is applied.

The Meaning of Proportionality for the Purposes of the ECHR

In the case law of the ECHR the proportionality principle is primarily used in applying the exceptions which the Convention allows in respect of the basic rights protected by it.[30] Those rights may indeed only be subject to such limitations "as are prescribed by law and are necessary in a democratic society in the interests of public safety, for the protection of public order, health or morals, or for the protection of the rights or freedoms of others" (as in Article 9 relating to the freedom of thought, conscience and religion, and in Article 11 relating to the freedom of assembly and association).

An example of how proportionality is applied is the judgment of the European Court of Human Rights in *Open Door*[31] relating to measures, taken on the basis of Article 40.3.3° of the Irish Constitution, declaring the dissemination of information concerning the identity and location of abortion clinics in the UK to be unlawful. Those measures were of the same type (injunctions to cease dissemination) as the measures on which the ECJ was requested to give a preliminary ruling in the *Grogan* case,[32] there from the viewpoint of their compatibility with Article 59 EC on free movement of services.[33] The European Court of Human Rights, having noted the Irish Government's acceptance that the injunction interfered with the applicants' freedom to impart information as guaranteed by Article 10(1) of the ECHR,[34] went on to examine whether the injunction fell under the exceptions contained in Article 10(2). In so doing, it had to establish *inter alia* whether the restriction which it accepted pursued "the legitimate aim of the protection of morals" (thus side-stepping the Irish government's argument that it pursued the protection of the "rights of others" including the unborn[35]) and was necessary in a democratic society. In that context the Court, as usual, applied the proportionality principle according to which it "must determine whether there existed a pressing social need for the measures in question and, in particular, whether the restriction complained of was proportionate to the legitimate aim pursued . . .".[36] Being struck by the "sweeping

[30] See J. McBride, "Proportionality and the European Convention on Human Rights", this vol. See Arts. 8, 9, 10 and 11 of the Convention. The principle is also applied in respect of the non-discrimination provision contained in Art. 14.

[31] *Open Door Counselling Ltd & Dublin Well Woman Centre* v. *Ireland* (1993) 15 EHRR (1) 244. For an excellent comment, see the notes, under excerpts from the judgment, in R.A. Lawson and H.G. Schermers, *Leading Cases of the European Court of Human Rights* (Nijmegen, Ars Aequi Libri, 1997), at 478 ff., particularly nn. 23–28.

[32] Case C–159/90 *SPUC* v. *Grogan* [1991] ECR I–4685.

[33] The ECJ avoided the issue in *Grogan* by holding that the relation with Art. 59 was too tenuous: see para. 24. The AG (as I then was) examined the issue of proportionality of the national measures, both under EC and ECHR law, at [1991] ECR I–4703, paras. 27–29 and 35–38.

[34] Judgment of 29 Oct. 1992, Publications ECHR, Series A vol. 246–A, at para. 55.

[35] *Ibid.*, at para. 63.

[36] *Ibid.*, at para. 73.

nature of the restriction", the Court (also relying on other factors) found the restriction to be "disproportionate to the aims pursued".[37]

Again, this is not the place to pursue this analysis further. Suffice it to emphasise the resemblance of the case law of both supra-national courts when the test of proportionality is applied to assess the scope of application of basic rights (as under the ECHR) and or fundamental freedoms (as under the EC Treaty) in relation to restrictions imposed thereon by national legislation. Under the ECHR the test operates to find out whether the imposition on the basic right is necessary in a democratic society, and therefore corresponds to a (legitimate) pressing social need for the national measures in question. Under EC law the test operates to establish whether the restriction on the fundamental right of freedom corresponds to the importance of the (legitimate) national aim pursued, and if it is necessary for the achievement of that aim.[38]

PROPORTIONALITY IN GERMAN PUBLIC LAW AS COMPARED TO "PROPORTIONALITY" IN FRENCH PUBLIC LAW[39]

In German law the "requirement of proportionality is not confined only to administrative measures. . . . Proportionality has acquired constitutional status and applies to legislative measures as well. When a statute is enacted in breach of the principle of proportionality, then the statute in question is unconstitutional and therefore invalid" (unless the statute in question is equal to, or higher than, the principle of proportionality[40]). Proportionality is an unwritten constitutional principle which plays an important role in the case law of the German constitutional Court.[41] It is based on the "*Rechtsstaatsprinzip*" according to which a citizen is entitled to a fundamental right or freedom against the State and is considered to pertain to the essence of the fundamental rights themselves in that the principle restricts the limitations imposed upon such rights.[42]

The "three-pronged" approach referred to above finds its origin in German law. It is well established now, and well documented in the Constitutional Court's case law,[43] that the principle contains three elements: suitability, necessity and proportionality *sensu stricto*, according to which the state measure con-

[37] Judgment of 29 Oct. 1992, Publications ECHR, Series A vol. 246–A, at para. 80.

[38] See E. Ellis and T. Tridimas, *Public Law of the European Community: Text, Materials and Commentary* (London, Sweet & Maxwell, 1995), at 549. See also on proportionality in general P. Craig and G. de Búrca, *EC Law* (2nd edn., Oxford, Clarendon Press, 1998), at 349–57, and G. de Búrca, "The Principle of Proportionality and its application in EC Law" (1993) 13 *YEL* 105.

[39] I have been able to draw on a wealth of information from two recent books: N. Emiliou, *The Principle of Proportionality in European Law: A Comparative Study* (London, Kluwer Law International, 1996) and A. de Moor-van Vugt, *Maten en Gewichten. Het evenredigheidsbeginsel in Europees perspectief* (Zwolle, W.E.J. Tjeenk Willink, 1995).

[40] Emiliou, n. 39 above, at 24.

[41] *Ibid.*

[42] De Moor-van Vugt, n. 39 above, at 20.

[43] See the thorough overview in Emiliou, n. 39 above, at 26–37.

cerned must be suitable for the purpose of facilitating or achieving the pursued objective; it must also be necessary in that no other instrument may be at the authority's disposal which is less restrictive of freedom, and it may not be disproportionate to the restrictions which it involves.[44] In the words of the Constitutional Court:

> The intervention must be suitable and necessary for the achievement of its objective. It may not impose excessive burdens on the individual concerned, and must consequently be reasonable in its effect on him.[45]

This "three-pronged" approach applies to both the enactment of laws and the application of the law by the administration, assuming that the administration has been granted a certain amount of discretion.[46] By virtue of the proportionality principle the latter can be so reduced in scope that only a particular decision will remain legitimate.[47]

It should be noted that the last two elements of proportionality (necessity and proportionality *sensu stricto*) involve the weighing of instruments as well as aims pusued thereby in that two or more measures or instruments which are suitable to pursue a given aim, and the interest it seeks to protect, are first weighed against each other in light of another interest protected, and therefore aimed at, by another rule or measure (for example, a constitutionally protected right), whereupon the mean or instrument retained is then examined on its own to see whether it does not impose an excessive burden on that other interest.[48] The terms of reference to carry out such balancing cannot be found, however, in the principle of proportionality itself, but must be found in the objective order of values laid down in the Basic Law and implementing legislation,[49] for indeed:

> the framers [of the *Grundgesetz*] are said to have arranged these values in a hierarchical order, the most important being a "free democratic basic order", coupled with the principle of "human dignity". These values include certain fundamental principles of government and the basic human rights.[50]

Weighing interests or objects protected by law ("*Rechtsgüter*") occurs not only in the framework of proportionality *sensu stricto*. There are many other doctrines in German law which involve such balancing, such as the "*Prinzip der praktischen Konkordanz*": in the case of conflicting constitutionally protected *Rechtsgüter*, a practical balance must be sought between them, so that both

44 J. Schwarze, n. 1 above, at 687.

45 BVerfGE 63, at 144. Cited by Schwarze, n. 1 above, at 687.

46 Thus, e.g., in respect of immigration authorities exercising their discretion to expel a foreigner on the ground of a criminal conviction: "the harm associated with the expulsion must not be disproportionate to the desired end" 60 BVerwGE 75, cited in English version by Emiliou, n. 39 above, at 35.

47 Schwarze, n. 1 above, at 689–90, who also refers to case law of the Constitutional Court stating that the proportionality principle must be observed in court decisions concerning conflicting provisions of private law: BVerfGE 35, 202.

48 De Moor-van Vugt, n. 39 above, at 27–8.

49 Also Emiliou, n. 39 above, at 33.

50 *Ibid.*

values are ensured as much as possible and that no more limits are imposed on either of them than is needed to reconcile both.[51]

Proportionality plays an important role in German law in the area of basic rights where legislative action is reviewed by the Federal Constitutional Court (BVerfG) and in the area of administrative discretion, at the initiative mainly of the Federal Administrative Court (BVerwG). In the first area the Constitutional Court holds that, whenever the legislator has been formally empowered, in view of protecting other *Rechtsgüter*, to pass laws restraining a constitutional freedom, such as personal liberty, the legislator's power is limited by the principle of proportionality. The Court has held, for example, that, although section 112, paragraph 4, of the Code of Criminal Procedure empowers the courts to issue warrants, the facts of the specific case were such as to allow the purpose of bringing a suspect to trial to be secured by other less restrictive means.[52] The use of proportionality in this respect has been the object of criticism, however, in that the principle was seen to be stretched beyond acceptable limits.[53] An example is provided by a case in which the Court held by a majority of five to three that the prosecution, under the West German Criminal Code, of East German spies who had committed the offence from East German territory (and not, then, on the territory of the Federal Republic) violated the principle of proportionality.[54] The majority reached that conclusion in light of the "unique situation" that the state protecting and supporting the spies had ceased to exist, and having regard to the purposes which could legitimately be pursued through criminal law.[55]

In the area of administrative acts, proportionality is mainly used to control discretionary powers regarding which the Constitutional Court held, as early as 1959, that:

> the rule of law requires that the administration can interfere with the rights of an individual only with the authority of law and that the authorization is clearly limited in its contents, subjects, purpose and extent so that the interference is measurable to a certain extent, foreseeable and calculable by the citizen.[56]

[51] Schwarze, n. 1 above, at 690. See also, with respect to the freedom to choose and exercise a professional activity, the "*Drei-Stufentheorie*" following the *Pharmacies* judgment in BVerfGE 7, 377. See further De Moor-van Vugt, n. 39 above, at 32–3, who also mentions the "*Wesentlichkeitstheorie*", according to which it is for the legislature to take all essential decisions, and to make its viewpoint known, in the area of basic rights. Where the Basic Law empowers the legislature to set limits to a specific basic right, the legislator may use that power (subject to the proportionality principle which, as said above, also applies to legislative acts). See further Emiliou, n. 39 above, at 53.

[52] BVerfgE 19, 343, mentioned by Emiliou, n. 39 above, at 56.

[53] Schwarze, n. 1 above, at 691.

[54] [1995] NJW 1811 notated by C. Arndt, at 1803, reported by G. Nolte and P. Rädler in (1995) 1 *EPL* 501.

[55] *Cf. ibid.*, who at 502–3 assert that the dissenting judges rightly thought that, instead of using the principle of proportionality, the court should have applied to criminal legislation the well-established balancing test developed for retroactive non-criminal legislation.

[56] Cited in English in Emilou, n. 39 above, at 63. Emiliou also notes, at 62, that according to the Court's case law laws are contrary to the Constitution when granting discretionary power without providing guidelines for its exercise.

These propositions have now been enacted in the 1976 Law of Administrative Procedure which provides in paragraph 113:

> If an administrative authority is authorized to act in its discretion, it has to exercise its discretion in accordance with the purpose of the authorization and the legal limits of the discretion have to be observed.[57]

Those limits consist in a prohibition to act, on the one hand, in excess of discretion (acting *ultra vires*) and, on the other hand, in abusing discretion, objectively or subjectively. Objective abuse results from the non-observance or violation of constitutional or other legal principles, such as the principle of proportionality.[58] In that respect "the three elements contained in the . . . principle also come into their own where statutes are applied by the administration in individual cases", in which case, as already mentioned above, the amount of discretion granted to the administration "can be so reduced in scope by the proportionality principle that only a particular decision will remain legitimate".[59]

Examples of how the proportionality principle is used to check the internal limits on discretionary powers are given by Schwarze:

> Thus, for example, exceptions must be granted to a general prohibition ordered by the police force [in that case a ban on receiving parcels for certain categories of remand prisoners] where such a prohibition, in the absence of genuine danger, is not absolutely necessary. On the other hand, the police may take drastic measures even in case of minor offences, where such infringements have increased in frequency and cannot be prevented in any other way.[60]

Another recent example is a decision of the Federal Administrative Court on the validity of low-level flights by the German airforce which were challenged for disproportionately disregarding the interests of affected local communities and citizens.[61] In that case the court confined its judicial review to securing that the Ministry of Defence, when determining the areas and conditions of these flights, had taken into account all relevant circumstances and considered adequately the public interest in noise protection. By thus granting the Ministry a margin of appreciation which, as observed, "is usually limited to decisions in planning law", the Federal Administrative court "departed from the normal standards of judicial review . . .".[62] Obviously, this limited application of proportionality is to be contrasted with the far-reaching application of the principle by the Constitutional Court regarding legislative acts, for example in the aforementioned espionage case.

In view of this, and notwithstanding the extensive analysis of proportionality in German case law and doctrine, it has been observed that there is no general

57 Thus Emiliou, n. 39 above, who also refers to (and quotes in English) para. 114 of the Law of Administrative Courts.

58 Emiliou, n. 39 above, at 63–4.

59 Schwarze, n. 1 above, at 689.

60 *Ibid.*, at 689 referring to BVerfGE 34, 384 respectively BVerwG in [1974] NJW at 807.

61 [1995] JZ 510, cited and briefly discussed by Nolte and Rädler, n. 54 above, at 503.

62 *Ibid.*

agreement on basic points regarding the definition and scope of proportionality, or even terminology,[63] and that wide-ranging criticisms have sometimes been levelled at the principle.[64]

In French law proportionality (a nomenclature which is rarely used in the case law of the Conseil d'Etat (CE)) is not regarded as a general principle of public law. That is not to say that, where conceived as a concept governing the relations between citizens and public authorities (namely to limit state interferences with individual rights), it is unfamiliar to the French legal tradition.[65] Actually the concept is used in different forms in a variety of situations.[66] This contrast with the position under German law is attributable to important structural differences between German and French public law. Whilst the concept is based in German law on the "*Rechtsstaat*" principle and, as such, is closely linked to the protection of the citizens' basic rights and freedoms, French administrative law takes a different point of departure, which is the need for administrative decisions to be taken in accordance with the law, as prescribed by the *principe de légalité*.[67] This principle used to be understood as *légalité externe*, meaning that judicial review has "little to do with the core of the decision, with its substantive aspect".[68] Only during the twentieth century did the willingness of the CE grow to extend its review to the *légalité interne* involving a review of the contents, the motives and the purpose of the administrative act.[69] But, as suggested above, there are various categories of control to be distinguished, depending on whether the administration acted by virtue of tied or discretionary powers: in the first case the control is normal; in the second it is minimal, in that the act is only quashed when the administration has submitted an "*erreur manifeste d'appréciation*".[70]

The "principle" of proportionality was first developed in the legal writings of authors such as Eisenmann and Braibant after the Second World War and concerned the question whether the administrative act was appropriate to attain a certain result and whether it was necessary so to do.[71] It was further developed in the 1970s[72] and applied in special circumstances involving a more thorough

[63] Emiliou, n. 39 above, at 25.

[64] Schwarze, n. 1 above, at 691.

[65] M. Fromont, "Le principe de proportionnalité" [1995] *AJDA* 156, at 156.

[66] *Ibid.* See also S. Boyron, "Proportionality in English Administrative law: a faulty translation?" (1992) 12 *OJLS* 237, at 241–5.

[67] See De Moor-van Vugt, n. 39 above, at 41 and Boyron, n. 66 above, at 239.

[68] See Boyron, n. 66 above, at 248, where the grounds to control external legality are mentioned.

[69] *Ibid.* The grounds to control internal legality, enumerated there, imply various controls of the application of law to the facts.

[70] Boyron, n. 66 above, at 241–3.

[71] De Moor-van Vugt, n. 39 above, at 45, citing Eisenmann's lectures on "Les actes juridiques de droit administratif", 1956–7, at 479. And see G. Braibant, "Le principe de proportionnalité", *Mélanges offerts à Marcel Waline* (Librairie Genérale de Droit et de Jurisprudence, Paris, 1974).

[72] M. Guibal, "De la proportionalité" [1978] *AJDA* 477; M. Letourneur, "L'erreur manifeste d'appréciation dans la jurisprudence du Conseil d'Etat français", *Miscellanea Ganshof van der Meersch* (Brussels, Bruylant, 1978) vol. III; J.P. Costa, "Le principe de proportionnalité dans la jurisprudence du Conseil d'Etat" [1988] *AJDA* 434. More recently see X Philippe, *Le contrôle de proportionnalité dans les jurisprudences constitutionelle et administrative françaises* (Paris, Economica, 1994).

control, as in the case of policing measures or of emergency situations, or a more varied control, as in the case of the so-called doctrine of *bilan coût-avantages*.

Because of the variety of situations in which the concept is applied it remains altogether a "rather vague notion . . . facilitat[ing] an all embracing meaning without clear boundaries".[73] As one author puts it: "[it] is sometimes difficult to apply imposing limits on its efficiency"[74] or as another author writes: "[it] needs careful handling; it requires circumspection and agility from those who apply it, failing which it risks transforming the judge into an administrator".[75]

From the viewpoint of a UK lawyer, it must be interesting to note that French law uses the concept, or rather the word, "*proportion*" in different situational contexts. One of the most important areas of application is, as already observed, the area of fundamental rights and freedoms, particularly in respect of policing measures taken to protect the "*ordre public*" which often entail restrictions on the exercise of personal freedom. Thus, for example, in the famous *Benjamin* case, the CE held a decree issued by a mayor prohibiting a conference to be illegal on the grounds that "the possibility of disturbances did not present such a degree of seriousness that he could not, without prohibiting the conference, have maintained order by issuing policing measures that it was [the mayor's] duty to take".[76] In other words the relationship between the restrictions on personal freedom and the damage resulting from serious disturbances was out of proportion, since the measure could have been replaced by less drastic policing measures, such as increasing the number of policemen.

A very special application of proportionality, so much that some authors believe it to be a different concept,[77] is the theory of "*bilan-coût-avantages*", which is used in connection with expropriation for reasons of "*utilité publique*". The landmark decision is the judgment of the CE in *Ville Nouvelle Est* relating to the building of new faculties of law and letters for the University of Lille, involving the building of a whole academic and residential complex (a whole new town adjoining the faculty buildings) and necessitating the demolition of 88 only recently constructed houses.[78] Following the advice given by its *commissaire du gouvernement* Braibant, the CE ruled "that an operation can only be legally declared to be of *utilité publique* if violations of private property, the financial cost and possibly the disadvantages of a social nature which it entails are not excessive having regard to the interest which it presents".[79] Although the

[73] Emiliou, n. 39 above, at 89.

[74] Costa, n. 72 above, at 437.

[75] J. Lemasurier, "Expropriation: 'Bilan-coût-avantages' et nécessité publique" [1979] *Rev. Adm.* 502, cited in English translation by Emiliou, n. 39 above, at 91.

[76] CE, 19 May 1933, Leb., 541 as cited in English translation by Emiliou, n. 39 above, at 98. See also Schwarze, n. 1 above, at 680–1. Both authors, as well as Fromont, n. 65 above, at 162, cite other and more recent cases. See also further case law in L.N. Brown and J.S. Bell, *French Administrative Law* (5th edn., Oxford, Clarendon Press, 1998), at 233–5.

[77] See, e.g., Fromont, n. 65 above, at 163–4. Brown and Bell, n. 76 above, treat it, at 263, as an expression of the doctrine of manifest error in assessment of the facts.

[78] CE, 28 May 1971, Leb. 409, with conclusions by Braibant.

[79] In English translation in Emiliou, n. 39 above, at 105.

CE assessed the project, and its impact under the circumstances, in light of the legal concept of *utilité publique*, it is clear that the decision marks "a remarkable extension of judicial control".[80] It is also clear, though, that a court should only intervene "above a certain threshold, in cases where a social or financial cost is abnormally high and has not been justified".[81] In its later judgment in *Sté civ. St. Marie de l'Assomption* the CE extended the doctrine of *bilan* to include also the balancing between public interests.[82] It ruled:

> An operation can only be legally declared as being of utilité publique if the harm done to private property, the financial cost and possibly disadvantages of social nature, or the harm done to other public interests is not excessive having regard to the interests which it presents.[83]

It should not come as a surprise that the doctrine of *bilan* has found another important field of application in the area of environmental protection. By virtue thereof French law has required an "*étude d'impact*" in the event of a *governmental* project of environmental importance, even before EC Directive 85/337 made an environmental impact statement compulsory for all major land-use projects.[84]

It is not only the Conseil d'Etat but also the Conseil Constitutionnel which uses the concept of proportionality, without acknowledging the existence of the "principle" as such, in its case law relating to the validity of legislative acts imposing excessive restrictions on rights of individuals.[85] In a "seminal decision of 1971 [in which the Conseil decided] on the substantive constitutionality of statutes passed by Parliament",[86] the Conseil Constitutionnel declared a statute unconstitutional which restricted the freedom to create an association: the imposition of controls before an association could come into existence was

[80] In English translation in Emiliou, n. 39 above, at 105.

[81] *Commissaire du gouvernement* Braibant, cited by Emiliou, n. 39 above, at 105.

[82] CE, 20 Oct. 1972, Leb. 657.

[83] See the English version of Emiliou, n. 39 above, at 107, where many more recent decisions are reported. In the article cited in n. 65 above, Fromont emphasises the differences between the classic application of proportionality in the area of basic rights and the theory of *bilan coût-avantages*: "*dans la jurisprudence dite du bilan, le juge abandonne une conception binaire des relations administration-citoyen* (*intérêt public-liberté*) *et adopte une conception multipolaire des relations dans lesquelles s'insèrent l'autorité administrative qui agit*: *plusieurs intérêts s'affrontent, plusieurs intérêts privés* [. . .] *et plusieurs intérêts publics*", at 164.

[84] For all this see Emiliou, n. 39 above, at 110–11.

[85] Boyron, n. 66 above, reports at 258 that "the *Conseil Constitutionnel* was created (in 1958) to ensure that the Constitution is respected by . . . three categories of texts ('*lois organiques*', international agreements and ordinary statutes), and more precisely, to regulate the relationship between Parliament and Executive in order principally to prevent Parliament, which only possesses competence in a limited number of areas, from trespassing on the sphere reserved to the Executive". In that connection she emphasises that the French legal system, in contradistinction to the UK legal system, "has shifted its emphasis from the principle of supremacy of Parliament to that of separation of powers" (*ibid.*). For a short description of the composition and jurisdiction (of an adjudicative or an advisory nature) of the Conseil, see C. Dadamo and S. Farran, *The French Legal System* (2nd edn., London, Sweet & Maxwell, 1996), 111–13.

[86] Boyron, n. 66 above, at 258–9.

destroying the freedom of association itself.[87] And in later decisions legislative provisions have been invalidated for having issued "a sanction which could have, in many cases, a manifestly disproportionate character" or "a sanction manifestly disproportionate in relation to the facts capable to support such measures".[88]

A (superficial) comparison of German and French law on proportionality shows that the acceptance of the test is far from the same under both legal systems. That relates as well to form and substance, and even denomination. In German law proportionality is a well known concept of which the scope, the elements and the functioning are rather well defined in the case law of the higher courts. That is particularly true for the case law of the Constitutional Court as regards the validity of statutes imposing limitations on basic rights and fundamental freedoms of citizens. It is applied on the basis of, and in accordance with, an objective order of values which is derived from the Basic Law and implementing legislation. Proportionality is a tool to balance conflicting values in order to reconcile them as much as possible in practice. It is an integral part of the concepts of *Rechtsstaat* and democracy and, as such, applied generally to all public acts, of a legislative or administrative nature, as well as in private relations.

French law takes a more pragmatic approach. Proportionality is not a general principle of public law, and is certainly not well defined in the case law of the courts. It is used in the form of a vague concept of proportion in several fields of the law to gauge the regularity of administrative action and, to a much lesser extent, to examine the constitutionality of legislative acts. The use of proportionality in administrative law has grown hand in hand with the acceptance and broadening of the control of the *légalité interne*, that is to say, of motives, purpose and content of administrative action, following the ever increasing intervention of public authorities in numerous areas of societal life, not least in the economic sector. As a result, the CE's traditional reluctance, embodied in the concept of *légalité externe*, to control the *opportunité* of administrative action has gradually ebbed away to make room for a more extensive balancing of interests, albeit that the judicial review differs in intensity depending on the more or less discretionary nature of the exercise of power as well as on the importance of the protected interest and the complexity of the interests involved.[89]

[87] Decision of 16 July 1971 cited by Boyron, n. 66 above, at 258, n. 96.

[88] Cited, in French, by Fromont, n. 65 above, at 164. At 165 other decisions are cited relating to interferences with constitutional rights applying, according to Fromont, an even stricter proportionality test.

[89] Thus in the case of assessing the *utilité publique* character of a vast expropriation project as in *Ville Nouvelle Est*, the CE will only interfere when there is a manifest disproportion, that is an excessive imbalance between advantages and drawbacks of the reviewed measure. Contrariwise, in the area of impact of policing measures on basic citizen's freedoms, as in *Benjamin*, the review is less extensive, since fewer factors have to be taken into consideration, but at the same time more intensive, that is to say, more inclined to set the measure in question aside. See further Emiliou, n. 39 above, at 112.

Obviously, the differences between German and French laws flow from deeper differences in mentality and constitutional structures: in mentality, in that German legal reasoning is, on the whole, more principled (and categorical) while French legal reasoning is more pragmatic (and factual). As to constitutional structures, the German State is a federal one which needs an umpire to decide conflicts of competences between federal and national public authorities and impositions of these different layers of state power on the private sphere of citizens, whereas the French State is still a highly centralised one based on a concept of separation of powers, with a strong centralised executive branch, as compared with a legislative branch which has only limited powers, and a judicial branch which, although it is not allowed to judge the *opportunité* of administrative or legislative acts, tends to monitor closely their *légalité*, *externe* and *interne*.[90]

PROPORTIONALITY IN BELGIAN AND DUTCH PUBLIC LAW

Until the creation of the Court of Arbitration in 1980 (see below), the notion of proportionality played a limited role in the case law of the Belgian Council of State (empowered, also after the creation of the Court of Arbitration, to review the legality of administrative acts). It was applied mainly in disciplinary cases, where the Council of State, in reviewing the imposition of a sanction on the ground of *ultra vires*, held that it must also assess whether the disciplinary sanction imposed was not beyond all proportion to the offence committed.[91] Thus, in a 1980 judgment of the Council of State relating to the annulment of a civil servant's dismissal, the Council decided:

> that, although the Council was not entitled to substitute itself for the relevant authority to determine a (disciplinary) sanction to be imposed on the employed person for proven but not yet punished facts, it had nonetheless to examine whether the facts were so serious as to merit a disciplinary sanction, and whether the sanction imposed was out of proportion to the facts. In other words, the disciplinary authorities were bound to observe the "proportionality principle", which requires the sanction to be reasonably proportionate to the punishable facts, to be justifiable and not to appear arbitrary.[92]

Obviously, the weighing of interests involved in these disciplinary cases is of a limited nature, and not comparable at all to the balancing of interests by the French Conseil d'Etat, for example, in expropriation cases (above), for which there is no counterpart in the case law of the Belgian Council of State.

[90] See also Boyron, n. 66 above, at 258–9.

[91] For an early decision see Judgment no. 17,101 of 26 June 1975, *Depelchin*, mentioned in Schwarze, n. 1 above, at 697–8 with references to other judgments and to articles of F. Delpéree and L.P. Suetens.

[92] Judgment no. 20,116 of 19 Feb. 1980, *Decock*, reproduced in (1979/80) Rechtskundig Weekblad, 2757–2762 and also referred to, and quoted, in Schwarze, n. 1 at p. 698.

From 1970 onwards the Belgian constitutional structure has been thoroughly changed, in the course of a devolutionary process in four stages of which the most recent one of 1993 has transformed Belgium into a federal state (Article 1 of the co-ordinated Constitution). In the process of that reform a Court of Arbitration was set up whose powers were gradually extended.[93] Its present jurisdiction is to review legal norms enacted by the different federal and regional legislatures from a viewpoint of allocation of legislative powers but also from a viewpoint of compliance of legislative acts (including acts giving assent to a Treaty) with the principles of equality and non-discrimination and with the constitutional protection of education. Despite these limitations the Court (assuming the role of a genuine constitutional court) has interpreted its competence extensively applying "the principles of equality and non-discrimination to all constitutionally guaranteed rights and liberties and even to all rights and liberties which are guaranteed by self-executing international treaties".[94]

The Court also "considers itself competent to review all legislative discrimination, even outside the field of education".[95] Direct applications for annulment can be brought by any natural or legal person having an interest in annulment. Moreover, all courts and tribunals may, and those who are to decide at last instance must, ask the Court of Arbitration for a preliminary ruling on the question whether a (federal or regional) legislator has acted *ultra vires*, or has violated the principles of equality and non-discrimination.[96]

It is in the exercise of this legislative review that the Court of Arbitration uses a proportionality principle both in a context of allocation of legislative powers and in a context of compliance with constitutional rights. In the first context the principle limits the competence of one or another legislator. An illustration of that is the federal law imposing eco-taxes by virtue of the general competence of the federal legislator to levy taxes but affecting, and intended to affect, the environment and disposal of waste which are regional competences. According to the Court of Arbitration the federal legislature must, in such an instance, act in compliance with the proportionality principle, meaning that it may not make the exercise of regional legislative powers "impossible or excessively difficult".[97] Although the imposition of eco-taxes affects the competences of the Regions, the federal legislature may nevertheless intervene, the Court said, because of the

[93] The "low profile" denomination of the Court reflects the initial role for the Court to act primarily as a referee between legislators. During the later major reforms of the Constitution, and also due to the Court's own jurisprudence, the Court of Arbitration took the role of a fully-fledged Constitutional Court: see P. Peeters, "The Judiciary. The Court of Arbitration" in G. Craenen (ed.), *The Institution of Federal Belgium, An Introduction to Belgian Public Law* (Leuven, Acco, 1996), at 125–6.

[94] *Ibid.*, at 128.

[95] *Ibid.*

[96] *Ibid.*, at 129–30.

[97] See further A. Alen, *Handboek van het Belgisch Staatsrecht*, syllabus (Deventer, Kluwer, 1995), Nos 798 and 815 referring to the eco-tax judgments of the Arbitration Court in Cases 4, 6, 8, 9 and 10/95 of 2 Feb. 1995, [1995] AA 39 with extracts in [1995] *JT* 470. The quoted words figure sub B.5.6 of the judgments, in AA, at 59; JT, at 470.

necessity to preserve the (Belgian) economic and monetary union[98]; regional measures which would subject the marketing of products to different conditions would indeed jeopardise the free movement of goods and the free competition within the integrated Belgian market. After having said that the Court emphasised again that "the intervention of the federal legislator would have been disproportionate if it had resulted in taking away from the regions competences assigned to them by the Constitution or by virtue thereof".[99]

The second context in which the Court of Arbitration has used the proportionality principle is in reviewing legislative acts for non-compliance with the principles of equality and non-discrimination and, through these principles, with constitutionally protected basic rights (including those laid down in directly effective Treaty law). In this context the Court of Arbitration used the proportionality principle for the first time in its judgment of 13 October 1989[100] relating to a legislative provision requesting persons working in a laboratory for clinical biology to become members of a company. This obligation was imposed by law to combat over-consumption in that sector. The Court of Arbitration found it to be inconsistent with the constitutional freedom of association to "impose on both companies and persons an obligation which, although related to the aim pursued by it, is nonetheless disproportionate to it since the provision (under review) affects the freedom of association too much".[101]

As can be seen, the Court of Arbitration uses proportionality in this connection to determine whether there has been an infringement of the equality and non-discrimination principles. Equal treatment of persons who find themselves in essentially different situations is only justified where there are reasonable grounds for it. In a judgment of 13 January 1994, it was said that the existence of such grounds must "be assessed taking into account the aim and the effects of the disputed measure and the nature of the relevant principles; the principle of equality is violated if it has been established that there is no reasonable propor-

[98] In its landmark judgment, No. 47/88 of 25 Feb. 1988 ([1988] AA 223; also in [1987–8] RW at 1311) relating to the validity of a Walloon Decree imposing a tax on the transfer of water to the Brussels and Flemish regions, the Arbitration Court declared that such legislative act was inconsistent with Belgian economic and monetary union, that is to say an institutional framework of an economy characterised by an integrated market and unity of currency. The existence of such a union was derived from the new constitutional structure. For a comment, see C. Vanderveeren, "Over leefmilieu en fiscaliteit in het raam van de economische en monetaire unie, Commentaar bij het arrest van het Arbitragehof van 25 februari 1988" [1988–9] *RW* at 345.

[99] Sub. B.5.8 of the judgments. In German law, it is not the proportionality principle, but rather the principle of *Bundestreue*, which is used to reach the same result. By virtue of that principle it is for the federal and the national authorities to take the others' competences into account. In BVerfGE 4, at 141, it is said: "[a] federal State can only exist when the Federation and the States take note in their mutual relationship that the degree in which they may use their formal competences is determined by mutual consideration ('*gegenseitige Rücksichtnahme*')". For a thorough comparison of Belgian and German law in that respect, see A. Alen and P. Peeters, "Bundestreue in het Belgisch grondwettelijk Recht" [1989–90] RW 1122, where the above quotation in the German original is reproduced at 1144, n. 332.

[100] Judgment no. 23/89, BS 8 Nov. 1989, 18,386; also in [1989] TRV 527.

[101] At B.2.9 of the judgment.

tional relation between the measures employed and the aim pursued".[102] However that may be, in applying the proportionality principle the Court remains very conscious of the fact that it should not enter into an examination of the *opportunité* of the (legislative) acts under review. A consequence of this is that (in contrast to the ECJ) it does not examine whether the aim could also have been pursued by an alternative (legislative) measure. It examines only whether there exists a manifest disproportion between aim and means.[103]

In Dutch law the proportionality principle was traditionally applied to the imposition of (punitive or compensatory) sanctions.[104] More important, however, is the role which it was called on to play later on regarding administrative decision-making in general. In that respect two kinds of decision-making can be distinguished: laying down generally binding rules, on the one hand, and taking individual decisions, on the other hand. Article 3:4, first paragraph, of the 1992 *Algemene Wet Bestuursrecht* (*Awb*: General Statute on Administrative Law) provides for both kinds of administrative decision-making that "the public organ must weigh all interests directly involved in the decision, in so far as a statutory provision or the nature of the power exercised does not contain a limitation". The second paragraph of Article 3:4 states that "the harmful consequences which the decision would have for one or more interested parties may not be disproportionate to the aims pursued by the decision". It is noted that the concept of proportionality constitutes the basis for this legal provision together with the related principle of carefulness (*zorgvuldigheid*) and the prohibition of arbitrariness (*willekeursverbod*).[105] Before the 1992 Act proportionality is said to have been "concealed behind [those] other general principles of administrative law". In practice, however, it was already applied in accordance with the concepts as developed in German and Community law.[106]

As for the making of generally binding rules, Article 3:4 (read together with Article 3:1) Awb applies, more particularly, to the activities of all administrative authorities (as defined in Article 1:1), not those of the legislator, however, whose acts are not subjected to judicial review in the Netherlands.[107] With regard to such rule-making activities, further guidelines (*aanwijzingen*) have been given in

102 Judgment no. 1/94 (*Biorim*) [1994] AA 1. The principle is also used by other high courts, such as the Court of Cassation in a judgment of 5 Oct. 1990, [1990–1] *RW* 330 relating to unequal treatment in tax matters. The Court, following in the footsteps of the Court of Arbitration, held that unequal treatment "must be tested against the aims and the effects of the tax imposed and against the reasonableness of the relation between the measure employed and the aim pursued".

103 P. De Ridder, "De beperkte toetsing van het gelijkheidsbeginsel door het Arbitragehof" [1990–1] *RW* 481, at 490. For a recent application see the judgment of the Court of Arbitration of 21 Mar. 1996 in case 21/96, [1996] AA 203, under B.4 and B.6.

104 See De Moor-van Vugt, n. 39 above, at 153–253. Until the enactment of Art. 3:4 Awb (see below) the requirement of proportionality (*evenredigheid*) was laid down in Art. 58, para. 3, of the 1929 *Ambtenarenwet* (Act on civil servants).

105 *Ibid.*, at 211.

106 *Ibid.*, at 267–8 and 278.

107 Legal doctrine holds, however, that the legislator proper is also bound to comply, of its own initiative, with the principle of carefulness which implies the duty to take account of all interests involved, and to weigh them carefully: see De Moor-van Vugt, n. 39 above, at 215.

a Decree of the Prime Minister competent for General Affairs, for all regulations falling under the responsibility of a Minister.[108] In guidelines 13 and 14 it is specified that, in choosing a specific regulation, the authority's aim must be to limit the burdens for citizens, enterprises and institutions as much as possible (unless the regulation precisely purports to impose such burdens) and that the burden for the administration must also be limited to the extent possible.[109]

Of the three elements (suitability, necessity and proportionality *sensu stricto*) which German law, and to a certain extent Community law, distinguish in the concept of proportionality, the first two, which are intended to ensure a fair relation between the aim pursued by the regulation and the means employed, are said to be of special importance for decision-making in general, and law-making in particular; the third element, involving the weighing of other interests as well, is held to be especially important for individual decisions.[110] However, the three elements are not always clearly distinguished. It is worthwhile in this connection to retrace the evolution before the enactment of Article 3:4 Awb.[111] Until 1976 when the *Wet Arob* (Judicial Review of Administrative Action Act) was enacted, it was for the *civil courts*, and the Hoge Raad as court of final appeal, to protect citizens against adverse administrative decisions. In the *Doetinchem* judgment of 25 February 1949[112] the Hoge Raad developed, to that effect, the arbitrariness ("*willekeur*") test holding (in F. Stroink's English translation[113]):

> that there could be cause for the court to intervene, if the requisition [of living accommodation, F.S.] was to be viewed as an arbitrary act; that there is such an act [if it] must be assumed that the requisitioning authority could not reasonably have decided to requisition considering the interests that had to be taken into account, and therefore a weighing of these interests must be assumed not to have taken place; however, that there is no such case at issue, because there is a possibility that fair minded people may come to opposite results when weighing these opposite interests involved in the case at hand.

It is clear that this test, also called the "reasonableness" test, bears much resemblance to the English Court of Appeal's *Wednesbury* test.[114]

In the aforementioned 1976 *Wet Arob*, the test of unreasonableness, as developed by the Dutch Supreme Court, was incorporated as one of the four grounds for judicial review in Article 8(1)(c), which provides that appeals can be lodged on the ground "that the administrative organ could not have reasonably reached

[108] De Moor-van Vugt, n. 39 above, at 213.

[109] *Ibid.*, at 213–14. Guideline 15 repeats the second para. of Art. 3:4 AWB.

[110] *Ibid.*, at 231 and 277.

[111] For an overview see F. Stroink, "Judicial Control of the Administration's Discretionary Powers (le bilan exécutif—juge administratif)" in R. Bakker, A.W. Heringa and F. Stroink (eds.), *Judicial Control, Comparative Essays on Judicial Review* (Antwerp, Maklu Utrecht, 1995). See also J.B.J.M. Ten Berge, *Besturen door de overheid* (Deventer, Tjeenk Willink, 1997), at 320–1.

[112] [1949] NJ 558.

[113] N. 111 above, at 82.

[114] See T. Koopmans, *Vergelijkend Publiekrecht* (2nd edn.; Deventer, Kluwer, 1986), at 121.

its decision upon considering the interests involved". One author observes: "it is noteworthy that the *administrative courts* have seized on this challenge ground to start testing more intensively".[115] For, indeed, the test of unreasonableness has been used later on to review an administrative decision (as the Court of Appeal had done itself in the judgment quashed by the Hoge Raad in *Doetinchem*) if it disproportionately harmed the interests of others, or if there was too large a disproportion between the protected and the harmed interest[116] (see further below[117]).

Parallel to, and closely intertwined with, the foregoing reasonableness test, another principle, the principle of substantive carefulness (*materiële zorgvuldigheid*) came to the fore. According to this principle, as laid down in the case law of the Council of State, the public authority concerned has not acted with due care when the aim pursued by it could be equally achieved by less coercive measures, since it is for the administration to take a decision which is the least burdensome for the person concerned.[118] Together with the legislative application of the proportionality principle in the 1929 Act on civil servants,[119] all this has led to the enactment of the aforementioned Article 3:4 Awb. It has also led to the acceptance by many of proportionality as a general principle of law and of its three constitutive elements of suitability, necessity and proportionality *stricto sensu* mentioned above.[120]

There are two particularities in Dutch law which merit special comment. The first lies in the ability of the courts to oblige the administration to make reparation, in the form of pecuniary compensation (or in another form), when a measure taken in the general interest, and for which no other equally efficient measure is available, leads to disproportionate harm to specific interests of some individuals.[121] In other words, compensation is a factor which allows an administrative decision to be saved from illegality, and thus to be kept in force, in that it remedies the unbalanced character of the decision.[122] As already observed, the legal basis for it can be found, according to some, in the proportionality principle laid down in paragraph 2 of Article 3:4 Awb, and more specifically in the

[115] Stroink, n. 111 above, at 83, emphasis supplied.

[116] See Ten Berge, n. 111 above, at 320; see also De Moor-van Vugt, n. 39 above, at 216, and particularly the reference to Hoge Raad, 18 Jan. 1991, which is referred to below.

[117] However, in recent case law, the highest administrative court, the Council of State, has again shown greater caution in applying the rule of Art. 3(4)(2) emphasising the wording of that legal provision which uses a double negative ("the decision . . . may *not* be *dis*proportionate", emphasis added): see the Council of State judgment of 9 May 1996 [1996], JB 158, with note by F. Stroink. See also the comment of F. Stroink, "Evenredigheid en belangenafweging" in Damen *et al.* (eds.), *Rechtspraak Bestuursrecht 1995–1996*, 1997, at 157.

[118] Ten Berge, 111 above, referring at 321 to R.I.G.M. Widdershoven *et al.*, *Bestuursrechtspraak in milieugeschillen* (Zwolle, Tjeenk Willink, 1991), at 180.

[119] See n. 104 above.

[120] Ten Berge, n. 111 above, at 322, who adheres to De Moor-van Vugt's analysis. But see P. Nicolaï, *Beginselen van behoorlijk bestuur* (Deventer, Kluwer, 1990), at 92 and 240.

[121] For a recent application, see Hoge Raad, 18 Jan. 1991 [1991] AB 241.

[122] De Moor-van Vugt, n. 39 above, at 245.

third element, that is to say, proportionality *sensu stricto*.[123] Others believe that the legal basis is to be found in the unwritten principle of "*égalité devant les charges publiques*" (as it is called in French law) which is derived from the aforementioned principle of carefulness.[124] Whether compensation is finally due depends on a variety of factors, such as the nature and weight of the general and individual interests involved, the nature and extent of the harm inflicted on the individual interests involved, and on similar interests of other individuals, whether the harm is to be regarded as part of the normal societal or entrepreneurial risk and therefore to remain uncompensated, or whether there are other reasons for not compensating the injured person.

The second peculiarity follows from Article 8: 72, paragraph 4, Awb, which allows an administrative court to rule that its judgment replaces the administrative decision quashed by it. In the memorandum accompanying the Awb, it is pointed out that the court may solely deal with the matter itself when only one decision is correct under the law.[125]

LESSONS TO BE DRAWN: PROPORTIONALITY, A NOTION IN SEARCH OF PRECISION

1. The foregoing overview shows that proportionality is about weighing conflicting interests involved in, and at the occasion of, the pursuit of a regulatory aim and the deployment of appropriate regulatory means. That means that the interests to be weighed against each other have to be inventorised, that it has to be determined whether they are legitimate, and that an order of prioritisation amongst those interests is somehow to be established. It is doubtful whether, in any legal system, these questions can be determined by the courts exclusively. Up to a certain point, they will have to be resolved by the legislature proper or, if proportionality is to play a role in respect of acts emanating from the legislator proper (as in Germany, France and Belgium), by the constitutional legislature. Obviously, countries which, like the UK, do not have a written Constitution including a Bill of Rights may have difficulty in meeting this preliminary condition for the proportionality test to apply.[126] Of course, even when this preliminary condition is fulfilled, courts must still play a role in interpreting, implementing and completing the legislative or constitutional provisions to determine the interests involved, and to weigh them in light of the specific circumstances of the case.

[123] De Moor-van Vugt, n. 39 above, at 245.

[124] See H.D. Van Wijk en Konijnenbelt, *Hoofdstukken van administratief recht* (s-Gravenhage, *VUGA*, 1996), nr. 35.

[125] See further Stroink, n. 111 above, at 84.

[126] That may change when the Human Rights Bill, introduced in the House of Lords on 27 Oct. 1997 and at the time of writing passing through its Commons stages, becomes law. When that happens, UK courts will be required, so far as possible, to interpret domestic legislation in a way that is compatible with Convention rights. Judges will be able to strike down or set aside secondary legislation that is found to be incompatible with the Convention. See further D. Feldman, "Proportionality and the Human Rights Act 1998", this vol.

2. To determine whether proportionality is to play a role in a given constitutional or legislative structure, the first question to be resolved is whether, in which context and to what extent, the judicial branch is allowed to interfere with rule-making and/or decision-taking of the legislative and executive branches. In federal States such as Germany or Belgium, and also in the European Community, in which an allocation of (legislative, executive and judicial) power is to be established at, and between, different levels of jurisdiction, the proportionality principle will already play a role in the allocation or exercise of powers (together eventually with the subsidiarity principle as in the European Community) or with some principle of loyalty, as in Germany *and* the EC), and, therefore, at the *legislative* level proper. In such a constitutional set-up, proportionality will also have a greater chance of being used in the protection of basic rights and fundamental freedoms of individuals, because of the existence in such legal systems of a Constitutional Court (as in Germany) or a court fulfilling the same function (as in Belgium and the EC), which court will ensure that the citizens' basic rights and freedoms are safeguarded against the exercise of legislative powers at the various levels of the constitutional structure. In such legal systems, the Bill of Rights enshrined in the ECHR will normally have a larger impact than in others, as it will be used to strengthen, or implement, the national Bill of Rights, and *vice versa*.

In all of the legal systems examined herein, some requirement of proportion(ality) operates in the area of judicial review of *administrative* acts in view of protecting the (basic and other) rights and freedoms of individuals against the exercise by the various public authorities of their power to lay down regulations or to take individual decisions. Such a requirement of proportion (or of moderation), mainly in the exercise of administrative powers containing a margin of discretion, may imply the less intensive form of unreasonableness (as under the English *Wednesbury* principle)[127] or of arbitrariness (as under the Dutch *Doetinchem* ruling) or, on the contrary, the more intensive form of proportionality. According to the first concept "a discretionary decision of a public authority should be quashed by the courts only if it is 'so unreasonable that no reasonable authority could ever come to it', whereas the principle of proportionality, as it has been developed in EC and ECHR case law, holds that the decision of a public body should be quashed only if its adverse effects on a legally protected interest or right go further than can be justified in order to achieve the legitimate aim of the decision".[128] The difference between the two concepts (unreasonableness and proportionality) is not always that clear, however. That is especially the case when the principle of proportionality is formulated in terms of a lack of proportion, that is to say, disproportion, and a distinction is made, in the application of the principle, between a less intensive control, on the basis of what is (clearly) disproportionate, and a more purposive control, on the

[127] *Associated Provincial Picture Houses Ltd* v. *Wednesbury Corporation* [1948] 1 KB 223.

[128] G. de Búrca, "Proportionality and *Wednesbury* Unreasonableness: The Influence of European Legal Concepts on UK Law" (1997) 3 *EPL* 561, at 562.

basis of what is regarded to be proportionate, or commensurate, to the aim pursued.[129]

The choice between the variant forms of proportionality is closely related to the idea of sovereignty of Parliament, as in English law,[130] in contradistinction to the concept of separation of powers, which, as in French law, has worked to the advantage of the Executive.[131] The latter concept turns, in substance, on the question of to what extent the judiciary is allowed to enter the core of administrative decision-making by virtue of checking the legality thereof, as is illustrated in French law by the distinction between *opportunité* and *légalité* (whereby the concept of *légalité* has slowly evolved from a narrow concept of *légalité externe* to a broad concept including *légalité interne*). In countries with a federal constitutional structure (such as the Federal Republic of Germany) proportionality plays an important role, as already observed, in the case law of the Constitutional Court which tends to protect the citizens' basic rights within a complex system of institutional equilibria. A consequence of this is that the judicial review of administrative acts tends to take place as well within a framework of principles of *Rechtsstaat* and democracy (or in the EC in light of the so-called democratic deficit) whereby the emphasis is shifted from the legality of the administrative act (as in France) to the protection of the rights of citizens. However that may be, the impact of the case law of the European Court of Human Rights, and of the proportionality principle inherent therein, may contribute to give effect to the same shift in emphasis also in countries where the review of legislative action is not in centre stage in judicial review.

3. Proportionality remains a vague concept. Even when it is regarded as a general principle of public law, as in Germany, its scope of application and its constitutive elements are not laid down in statutory provisions. They are defined, at best, in case law and legal writings, and therefore lack precision and clarity. Thus, for example, in the case law of the ECJ we have seen that there is no consensus even on how to define the concept, whether it contains two or three elements and whether (and, if so, to what extent) it has a different content depending on the situation, that is to say, primarily on the nature of the interests involved.

That brings us to the question whether proportionality can be defined in general. This is doubtful, given the ambiguity which pervades the three constituent elements of proportionality and the uncertainty as to which interests have to be taken into account: is it only the interest pursued by the specific regulatory aim of the provision under review (for example, in the ECJ's *Hauer* judgment,[132] the necessity to limit wine production) and in light of that, the means or instruments used to attain such aim (in that case the temporary prohibition on planting new vines)? Or do the underlying and more basic interests involved also have to be

[129] Van Wijk en Konijnenbelt, n. 124 above, at nr. 36.

[130] De Búrca, n. 128 above, at 567.

[131] Boyron, n. 66 above, at 258.

[132] Case 44/79 *Hauer* v. *Rheinland Pfalz* [1979] ECR 3727.

taken into account (in that case the organisation of wine markets and the hindrance of intra-Community trade which it entailed, on the one hand, and the restriction of the right to property and the freedom to pursue a trade or profession, on the other hand)? And must the basic rights and fundamental freedoms of third parties (who are not the immediate addressees of the provision), as well as other public interests, also be taken into account?

If the most extensive approach is chosen, implying the weighing of all legitimate, directly and indirectly involved, specific and general, private and public interests, the three elements of proportionality achieve their broadest significance. This would mean, in relation to *suitability*, that the measure under review must be useful to attain properly the immediate regulatory aim *and* that it must not be out of proportion to that aim (in the sense that one "must not use a steamhammer to crack a nut"[133]); in relation to *necessity*, it would mean that the measure must be *necessary* to attain the specific aim in the sense that the aim will not come about by itself *and* that it must be indispensable, in the sense that the aim cannot be attained by other measures which are as useful and, at the same time, less harmful for other interests; and in relation to *proportionality sensu stricto* it would mean that the measure—although it is the most suitable and indispensable, as compared with other possible measures—must nonetheless be abandoned, or replaced by another less appropriate measure, because of a substantial adverse impact on *other* interests, so much so that the advantages for which it is preferred over other measures are out of proportion to the harm caused to those other interests.

Obviously, the more accurately the principle of proportionality is defined, the more intensive the judicial review effected thereby will also be. The mere distinguishing in the principle of different sub-tests (two or three), as compared with, for example, the undistinctive *Wednesbury* test of unreasonableness, will lead to a more rigorous review, just as (to use an example from the academic world) a student's achievement at an interview, or in an examination, will be more intensively assessed when three distinct questions are put to him (preferably in writing) and the three answers are separately checked, than when a global indistinctive, and therefore more intuitive, assessment is made.

4. The question of how sophisticated the proportionality principle must be, in its formulation and application, depends on the intensity of control the legal system in question wishes to exercise. That is dependent in turn, *in abstracto*, on the constitutional nature of the legal system concerned and on the nature of the acts to be assessed and, *in concreto*, on the importance of the interests involved and on the variety of interests to be taken into account. If, for example, the exercise of administrative power containing only a limited margin of discretion is involved which has a considerable impact on the direct addressee's personal freedom and does not very greatly affect other private or public inter-

[133] See Lord Diplock in *R.* v. *Goldstein* [1983] 1 WLR 151, at 155B.

ests, the control by virtue of proportionality will probably be intensive, to the extent that the reviewing court may come to the conclusion that another (or even, only one other) measure must be used. If, on the contrary, the exercise of broad legislative power comprising wide discretion is involved, affecting many other basic rights or substantial interests of a private or a public nature, then the principle of proportionality will normally be applied with moderation, so much so that it may be tantamount to the test of unreasonableness.

An illustration of the latter is the French theory of *bilan coût-avantages* where the concept of proportionality is used with extreme caution (in that the review of administrative decisions will only occur above a certain threshold, that is in cases of manifest misjudgment) taking account of the utmost complexity of the situation where several, often basic, interests of a private and public nature are to be weighed against each other. Also the ECJ's judgment in *Familiapress*[134] is rendered in such a complex situation since the balancing test, to be applied by the national courts, touches upon issues of such a diverse and complicated nature that the domestic court will probably be induced to apply a global test of "unreasonableness" rather than a fully-fledged proportionality test (as it is invited by the ECJ to do).

5. It will be apparent from the foregoing that the concept of proportionality is a general concept used in a variety of situations, which in turn accounts for the diversity and pluriformity of the concept itself. Since the concept relates to the exercise of administrative, and frequently also legislative, powers and leads to the imposition of limitations on such powers, and the aims which they pursue, as well as on basic rights and fundamental freedoms protected, or conversely affected thereby, it has a significant constitutional dimension. In view of these factors—diversity of situations, on the one hand, and importance of the (sometimes conflicting) interests involved, on the other hand—it would certainly be preferable to provide the principle with a firm legal basis, both in the law of the European Community (for example, by amending Article 3b(3) EC) and in the national legal systems. As to the latter, and in order to attain coherence in each national legal order between the application of the principle in matters falling within the range of Community law and in matters of a "purely national" nature, that is to say, falling outside that range, it would moreover be preferable that the principle be formulated in each EU Member State so far as possible in the same way as in Community law. The wording of Article 3.4, first and second paragraph, of the Dutch Awb[135] could serve as a model therefor, as it both emphasises, in paragraph 1, the need to weigh (and therefore first to inventorise) all interests *directly* involved[136] and, in paragraph 2, defines

[134] Case C–368/95 [1997] ECR I–3689, op. cit., n. 20.

[135] Including eventually the so-called theory of harm compensation applicable in Dutch law obliging the administration to provide compensation if certain individual interests are disproportionately harmed, above.

[136] The Art. continues: "in so far as a statutory provision or the nature of the power exercised does not contain a limitation".

(dis)proportionality in terms of comparing the aim pursued by the measure in question with the harmful consequences of the measure for one or more *interested parties*. Defining the "interests directly involved", and therefore the "interested parties", and determining the harmful consequences and their disproportionate character compared to the aim of the measure, is a task which is not beyond the possibilities of a court of law. The Dutch provision is also commendable because it goes further than the Dutch counterpart of the *Wednesbury* rule (that is to say, the *Doetinchem* rule) without stretching the concept of proportionality to its outer limits but allowing the courts, instead, to adapt the concept to the specific context of the litigation.

In the absence of legislative initiatives, it would be desirable that the Supreme Courts of the EC and of the Member States try at least to achieve some uniformity in their own jurisprudence.

6. Weighing conflicting interests, and thus giving priority to one interest over another, requires that the court of law called upon to carry out this balancing test be put in a position to hear the "interested" parties in order for them to discuss the comparative importance of the interests involved in the litigation. This refers to the so-called method of proceduralisation of the law which emphasises "*que l'universel n'est plus déterminable dans son contenu . . .* (*cette methode*) *ne nous livre plus un contenu du juste, du vrai, de l'authentique mais simplement se ramène aux conditions procédurales qui permettent de garantir un processus discursif et argumentatif*".[137]

The requirement of "proceduralisation" of the principle of proportionality may create difficulties at the level of European Community law in so far as the principle is applied, as it often is, in the course of a preliminary ruling procedure by the ECJ itself, since that procedure does not give all of the interested parties the chance to present and discuss their viewpoints before the Court. To hear those parties will then be a matter for the national court which has made the reference. In so far as that court must take into account the interest of the Community, it should be allowed to obtain information, in the course of the procedure before it, and therefore in accordance with its procedural rules, from the Community institution representing that interest.[138]

[137] See J. De Munck and J. Lenoble, "Les mutations de l'art de gouverner" at 18 of the mimeographed text reproduced in the materials for a conference held in Louvain-la-Neuve at the Journées J. Dabin, on 16–17 Oct. 1997 (not yet published).

[138] See, in the context of interim relief to be granted by the national court, the ECJ's judgment in Case C–334/95, *Krüger GmbH & Co. KG* v. *Hauptzollamt Hamburg-Jonas* [1997] ECR I–4517, at paras. 45–46.

Proportionality in Community Law: Searching for the Appropriate Standard of Scrutiny

TAKIS TRIDIMAS

THE PRINCIPLE OF PROPORTIONALITY AND ITS FUNCTION IN COMMUNITY LAW

At its most abstract level, the principle of proportionality requires that action undertaken must be proportionate to its objectives.[1] The notion of proportionality goes back to ancient times[2] but as a general principle of law in modern legal systems it is inspired by ideas underpinning liberal democracy, in particular, the concern to protect the individual *vis-à-vis* the State and the premise that regulatory intervention must be suitable to achieve its aims.[3] The principle was developed in continental legal systems, especially in Germany and France, in the twentieth century. Its development as a ground of review can be seen as the judiciary's response to the growth of administrative powers and the augmentation of administrative discretion.[4] The principle finds only limited expression in the Treaty of Rome[5] but has been developed by the Court as a fundamental principle deriving from the rule of law[6] and requiring in particular that "the individual should not have his freedom of action limited beyond the degree necessary

[1] This contribution borrows elements from my article "The Principle of Proportionality in Community Law: From the Rule of Law to Market Integration" (1996) 31 *The Irish Jurist* 83 and from my forthcoming book: *The General Principles of EC Law*, (OUP, 1999).

[2] The spirit of the principle is encapsulated in the ancient Greek dictum "*pan metron ariston*".

[3] J. Schwarze, *European Administrative Law* (London, Sweet & Maxwell, 1992), at 679.

[4] In German law it is known as *Verhaltnismässigkeit* and, according to the case law of the Federal Constitutional Court, it underlies certain provisions of the Basic Law. For a review of the principle in the laws of the Member States, see Schwarze, n. 3 above, at 680 ff. For the latest review in Community law see N. Emiliou, *The Principle of Proportionality in European Law* (London, Kluwer, 1996); see also T. Tridimas, "The Principle of Proportionality", n. 1 above; and G. de Bùrca, "The Principle of Proportionality and its Application in EC Law" (1993) 13 *YEL* 105. For the application of the principle in the European Convention of Human Rights, see Schwarze, n. 3 above, 704 ff.; C. Picheral and A.D. Olinga, "La théorie de la marge d'appréciation dans la jurisprudence récente de la Cour européenne des droits de l'homme" [1995] *R.Trim Dr.Homme* 567; L. Adamovich, "Marge d'appréciation du législateur et principe de proportionnalité dans l'appréciation des restrictions prévues par la loi au regard de la Convention européenne des droits de l'homme" [1991] *R. Trim.Dr. Homme* 291.

[5] See Art. 3b(3). Among the provisions which have been held in the case law to incorporate the principle are Arts. 40(3), 115, 213 and those providing for derogations to the fundamental freedoms, i.e. Arts. 36, 48(3), 56, 66.

[6] Case 4/73 *Nold* v. *Commission* [1974] ECR 491, at 513–14, *per* Trabbucchi AG.

in the public interest".[7] Although the principle is particularly important in the field of economic law, in its case law the Court has applied it in diverse areas including, for example, remedies and interim measures,[8] and external trade,[9] so that it now permeates the whole of the Community legal system. As Jacobs AG has stated "there are few areas of Community law, if any at all, where [the principle of proportionality] is not relevant".[10] The only cases where the Court appears reluctant to apply the principle is where it is invoked in an attempt to justify a failure to comply with Community law.[11] The principle is invoked by litigants more often than any other general principle of Community law.

The principle of proportionality applies both to Community and to national measures and covers both legislative and administrative action. In Community law, it is used particularly, although not exclusively,[12] in two contexts: as a ground of review of Community measures and as a ground of review of national measures affecting one of the fundamental freedoms.

It should be emphasised that the underlying interests which proportionality seeks to protect in each of the above cases are different. As a result, the intensity of review exercised by the Court varies considerably. Where proportionality is invoked as a ground of review of Community policy measures, the Court is called upon to balance a private against a public interest. The underlying interest which the principle seeks to protect is the rights of the individual but, given the discretion of the legislature, review of policy measures is based on the so-called "manifestly inappropriate test". The Court will not strike down a measure unless it considers that it is manifestly inappropriate to achieve its objectives. By contrast, where proportionality is invoked in order to challenge the compatibility with Community law of national measures affecting one of the fundamental freedoms, the Court is called upon to balance a Community against a national interest. The principle is applied as a market integration mechanism and the intensity of review is much stronger. It is based, at least in most cases, on the notion of "necessity" exemplified by the "less restrictive alternative" test.

The dual nature of proportionality sometimes gives rise to problems where the principle is applied by national courts. In *R.* v. *Chief Constable of Sussex, ex*

[7] Case 11/70 *Internationale Handelsgesellschaft* v. *Einfuhr- und Vorratsstelle Getreide* [1970] ECR 1125 at 1147, *per* Dutheillet de Lamothe AG.

[8] See e.g. Case C–12/95P *Transactiones Maritimas and Others* v. *Commission* [1995] ECR I–467; and C–149/95P(R) *Commission* v. *Atlantic Container Line and Others* [1995] ECR I–2165.

[9] See e.g. Case C–367/89 *Criminal proceedings against Aimé Richardt* [1991] ECR I–4621; [1993]; Case C–26/90 *Hauptzollant Hamburg-Jones* v. *Wünsche Handelsge-Sellschaft moH and Co KG* [1991] ECR I–4961; and Case 112/80 *Durbeck* v. *Hauptzollamt Frankfurt am Main-Flughafen* [1981] ECR 1095.

[10] Case C–120/94 *Commission* v. *Greece* (*FYROM Case*) [1996] ECR 1513, at 1533.

[11] Thus, in relation to state aids, the Court has held that the obligation to recover unlawful state aid with interest cannot in principle be regarded as disproportionate to the objectives of the provisions of the EC Treaty: Case 142/87 *Belgium* v. *Commission* (*Tubemeuse case*) [1990] ECR I–959, para. 66; Case C–305/89 *Italy* v. *Commission* (*Alfa Romeo case*) [1991] ECR I–1603, para. 41; and Case C–169/95 *Spain* v. *Commission* [1997] ECR I–135, para. 47.

[12] For other uses of the principle, see below.

parte International Trader's Ferry Ltd,[13] in issue was the decision of the Chief Constable to limit police assistance to the applicants to two days a week. Such assistance was necessary to facilitate the export of animals to other Member States, given that intense demonstrations by animal rights groups made exports impossible without police cover. The Court of Appeal, reversing the judgment of the Divisional Court, held that the need to ensure proper policing and to prevent crime were matters of public policy within the meaning of Article 36 and that, in view of the finite manpower and financial resources at the disposal of the Chief Constable, the restriction on exports resulting from his decision complied with the principle of proportionality. Kennedy LJ took the view that "outside of the field of human rights, proportionality should normally only be applied if the means are manifestly grossly out of balance in relation to the end sought"[14] and he stated that "[i]t is European law as well as domestic law that no court will interfere with [the Chief Constable's] decision unless it can be shown that he was plainly wrong".[15]

Although the result reached by the Court of Appeal in the circumstances of this case was correct, the above dicta should not be taken as representing the ECJ's case law on the application of proportionality to national measures that interfere with the fundamental freedoms. That case law normally requires a higher level of scrutiny than the Court of Appeal suggests.

The distinction drawn above between proportionality as the guardian of individual rights and proportionality as an instrument for economic integration does not mean that the two concepts are unrelated. In fact, the second incorporates the first. In *Kraus*,[16] as earlier in the *Beer case*,[17] the Court was adamant that, to be proportionate, a restriction on the exercise of a fundamental freedom must comply with essential procedural guarantees enabling the person concerned to assert his Community rights. In other words, freedom of movement and the rule of law are closely intertwined aspects of the same constitutional order.[18] In particular, the case law provides that, in order to meet the requirements of proportionality, a restriction on a fundamental freedom must be adequately reasoned and be subject to judicial review.[19]

[13] Court of Appeal: [1997] 2 All ER 65; Divisional Court: [1995] 4 All ER 364, noted by C. Barnard and I. Hare in (1997) 60 *MLR* 394. See also *R.* v. *Coventry City Council, ex parte Phoenix Aviation* [1995] 3 All ER 37.

[14] *Ibid.*, at 80.

[15] *Ibid.*, at 81.

[16] Case 19/92 *Kraus* v. *Land Baden-Württemberg* [1993] ECR I–1663.

[17] Case 178/84 *Commission* v. *Germany* [1987] ECR 1227.

[18] This evinces the influence of the so-called "ordoliberal" tradition of the Freiburg school on the Community legal system.

[19] See further Case 222/86 *UNECTEF* v. *Heylens* [1987] ECR 4097; Case C–340/89 *Vlassopoulou Ministeriam für Justiz, Bunder- und Europaangelegenheiten Baden-Würtemburg* [1991] ECR I–2357; Case C–104/91 *Borrell and Others* [1992] ECR I–3003; and Joined Cases C–65 and 111/95 *The Queen* v. *Secretary of State for the Home Department, ex parte Mann Singh Shingara and Abbas Radiom, Gebbard* [1997] All ER (EC) 577; see also Case C–189/95 *Franzén*, judgment of 23 Oct. 1997, paras. 50–51.

WHAT DOES PROPORTIONALITY ENTAIL?

The principle of proportionality requires that a measure must be appropriate and necessary to achieve its objectives. According to the standard formula used by the Court, in order to establish whether a provision of Community law is consonant with the principle of proportionality, it is necessary to establish whether the means it employs to achieve the aim correspond to the importance of the aim and whether they are necessary for its achievement.[20] Thus, the principle comprises two tests: a test of suitability and a test of necessity. The first refers to the relationship between the means and the end. The means employed by the measure must be suitable, namely reasonably likely, to achieve its objectives. The second is one of weighing competing interests. The Court assesses the adverse consequences that the measure has on an interest worthy of legal protection and determines whether those consequences are justified in view of the importance of the objective pursued. It has been said that the application of the principle of proportionality entails in effect a three-part test.[21] First, it must be established whether the measure is suitable to achieve a legitimate aim (test of suitability). Secondly, it must be established whether the measure is necessary to achieve that aim, namely, whether there are other less restrictive means capable of producing the same result (the least restrictive alternative test). Thirdly, even if there are no less restrictive means, it must be established that the measure does not have an excessive effect on the applicant's interests (proportionality *stricto sensu*). The tripartite test has received some judicial support,[22] but in practice the Court does not distinguish in its analysis between the second and the third tests. Also, as will be shown, in some cases the Court finds that a measure is compatible with proportionality without searching for less restrictive alternatives, or even where such alternatives seem to exist. The essential characteristic of the principle is that the Court performs a balancing exercise between the objectives pursued by the measure in issue and its adverse effects on individual freedom.

The application of the tests of suitability and necessity enables the Court to review not only the legality but also, to some extent, the merits of legislative and

[20] See e.g. Case 66/82 *Fromançais* v. *Forma* [1983] ECR 395, para. 8; Case 15/83 *Denkavit Nederland* v. *Hoofdproduktschap voor Akkerbouwprodukten* [1984] ECR 2171, para. 25; Case 47/86 *Roquette Frères* v. *ONIC* [1987] ECR 2889, para. 19; Case 56/86 *Société pour l'exportation des sucres* [1987] ECR 1423, para. 28; Case 291/84 *Zuckerfabrik Bedburg* v. *OBEA* [1987] ECR 49, para. 46; Case C–358/88 *Oberhausener Kraftfutterwerk Wilhelm Hopermann GmbH* v. *Bundesanstalt für landwirtschaftliche Marktordnung* [1990] ECR I–1687, para. 13. See also F.G. Jacobs, "Recent Developments in the Principle of Proportionality in European Community Law" and W. van Gerven, "The Effect of Proportionality on the Actions of Member States of the European Community: National Viewpoints From Continental Europe", this vol.

[21] de Búrca, n. 4 above, at 113. See also C. Tomuschat, "Le principe de proportionnalité: Quis iudicabit?" (1977) 13 *Cah. dr. eur.* 97.

[22] See the Opinion of Van Gerven AG in Case C–159/90 *SPUC* v. *Grogan* [1991] ECR I–4685 and the Opinion of Mischo AG in Case C–331/88 *Fedesa and Others* [1990] ECR I–4023, at 4051, discussed below.

administrative measures. Because of that distinct characteristic, proportionality is often perceived to be the most far-reaching ground of review, the most potent weapon in the arsenal of the public law judge. It will be noted however that much depends on how strictly a court applies the tests of suitability and necessity and how far it is prepared to defer to the choices of the authority which has adopted the measure in issue. As already stated, in Community law, far from dictating a uniform test, proportionality is a flexible principle which is used in different contexts to protect different interests and entails varying degrees of judicial scrutiny. Subject to this caveat, it is correct to say that in general the principle of proportionality goes further than *Wednesbury* unreasonableness and facilitates the application of higher standards of judicial scrutiny than those traditionally followed by English courts.[23]

THE DEVELOPMENT OF THE PRINCIPLE IN COMMUNITY LAW

As a ground of review, the principle of proportionality was first developed by the Court to counterbalance the effects of market-regulation measures restricting economic freedom adopted under the ECSC Treaty. In *Fédéchar* v. *High Authority*[24] decided in 1956, the Court referred to "a generally-accepted rule of law" according to which the "reaction by the High Authority to illegal action must be in proportion to the scale of that action". The principle was applied in early years also in staff cases.[25] It was not until 1971, however, that proportionality was expressly relied on by the Court in *Internationale Handelsgesellschaft*.[26] The distinctive characteristics of proportionality, which the Court elaborated in subsequent cases, were laid down in the judgment in that case. After *Internationale Handelsgesellschaft*, the application of the principle as a ground of review gradually expanded beyond administrative and executive discretion to cover policy measures of general application.

The development of the principle as a ground of review of national measures followed a somewhat different pattern. Already at an early stage, the case law made it clear that a national measure could not take advantage of a derogation from the fundamental freedoms, unless it was strictly necessary.[27]

[23] In *R.* v. *Home Secretary, ex parte Brind* [1991] 1 AC 696, the House of Lords declined to accept the principle of proportionality as a ground of judicial review. But see *R.* v. *Secretary of State for the Environment, ex parte NALGO* (1992) 5 Admin.LR 785, at 799–801. For a discussion of the principle in English law, see P. Craig, *Administrative Law* (London, Sweet & Maxwell, 3rd edn., 1994), at 411 ff.; S. de Smith, H. Woolf and J. Jowell, *Judicial Review of Administrative Action* (London, Sweet & Maxwell, 1998), at 593 ff. See also J. Jowell and A. Lester, "Proportionality: Neither Novel nor Dangerous" in (1988) *CLP Special Issue, New Directions in Judicial Review* 51; and S. Boyron, "Proportionality in English Administrative Law: A Faulty Translation?" (1992) 12 *OJLS* 237.

[24] Case 8/55 *Fédération Charbonnière Belgique* v. *High Authority* [1954–56] ECR 292, at 299.

[25] See e.g. Case 18/63 *Wollast* v. *EEC* [1964] ECR 97, at 99.

[26] Case 11/70 *Internationale Handelsgesellschaft* v. *Einfuhr- und Vorratsstelle Getreide* [1970] ECR 1125. See also Case 25/70 *Einfuhr- und Vorratsstelle* v. *Koster* [1970] ECR 1161 and Case 26/70 *Einfuhr- und Vorratsstelle* v. *Henck* [1970] ECR 1183.

[27] See e.g. Case 41/74 *Van Duyn* v. *Home Office* [1974] ECR 1337.

Proportionality however began to acquire particular importance in the early 1980s. Two reasons account for that development. The first relates to the increase in litigation. As national jurisdictions became more familiar with Community law, litigation before the Court of Justice increased, and so correspondingly did reliance on proportionality as a ground of challenge of national measures. The second reason relates to a fundamental shift in judicial policy. The extension of Article 30 to encompass non-discriminatory national measures, firmly established in the seminal *Cassis de Dijon* judgment,[28] brought a vast range of national provisions within the scope of that provision, which hitherto were considered "safe" from the point of view of Community law. The emancipation of Article 30 from the notion of discrimination elevated proportionality to the determining criterion of compatibility with Community law. Similar developments followed in the context of the free movement of services and persons.

REVIEW OF COMMUNITY MEASURES: MARGINAL REVIEW

The principle of proportionality has exerted particular influence in the field of agricultural law. In effect, the fundamental difficulty which the Community's political institutions, and reflectively the Court, have encountered in the sphere of the common agricultural policy is how to allocate burdens in declining and oversupplied markets. Proportionality has been applied primarily to the following types of measures:

—market regulation measures involving choices of economic policy;
—the Community deposit system;
—measures imposing charges, sanctions and penalties.

In relation to market regulation measures, the Court applies a loose test of proportionality. Although it is prepared to assess whether a measure is appropriate and necessary in view of all relevant circumstances and to scrutinise the way the institution concerned has exercised its discretion, where it comes to the adoption of legislative measures involving economic policy choices, it will defer to the expertise and the responsibility of the adopting institution exercising "marginal" rather than "comprehensive" review. In *Fedesa*,[29] it held that the lawfulness of the prohibition of an economic activity is subject to the condition that the prohibitory measures are appropriate and necessary in order to achieve the objectives legitimately pursued by the legislation. Where there is a choice between several appropriate measures, recourse must be had to the least onerous, and the disadvantages caused must not be disproportionate to the aims pursued. The Court qualified that principle, however, by stating:

[28] Case 120/78 *Rewe-Zentral AG* v. *Bundesmonopolverwaltung für Branntwein* [1979] ECR 649.
[29] Case C–331/88 *Fedesa and others* [1990] ECR I–4023, para. 13.

> with regard to judicial review of compliance with those conditions it must be stated that in matters concerning the common agricultural policy the Community legislature has a discretionary power which corresponds to the political responsibilities given to it by Articles 40 and 43 of the Treaty. Consequently, the legality of a measure adopted in that sphere can be affected only if the measure is manifestly inappropriate having regard to the objective which the competent institution is seeking to pursue.[30]

The expression "manifestly inappropriate"[31] delineates what the Court perceives to be the limits of judicial function with regard to review of measures involving choices of economic policy. In fact, the test is rather reminiscent of that which the Court is directed to follow under Article 33(1) of the ECSC Treaty.[32] The test grants to the Community institutions ample discretion and applies to both aspects of proportionality, i.e. suitability and necessity. Although in a number of cases the suitability and effectiveness of a measure have been contested,[33] argument concentrates usually on the requirement of necessity. Necessity is more important because, in applying the principle of proportionality, the Court does not act as an appellate body exercising full-scale review of the merits but is concerned primarily with the restrictive effects of the measure on the freedom of the individual. The enquiry whether such restrictive effects are justified centres on their necessity to achieve the objective in view. In practice, review of suitability is closely linked to review of necessity and a measure which is clearly unsuitable to achieve its objectives cannot be justified and will be struck down by the Court.[34] In assessing whether a measure is suitable to achieve its objectives, it is relevant to consider the actual effects of the measure. But the fact that a measure has failed to attain its objectives in practice does not mean that it is manifestly inappropriate. The Court has held that the

[30] *Ibid.*, para. 14. See also Case 265/87 *Schräder* v. *Hauptzollamt Gronau* [1989] ECR 2237, paras. 21–22; and Case 179/84 *Bozetti* v. *Invernizzi* [1985] ECR 2301, para. 30.

[31] In other cases the Court has stated that the measure must not be "patently" or "manifestly unsuitable" to achieve its objectives. See Case 138/78 *Stölting* v. *Hauptzollamt Hamburg-Jonas* [1979] ECR 713, para. 7; and Case 59/83 *Biovilac* v. *EEC* [1984] ECR 4057, para. 17.

[32] Art. 33(1) defines the jurisdiction of the Court in actions for judicial review against acts of the High Authority. It provides that "the Court may not . . . examine the evaluation of the situation, resulting from economic facts or circumstances, in the light of which the High Authority took its decision or made its recommendations, save where the High Authority is alleged to have misused its powers or to have manifestly failed to observe the provisions of this Treaty or any rule of law relating to its application". In Case 6/54 *Netherlands* v. *High Authority* [1954–56] ECR 103, at 115, the Court held that "the term 'manifest' within the meaning of Article 33 presupposes that a certain degree is reached in the failure to observe legal provisions so that the failure to observe the ECSC Treaty appears to derive from an obvious error in the evaluation . . . of the situation in respect of which the decision was taken".

[33] See e.g. *Stölting*, n. 31 above; *Schräder*, n. 30 above; and see Joined Cases C–133/93, C–300/93 and C–362/93 *Crispoltoni Fattoria autonoma Tabacchi & Donatab Srl* [1994] ECR I–4863.

[34] See e.g. Case C–368/89 *Crispoltoni* v. *Fattoria autonoma Tabacchi di Città di Castello* [1991] ECR I–3695. In that case the Court held that a measure which retroactively fixed maximum quantities was incapable of achieving its objective of limiting production since production decisions had already been taken by the producers before its adoption.

legality of a Community act cannot depend on retrospective considerations of its efficacy.[35]

In order to determine whether a measure is necessary, the Court is receptive to argument that the same objective may be attained by less restrictive means. The case law suggests however that, in relation to policy measures, the Court does not apply the less restrictive alternative test scrupulously, relying instead on some notion of reasonableness or arbitrary conduct. In *Fedesa*[36] it was claimed that the prohibition of certain hormones on health protection grounds was not necessary. The Court did not examine whether there were any less restrictive alternatives. It held that since the Council enjoyed discretion and had made no manifest error in considering that the prohibition was appropriate, it was also entitled to take the view that the objectives pursued could not be achieved by less onerous means. The less restrictive alternative argument has been unsuccessfully submitted in a number of other cases.[37]

The manifestly inappropriate test has been applied in particular to the following types of measures:

—measures seeking to control production;
—measures setting up a common organization of the market;
—measures prohibiting or restricting the use of certain products or substances;
—monetary compensatory amounts.[38]

PROTECTIVE MEASURES IN TRADE WITH THIRD STATES

Regulations setting up a common organisation of the market often contain provisions which enable the Community institutions to introduce appropriate measures in the event that imports from, or exports to, third States threaten to cause serious disturbances to the Community market.[39] The power to take protective measures is entrusted to the Commission which, in general, enjoys wide discre-

[35] Case 40/72 *Schroeder* v. *Germany* [1973] ECR 125, para. 14. See also Joined Cases C–133/93, C–300/93 and C–362/93 *Crispoltoni* [1994] ECR I–4863, discussed below, and Joined Cases C–267 to 285/88 *Wuidart and Others* v. *Latierie coopérative eupenoise* [1990] ECR I–435, para. 14.

[36] N. 29 above.

[37] See e.g. the cases referred to in n. 35 and also Case C–280/93 *Germany* v. *Council* (*Bananas case*) [1994] ECR I–4973; Case C–8/89 *Zardi* v. *Consorzio agrario provincale di Ferrara* [1990] ECR I–2515; and Case 138/79 *Roquette Frères* v. *Council* [1980] ECR 3333, *per* Reischl AG, at 3380 ff.

[38] For detailed discussion, see Tridimas, n. 1 above.

[39] See e.g. Council Reg. 1035/72 on the common organisation of the market in fruit and vegetables [1972] II OJ Spec. Ed. 437) and its implementing Council Reg. 2707/72 [1972] OJ Spec. Ed. 3); Council Reg. 516/77 on the common organisation of the market in products processed from fruit and vegetables [1977] OJ L73/1 and its implementing Council Reg. 521/77 [1977] OJ L73/28. Reg. 516/77 was replaced by Council Reg. 426/86 [1986] OJ L49/1. Reg. 521/77 was repealed, with effect from 1 July 1995 by Council Reg. 3290/94 on the adjustments and transitional arrangements required in the agriculture sector in order to implement the agreements concluded during the Uruguay Round of multilateral trade negotiations [1994] OJ L349/105.

tion. It is for the Commission to assess whether there is a risk of serious disturbance of the market and the Court will intervene only if the Commission has committed a manifest error of assessment.[40] In practice, a challenge to the Commission's evaluation of the market conditions is extremely unlikely to succeed. Also, it is for the Commission to choose the appropriate protective measures. Such measures may include the temporary suspension of imports, the imposition of levies, or the imposition of countervailing charges.[41] Such measures inevitably impose restrictions on the economic freedom of traders and are subject to the principle of proportionality.[42] The Court has held that a countervailing charge is not unlawful merely because it is set at a fixed rate, its legality being dependent on a whole range of factors, such as the prices charged for imports and the requirement of achieving the desired aim effectively.[43] The general principle however is that a charge may not be levied at a higher level than is necessary to achieve its objectives, and in a number of cases fixed-rate charges have been annulled. In *National Dried Fruit Trade Association*[44] Commission Regulation 2742/82[45] introduced a minimum import price for dried grapes from third countries together with a fixed-rate countervailing charge applicable if the minimum price was exceeded. The Court stated that the aim of the countervailing charge was to enforce the minimum price so as to ensure Community preference in the market for dried grapes and not to inflict an economic penalty on traders who had imported below the minimum price. It followed that the introduction of a single, fixed-rate countervailing charge, imposed even where the difference between the import price and the minimum price was very small, amounted to an economic penalty and infringed the principle of proportionality.[46]

[40] See e.g. Case C–205/94 *Binder* v. *Hauptzollamt Stuttgart-West* [1996] ECR I–2871, para. 17.

[41] In Case 345/82 *Wünsche* v. *Germany* [1984] ECR 1995 it was argued that a Commission regulation imposing a levy on the importation of preserved mushrooms was invalid on the ground that the enabling regulation of the Council provided for an exhaustive list of protective measures which did not include the imposition of an additional levy. The Court rejected that argument, stating that, since the enabling regulation authorised the Commission to take protective measures leading to a complete suspension of imports, the Commission was, *a fortiori*, entitled to adopt less restrictive rules. This has been confirmed in subsequent cases: see e.g. Case 291/86 *Central-Import Münster* v. *Hauptzollamt Münster* [1988] ECR 3679; and Case C–64/95 *Lubella* v. *Hauptzollamt Cottbus* [1996] ECR I–5105.

[42] Examples are given in the text. See further Case 52/81 *Faust* v. *Commission* [1982] ECR 3745, where the Court held that suspension of imports of mushrooms from certain third States was proportionate to achieve the dual objectives of stabilisation of the market and the implementation of a Community policy relating to external trade. Cf. Case 62/70 *Bock* v. *Commission* [1971] ECR 897. In *Lubella* v. *Hauptzollampt Cottbus*, n. 41 above, the Court found compatible with the principle of proportionality protective measures consisting in the introduction of a minimum import price and a countervailing duty on the import of sour cherries.

[43] Case 77/86 *The Queen* v. *Customs and Excise, ex parte National Dried Fruit Trade Association* [1988] ECR 757, para. 29.

[44] N. 43 above.

[45] [1982] OJ L290/28.

[46] [1988] ECR 757, at para. 32, and see also the reasoning of Slynn AG at 775. For the calculation of the countervailing duty following the partial annulment of the regulation by the Court see Joined Cases C–351, 352 and 353/93 *Van der Linde and Tracotex* v. *Minister Van Landbouw* [1995] ECR I–85.

The Court's approach towards fixed-rate charges is best illustrated by reference to the mushroom cases. In 1980 the Community market in mushrooms was threatened by imports from third countries at prices well below the cost prices prevailing in the Community. In order to protect the Community industry, Commission Regulation 3429/80 made the importation of preserved mushrooms above certain quantities subject to a levy referred to as an additional amount. The levy was imposed initially for a period of three months and had a fixed rate. It was set at approximately 150 per cent of the cost price of top quality mushrooms. In *Werner Faust*[47] and *Wünsche I*[48] the Court held that the Regulation infringed the principle of proportionality on two counts. First, it penalised particularly imported mushrooms of lower quality, since it was calculated on the basis of the price of top quality mushrooms.[49] Secondly, it did not enable the levy to be set at different levels according to the quality of the products and the circumstances in which they were imported. The Court pointed out that the objective of the regulation was not to penalise imports without a licence but to protect the Community market from serious disturbance. It came to the conclusion that the levy was set at such a high level as to constitute a considerable financial charge for importers and was therefore disproportionate in relation to the objective of the regulation.[50]

Werner Faust and *Wünche* illustrate a strict application of the principle of proportionality. They establish that, in applying protective measures, the Commission must choose the alternative which is least restrictive of commercial freedom. Whereas in *National Dried Fruit Trade Association* the fixed-rate charge was annulled because it was excessive in relation to its objectives, in *Werner Faust* and *Wünche* the levy was annulled because it imposed an excessive burden on the traders concerned. An interesting argument submitted by the Commission was that the levy satisfied the test of proportionality because it was less restrictive of trade than a complete prohibition of imports which the Commission was authorised to impose under the enabling Council regulations.

[47] Case C–24/90 *Hauptzollamt Hamburg-Jonas* v. *Werner Faust OHG* [1991] ECR I–4905.

[48] Case C–25/90 *Hauptzollamt Hamburg-Jones* v. *Wünsche Handelsgesellschaft mbH and Co. KG* [1991] ECR I–4939.

[49] Cf. *Binder*, n. 40 above; in that case, the Commission imposed a minimum price and a countervailing charge on the importation of strawberries from Poland. It was argued that the protective measures breached the principle of proportionality because the minimum price was the same, irrespective of the quality of the imported strawberries. The Court held that there was no breach of proportionality because, before the entry into force of the protective measures, the Polish authorities had agreed to ensure that their exporters would comply with a mean export price applicable to all products irrespective of quality. Also, the Polish authorities were not able to ensure that the quality of exported strawberries was checked and therefore Community customs authorities were unable to monitor that minimum prices linked to the quality of imported strawberries were respected.

[50] The Court followed identical reasoning in the third mushroom case: Case C–26/90 *Wünsche II* [1991] ECR I–4961. See also Case 95/75 *Effem* v. *Hauptzollamt Luneburg* [1976] ECR 361 where the Court held that the fixing of a standard export levy applicable irrespective of the quantity, whether negligible or substantial, of cereals in certain products used for animal feed infringed Community law. Although the judgment made no reference to the principle of proportionality, Reischl AG expressly referred to the principle: see [1976] ECR at 373.

The Court dismissed that argument, stating that the contested regulation was not intended to prohibit imports in excess of certain quantities. Rather, it left open the possibility of issuing import licences against payment of a levy even where those quantities were exceeded. Having opted for that solution, the Commission was required to comply with the principle of proportionality.[51] This reasoning evinces that whether a charge is proportionate is to be determined within the confines of the policy option chosen by the Commission. A charge imposed on the individual may not go beyond what is necessary to achieve the specific, avowed, objectives of the measure in issue. The fact that the institution which introduced the measure might have chosen a different measure, more restrictive of commercial freedom, does not justify the charge. As Jacobs AG vividly put it: "[t]he use of a cannonball to kill a fly cannot be defended on the ground that a nuclear missile might have been used instead".[52] The mushrooms judgments also highlight a second function performed by the principle of proportionality. Not only does it protect the individual but it also requires the Community administration to ensure consistency between the objectives sought and the means chosen. It thus contributes to the rationalisation and coherence of the policy-making process.

It may be thought that in *Werner Faust and Wünsche* the Court applied the principle of proportionality strictly because the enabling Council regulation, on the basis of which the Commission imposed the levy, expressly provided that the Commission could take protective measures only to such extent and for such length of time as was strictly necessary. That, however, was not of paramount importance. Subsequently, in *Hüpeden* v. *Hauptzollamt Hamburg-Jonas*[53] the Court applied the same reasoning and annulled a fixed charge on imports of mushrooms, applying the general principle of proportionality even though the enabling regulation did not incorporate a specific proportionality requirement.

Following the judgments in the mushrooms cases, the Commission reduced the levy with retroactive effect but maintained it at a fixed rate. Under the new rules, the levy was no longer calculated on the basis of top quality mushrooms but on the basis of grade 3 mushrooms which were of lower quality. The levy was reduced from 150 per cent to 90 per cent of the value of the mushrooms. But the new regulation fared no better. In *Pietsch* v. *Hauptzollamt Hamburg-Waltershof*[54] it was annulled as being contrary to the principle of proportionality. The starting point of the Court's reasoning was that the aim of the regulation was not to prohibit all imports beyond the quantities specified but to protect the Community market from disruption owing to excessive imports. Even though the level of the levy was reduced, it still amounted to two-thirds of the cost price of top quality Community mushrooms. The levy substantially

[51] *Werner Faust*, n. 47 above, at para. 21. See also Case C–295/94 *Hüpeden* v. *Hauptzollamt Hamburg-Jonas* [1996] ECR I–3375, para. 30.

[52] *Werner Faust*, n. 47 above, at 4926.

[53] Case C–295/94 [1996] ECR I–3375.

[54] Case C–296/94 [1996] ECR I–3409.

increased the cost of imported mushrooms and was thus equivalent to a substantive prohibition of imports. It clearly exceeded what was necessary to attain its objective and was therefore contrary to the principle of proportionality.

In the above cases the Court exercised high intensity review, scrutinising closely the Commission's means and objectives. An interesting aspect of *Pietsch* and *Hüpeden* is that they were decided by a three-member chamber. This is noteworthy for the following reason. In January 1995, when Austria, Finland and Sweden acceded to the Community, the number of judges was increased to 15. Since then, cases which involve issues of some difficulty have been heard by a five-member chamber. It is rare for a three-member chamber to annul a Community measure and it is arguable that the cases deserved a higher court formation.

OVERVIEW OF FACTORS TO BE TAKEN INTO ACCOUNT

It has become clear from the above analysis that, far from dictating a uniform test, proportionality is a flexible principle which is used in different contexts to protect different interests and entails varying degrees of judicial scrutiny. It is by its nature flexible and open-textured. The Court applies the test of suitability and the test of necessity with varying degrees of strictness depending on a number of factors. It may be helpful here to recapitulate by listing some of those factors. They include:

—*Power of appraisal.* The nature of the contested act and, in particular, the degree of discretion required are of decisive importance. The broader the power of appraisal that the adopting institution has, the less comprehensive the review exercised by the Court. In general, it can be said that the Court undertakes only marginal review in the following cases: in relation to legislative measures of economic policy broadly understood and in relation to measures the adoption of which requires complex economic and technical evaluations.

—*The restrictive effect of the measure and the type of interest adversely affected.* The more severely a measure affects private interests, the more difficult it is to establish its necessity. For example, a charge or a penalty entails a greater restriction on commercial freedom than the refusal of a subsidy or a benefit and imposes a higher burden on the authorities to justify it. By contrast, it seems that limited importance is attributed to whether the provision under which the contested measure was adopted incorporates a test of necessity, e.g. requires action only where it is strictly necessary.[55]

[55] See *Hüpeden* v. *Hauptzollamt Hamburg-Jonas*, n. 51 above; Case 5/73 *Balkan-Import-Export* [1973] ECR 1091.

—*The objective of the measure and the type of interest which the measure seeks to protect.* Thus, public health considerations may be accorded priority over economic interests,[56] as may nuclear safety[57] and public security considerations.[58]

—*Whether the same objective can be achieved by less restrictive measures.* The Court is open to argument that the same objective can be achieved by less restrictive means. But where policy measures are involved, the less restrictive alternative test gives way to the manifestly inappropriate test.

—*The treatment of comparable products or producers.* With a view to determining whether a measure is necessary, regard may be had to the way comparable situations are treated.[59] The principle of proportionality is closely linked to the principle of equal treatment and incorporates an element of participation.[60]

—*Whether the individual has suffered actual hardship as a result of the measure.*[61]

—*The temporary effect of the measure.* Measures restricting economic freedom may be easier to justify if they are only of limited temporal application.[62]

—*The urgency of the situation.* A pressing need to regulate the market may give wider discretion to the institution which introduces the act. The same applies to transitional measures urgently drawn to deal with an emergency.[63]

—*The technicality of the subject-matter and the degree of expertise required.* The Court is more reluctant to intervene in areas of legislative intervention which require a degree of technical expertise such as anti-dumping.[64]

THE ROLE OF NATIONAL COURTS

Where proportionality is invoked to challenge the validity of a Community act, it is for the Court of Justice to apply the principle and determine whether it is infringed by the contested act. But where proportionality is invoked in

[56] *Fedesa*, n. 29 above.

[57] Case C–308/90 *Advanced Nuclear Fuels* v. *Commission* [1993] ECR I–309.

[58] Case C–120/94 *Commission* v. *Greece (FYROM Case)* [1996] ECR 1513, *per* Jacobs AG.

[59] See e.g. Case C–256/90 *Mignini* SpA v. *AIMA* [1992] ECR I–2651.

[60] See e.g. Case 114/76 *Bela Mühle Josef Bergmann KG* v. *Grons-Farm GmbH and Co. KG* [1977} ECR 1211 and *Mignini*, n. 59 above.

[61] Case 138/79 *Roquette Frères* v. *Council* [1980] ECR 3333, paras. 29, 31, and Case 106/83 *Sermide* v. *Cassa Conguaglio Zucchero* [1984] ECR 4209.

[62] But see *Bela Mühle*, n. 60 above.

[63] *Balkan-Import-Export*, n. 55 above; Case 138/79 *Roquette Frères* v. *Council* [1980] ECR 3333, para. 27.

[64] See Egger, "The Principle of Proportionality in Community Anti-Dumping Law" (1993) *18 EL Rev 367*.

preliminary reference proceedings to assess the compatibility with Community law of a national measure, the final determination of the issue may be left to the national courts.[65] More specifically, in proceedings under Article 177, the Court has three options:

—It may decide that the national measure does not interfere excessively with a fundamental freedom[66];
—It may decide that the national measure interferes excessively with a fundamental freedom and is therefore in breach of the principle of proportionality[67];
—It may give guidelines on what the principle of proportionality requires, leaving it to the national court to apply the principle in the circumstances of the case. Such guidelines may vary in specificity.

Whether the principle of proportionality should be left to the national court to apply depends on the nature of the issue involved and the specific circumstances of the case. In some cases, because of the nature of the dispute, it will simply not be possible for the Court of Justice to apply the principle conclusively. That will be so, for example, where in issue is the severity of criminal penalties. Whether a penalty is proportionate may depend on factors such as the good faith of the accused which the Court of Justice, because of the limits of its jurisdiction, is not in a position to determine.[68] One area where the Court has left considerable discretion to national courts is measures restricting free trade in the interests of national security.[69] In other cases, the issue may not be straightforward and opinions may differ. In *Clinique*[70] the Court found that the prohibition imposed by German law on the marketing of products under the name "Clinique" was not justified on grounds of consumer protection, leaving no discretion to the national court. Advocate General Gulmann, however, took the view that such a conclusive answer by the Court would overstep the limits of its jurisdiction under Article 177 and urged the Court to leave the issue to the national court to decide giving only general guidelines.[71]

[65] In enforcement proceedings, it will be for the Court of Justice to determine conclusively whether the national law or practice in issue infringes Community law in the light of proportionality See e.g. Case 124/81 *Commission* v. *UK* (*UHT Milk case*) [1983] ECR 203; Case 193/80 *Commission* v. *Italy* (*Italian Vinegar case*) [1981] ECR 3019; and Case 178/84 *Commission* v. *Germany* (*Beer case*) [1987] ECR 1227.

[66] See e.g. Case C–384/93 *Alpine Investments* [1995] ECR I–1141 and Joined Cases 266 & 267/87 *R.* v. *Royal Pharmaceutical Society of Great Britain, ex parte Association of Pharmaceutical Importers* [1989] ECR 1295.

[67] See e.g. Case 215/87 *Schumacher* v. *Hauptzollamt Frankfurt am Main-Ost* [1989] ECR 617 and Case C–347/89 *Freistaat Bayern* v. *Eurim-Pharm* [1991] ECR I–1747.

[68] See e.g. Case C–367/89 *Criminal Proceedings against Aimé Richardt* [1991] ECR I–4621, para. 25.

[69] See, e.g. *ibid*., and Case C–83/94 *Leifer* [1995] ECR I–3231.

[70] Case C-315/92 *Verband Sozialer Wettbewerb* v. *Clinique Laboratories and Estée Lauder* [1994] ECR I–317, at 326–8, *per* Gulmann AG.

[71] N. 70 above.

In some cases, because of the discretion left to it, the national court will have a creative role to play in applying the principle. In *Piageme II*,[72] the Court held that it is for the national court to determine in each individual case whether labelling given in other than the language mainly used in the Member State or region where the goods are marketed can easily be understood by consumers. Considerable discretion was also left to the national court in *De Peijper*,[73] where it was held that the national rule in issue, which had the effect of impeding parallel imports, could not be maintained unless it was clearly proved that any other rule or practice less restrictive of trade between Member States would be beyond the means which could reasonably be expected of the national administration. Similarly, in *Wurmser*[74] the Court stated that, where a Member State requires an importer to ensure that the composition of imported products complies with health and safety regulations, the importer may discharge that obligation by producing a certificate concerning composition issued by the authorities of the Member State of production or by a laboratory approved by those authorities. Where the Member State of production does not require official certificates concerning composition of the product to be supplied the importer must be entitled to supply other attestations providing a similar degree of assurance. The Court concluded that it is for the national court to determine whether, having regard to all the circumstances of the case, the attestations provided by the importer are sufficient to establish that the latter has fulfilled his obligation to verify.

The approach of leaving considerable discretion to the national courts is not without drawbacks. The national court which made the reference may not get an answer to the question referred. Lengthy and costly litigation before the Court of Justice may prove inconclusive, or even of little help for the solution of the dispute. This was clearly illustrated in the protracted Sunday trading litigation.[75] Also, leaving the application of proportionality to the national court inevitably gives rise to differences in the application of Community law in the various Member States. Despite those problems, entrusting, where appropriate, national courts with the application of the principle is the correct policy. In determining the demarcation line between lawful and unlawful impediments to fundamental freedoms, national jurisdictions cannot be denied a role, and this is so for two reasons. The first is a practical one. As already stated, in some cases, national courts are better placed to perform the balancing exercise which is the essence of proportionality. The second reason is one of principle. The underlying objective of the case law is to achieve a balance between the need for uniform application of Community law and the need to respect the autonomy

[72] Case C–385/94 *Groupement Producteurs, Importateurs et Agents Généraux d'Eaux Minérales Etrangères, VZW (Piageme)* v. *Peeters NV* [1995] ECR I–2955. See also Case 27/80 *Criminal Proceedings against Anton Adriaan Fietje* [1980] ECR 3839 and Case 220/81 *Criminal Proceedings against Timothy Frederick Robertson* [1982] ECR 2349.

[73] Case 104/75 *Adriaan De Peijper Managing Director of Centraform BV* [1976] ECR 613.

[74] Case 25/88 *Criminal Proceedings* v. *Bonchara, Nee Wurmser* [1989] ECR 1105, at para. 19.

[75] See especially *Stoke-on-Trent CC and Norwich CC* v. *B & Q* [1991] Ch. 48 (Hoffmann J).

of Member States in areas where there is no Community harmonisation. That is best served by leaving, within certain limits, discretion to the national jurisdictions. It is submitted that overall the Court of Justice has not followed an inconsistent approach, leaving the issue to national courts to decide only where the latter are by virtue of objective criteria better placed to do so.[76] It will be noted that even where the Court of Justice does not give the referring court a conclusive answer for the solution of the dispute, its reference to the principle of proportionality by no means lacks relevance. However large the discretion left to the national court in a specific case, it is under an overriding obligation to perform a balancing exercise, paying due regard to the requirements of the fundamental freedoms. It is with this consideration in mind that the case law should be assessed. In effect, the Court infuses certain standards of judicial control and cultivates a propensity on the part of the national courts to "think federal". That is particularly important for English law, where proportionality is not traditionally recognised as a ground of review.

PROPORTIONALITY AS A PRINCIPLE GOVERNING THE EXERCISE OF COMMUNITY COMPETENCE

Article 3b(3) EC states that "[a]ny action by the Community shall not go beyond what is necessary to achieve the objectives of this Treaty". According to the prevailing view, Article 3b(3) does not add to the existing case law. It merely reiterates the importance of the principle of proportionality and grants it constitutional status.[77] The only difference seems to be one of emphasis. As a general principle of law, proportionality has been developed by the Court primarily with a view to protecting the individual from action by the Community institutions and by the Member States. By contrast, Article 3b(3) forms part of a system of provisions whose aim is to control the expansion of the Community legislative action and to seek to limit burdens on Member States rather than burdens on individuals. This is not to say that the protection of rights of the individual is excluded from the scope of Article 3b(3). The provision is understood to mean that "any burdens, whether financial or administrative, falling upon the Community, national governments, local authorities, economic operators and citizens, should be minimized and should be proportionate to the objectives to be achieved".[78]

[76] There are, however, exceptions. A case in the area of sex discrimination where it is submitted the issue should have been left to the national court to decide as suggested by the AG is Case C–457/93 *Lewark* [1996] ECR I–243. See also discussion of this case by E. Ellis in "The Concept of Proportionality in European Community Sex Discrimination Law", this vol.

[77] See K. Lenaerts and P. Van Ypersele, "Le principe de subsidiarité et son contexte: Étude de l'article 3B du traité CE" (1994) 30 *Cah. dr. eur.* 3, at 61; T.C. Hartley, *The Foundations of European Community Law* (4th edn., Oxford, Clarendon, 1998), at 148; Emiliou, op.cit., n. 4, at p. 401. But see V. Constantinesco, R. Kovar and D. Simon, *Traité sur l'Union Européenne* (Paris, Economica, 1995), at 113.

[78] European Council of Edinburgh, 11–12 Dec. 1992, Presidency Conclusions, Annex 1 to Part I A, *Agence Europe*, Spec.Ed., No. 5878*bis*, 13/14 Dec. 1992.

Proportionality is also incorporated by implication in the principle of subsidiarity. Article 3b(2) requires that the Community may take action "only if and in so far as" the objectives of the proposed action cannot be sufficiently achieved by the Member States. There are however differences between the two. First, the principle of subsidiarity comes into play at an earlier stage than the principle of proportionality.[79] It defines whether or not action must be taken at Community level. Proportionality, by contrast, comes into play only once it is decided that Community action is necessary and seeks to define its scope. The second difference is that Article 3b(2), which defines the principle of subsidiarity, applies only in cases where the competence of the Community is not exclusive, whereas Article 3b(3) applies also where the Community enjoys exclusive competence. Indeed, it seems that the reason Article 3b(3) was added by the Treaty of European Union was to ensure that the Community respects the interests of Member States not only where it exercises concurrent competence but also where it exercises its exclusive competence, which falls outside the scope of Article 3b(2).[80] A third difference was identified by Advocate General Léger in the *Organisation of Working Time Directive case*.[81] The Advocate General pointed out that subsidiarity determines whether Community action is to be set in motion, whereas proportionality defines its scope. From this he concluded that the first principle comes into play before the Community takes action, whereas the second comes into play after such action has been taken.[82] It is submitted however that Article 3b(3) lays down a principle which, like the principle of subsidiarity, is directed primarily, although not exclusively, at the political institutions of the Community and is designed to influence the legislative process *ex ante* i.e. at the stage of preparation of legislation.[83]

Article 3b(3) refers both to the extent and to the intensity of Community action. It requires Community action not to exceed what is necessary to achieve the objectives of the Treaty but does not itself limit those objectives, nor does it require their restrictive interpretation. The Conclusions of the Presidency of the European Council held in Edinburgh in December 1992 laid down guidelines for the adoption of Community legislation in the light of Article 3b(3).[84] The guidelines state *inter alia* that Community measures should leave as much scope for national decision as possible and that, while respecting Community law, care

[79] See Lenaerts and Van Ypersele, n. 77 above, para. 100 and G. Strozzi, "Le principe de subsidiarité dans la perspective de l'intégration européenne: une énigme et beaucoup d'attentes" (1994) 30 *RTDE* 373, at 379. Those texts received judicial recognition by Léger AG in Case C–84/94 *United Kingdom* v. *Council* [1996] ECR I–5755, at 5783.

[80] Lenaerts and Van Ypersele, n. 77 above, 62.

[81] Case C–84/94 *United Kingdom* v. *Council* [1996] ECR I–5755.

[82] *Ibid.*, at para. 126.

[83] This view is also shared by A. Dashwood, see "The Working Time Judgment in a Wider Perspective", in "The ECJ's Working Time Judgment: The Social Market Vindicated", *CELS Occasional Paper* No. 2, 30.

[84] See also now the Protocol on the application of the principles of subsidiarity and proportionality annexed to the EC Treaty by the Treaty of Amsterdam, on which see V. Constantinesco, "Le protocole sur l'application des principes de subsidiarité et de proportionalité" (1997) 33 *RTDE* 765.

should be taken to respect well-established national arrangements and the organisation and working of Member States' legal systems. Where appropriate, and subject to the need for proper enforcement, Community measures should provide Member States with alternative ways to achieve the objectives of the measures.[85] Where it is necessary to set standards at Community level, consideration should be given to setting minimum standards, with freedom for Member States to set higher national standards, not only in the areas where the Treaty so requires (e.g. Articles 118a, 130t) but also in other areas where this would not conflict with the objectives of the proposed measure or with the Treaty.[86] The Community should legislate only to the extent necessary. Other things being equal, directives should be preferred to regulations and framework directives to detailed measures. Non-binding measures such as recommendations should be preferred where appropriate. Consideration should also be given, where appropriate, to the use of voluntary codes of conduct.[87] Where difficulties are localised and only certain Member States are affected, any necessary Community action should not be extended to other Member States unless this is necessary to achieve an objective of the Treaty.[88] The last point is important because it brings to the surface the relationship between the principle of proportionality and the principle of equality of Member States. In its case law the Court has accepted that it is compatible with the principle of equal treatment for the Community to adopt rules which apply only to certain Member States, where that is objectively justified.[89] The European Council conclusions recognise that differences in infrastructure or the underlying conditions of Member States in specific sectors where Community action is envisaged may make intervention by the Community proportionate in relation to some Member States but disproportionate in relation to others.[90]

Before the Treaty on European Union came into force, the case law accepted that the principle of proportionality can be invoked by Member States as well as by individuals.[91] In one case, the Court rejected the argument that the principle of proportionality amounted to a "principle of minimum intervention" according to which, in interpreting Community measures, preference should be given to the interpretation which restricted Community intervention on Member States sovereignty to the minimum.[92] Proportionality as a principle governing the exercise of Community competence came to the fore in *Germany* v.

[85] See Conclusions, n. 78 above, para. (iii).

[86] *Ibid.*, para. (iv).

[87] *Ibid.*, para. (v).

[88] *Ibid.*, para. (vii).

[89] See e.g. Case 13/63 *Italy* v. *Commission* [1963] ECR 338 and Joined Cases C–181, 182 & 218/88 *Deschamps* v. *Ofival* [1989] ECR I–4381.

[90] Lenaerts and Van Ypersele, n. 77 above, at 67.

[91] See e.g. Case 116/82 *Commission* v. *Germany* [1986] ECR 2519 and Case 37/83 *Rewe-Zentrale* v. *Landwirtschaftskammer Rheinland* [1984] ECR 1229.

[92] Case 28/84 *Commission* v. *Germany* [1985] ECR 3097.

Council.[93] By Regulation 2186/93,[94] adopted under Article 213 EC, the Council required Member States to establish registers for statistical purposes containing information on commercial enterprises. The purpose of registers was to provide the Commission with reliable information so as to enable it to perform its various tasks. The German government argued that the Regulation infringed the principle of proportionality in two respects. First, it required the registration of certain data which were not necessary to achieve the objectives of the Regulation. Secondly, the financial and administrative costs in establishing and periodically updating the national registers were disproportionate by comparison to the potential benefits. The Court rejected both arguments. With regard to the first, it held that the information required to be included was statistically relevant. With regard to the second, it stated that the German government had not shown that the costs were "manifestly disproportionate" to the advantages resulting for the Community from the availability of reliable data regarding the structure of the economy throughout the Community.

The case was introduced before the Treaty on European Union came into force so that Article 3b(3) was not directly relevant. But there is no reason to suppose that the solution would now be different. It seems then that the Court will be reluctant to intervene unless it is shown that a measure manifestly goes beyond the objectives of the Treaty. The intensity of review is no different from when proportionality is applied for the protection of the individual to control the legality of policy measures.[95] This is confirmed by the *Organisation of the Working Time Directive case*[96] where the Court rejected the challenge of the United Kingdom to Council Directive 93/104[97] on grounds of breach of the principle of proportionality. The Court stated that, in making social policy choices, the Community legislature is required to make complex assessments and must be allowed wide discretion. Consequently, review is limited to examining whether the exercise of discretion has been vitiated by manifest error or misuse of powers or whether the institution concerned has manifestly exceeded the limits of its discretion.[98]

In the *Organisation of Working Time Directive case*, the United Kingdom objected to what it saw as the introduction of broad social policy measures by the back door, namely on the basis of Article 118a which deals with health and safety at work and authorises the adoption of directives by qualified majority as opposed to unanimity in the Council of Ministers. One of the arguments submitted by the government was that the measures for the organisation of working time provided in Directive 93/104, including minimum rest periods and maximum weekly working time, were disproportionate. The desired level of

[93] Case C–426/93 [1995] ECR I–3723.

[94] Reg. 2186/93 on Community co-ordination in drawing up business registers for statistical purposes, [1993] OJ L196/1.

[95] See also Case C–233/94 *Germany* v. *Parliament and Council* [1997] ECR I–2405.

[96] Case C–84/94 *United Kingdom* v. *Council* [1996] ECR I–5755.

[97] Dir. 93/104/EC of 23 Nov. 1993 concerning certain aspects of the organisation of working time [1993] OJ L307/18.

[98] *United Kingdom* v. *Council*, n. 96 above, at para. 58.

protection could have been achieved by less restrictive measures such as the use of risk assessments where working hours exceeded particular norms. The Court held that the measures of the directive contributed directly to the improvement of health and safety of workers within the meaning of Article 118a and were therefore suitable to attain their objectives. With regard to the test of necessity, the Court held that the Council had not committed a manifest error in considering that the objectives of Article 118a could be achieved be less restrictive measures. In reaching that conclusion, the Court placed particular emphasis on the flexibility of the directive. Its provisions were subject to several derogations thus leaving scope for adjustments at national level.

It is submitted that the Court's approach to exercising only marginal review in cases such as the *Organisation of Working Time Directive case* is correct. Proportionality seems a less suitable criterion for assessing whether Community action interferes unduly with Member State sovereignty than for assessing undue restrictions on individual freedom. Whether Community action is necessary or not is primarily a question of policy, not a question of law. It is likely that in most cases there will be a dearth of objective criteria on the basis of which the choices of the Community legislature may be assessed by a judicial body. Review therefore must necessarily be restricted to determining whether there is manifest error. By contrast, in such cases there is more scope for judicial intervention in determining whether the measure in issue is adequately reasoned and whether it has been adopted on the correct legal basis.

CONCLUSIONS

The above analysis has attempted to show the relative nature of the principle of proportionality in Community law. Far from dictating a uniform test, it is an open-textured principle which is used in different contexts to protect different interests, and it entails different degrees of judicial scrutiny. In applying the principle, the Community courts do not exercise full-scale review of the merits. But the Community judicature is prepared to exercise closer scrutiny than English courts. As Laws J put it, in European law, the limits of judicial review "lie further back". The decision-making body is required to demonstrate a substantive justification for its actions or, in other words, to "provide a fully reasoned case".[99] The contrast is sharper in certain areas, for example, in issues of public security where English courts are singularly reluctant to review executive decision-making[100] whereas the Court of Justice is prepared to hold an enquiry on grounds of proportionality.[101]

[99] *R.* v. *Ministry of Agriculture, Fisheries and Food, ex parte First City Trading Limited* [1997] 1 CMLR 250, at 279, *per* Laws J.

[100] See e.g. *R.* v. *Secretary of State for the Home Department, ex parte Cheblak* [1991] 2 All ER 319.

[101] See e.g. Case 72/83 *Campus Oil Limited* v. *Minister for Industry and Energy* [1984] ECR 2727 and Case C–83/94 *Leifer* [1995] ECR I–3231.

Unreasonableness and Proportionality in UK Law

PAUL CRAIG

There has been considerable discussion about whether proportionality should be recognised as a head of review in its own right, and the relationship between proportionality and *Wednesbury* review. The present paper is a contribution to this debate. The argument is structured in the following way.

The object of the first section is to clear the ground by making it clear that no one advocates substitution of judgment by the reviewing court, and that proportionality does not entail any such substitution. This is followed by an analysis of the present status of proportionality within UK law. The third section of the paper then examines in more detail than hitherto the meaning of the *Wednesbury* principle itself, and the way in which it has been applied by our courts. There is then an examination of the arguments for and against the recognition of proportionality as an independent ground of review. The conclusion reached is that proportionality should indeed be recognised now as a ground of review in its own right, and that the fears of those who are opposed to this step can be properly met.

THE LIMITS OF THE JUDICIAL ROLE: CLEARING THE GROUND

Before examining the relationship between proportionality and unreasonableness it might be helpful at the outset to clear the ground by stating what is not in dispute: it is not for the courts to substitute their judgment on the merits of the case for that of the primary decision-maker. It should be stressed that this is accepted by all, even those who are in favour of the recognition of proportionality as an independent head of review in its own right. Our basic conceptions of political theory and the allocation of governmental functions are against any such substitution of judgment. Decisions as to political and social choice are made by the legislature, or by a person assigned the task by the legislature. To sanction general judicial intervention simply because the court would prefer a different choice from that of the administrator runs counter to this fundamental assumption, and would entail a re-allocation of power from the legislature and bureaucracy to the courts. The courts in the UK are fully aware of this.

This is exemplified by *R.* v. *Cambridge Health Authority, ex parte B.*[1] The applicant, B, was a 10-year-old girl who was extremely ill. She had received varying treatments for this illness, including a bone marrow transplant, but the treatment had not proven to be effective. As a result the hospital, on the advice of the relevant specialists, decided that B had only a short time to live and that further major therapy should not be given. B's father sought the opinion of two further specialists who thought that a second bone marrow transplant might have some chance of success. Such treatment could, however, only be administered privately because there were no beds in the National Health Service public sector within a hospital which could carry out such therapy. The proposed treatment would take place in two stages, the first of which would cost £15,000 and have a 10–20 per cent chance of success; the second stage would cost £60,000 with a similar 10–20 per cent chance of success. B's father requested the health authority to allocate the funds necessary for this therapy. It refused to do so, given the limited nature of the funds at its disposal and the small likelihood that the treatment would be effective. B's father then sought judicial review of this decision. This application succeeded in part at first instance, but the decision was overturned by the Court of Appeal.

Sir Thomas Bingham MR recognised the tragic nature of B's situation, but stressed also that the courts were not the arbiters of the merits in cases of this nature. It was not for the courts to express any opinion as to the likely success or not of the relevant medical treatment.[2] The courts should, said the Master of the Rolls, confine themselves to the lawfulness of the decision under scrutiny. The basic rationale for the health authority's refusal to press further with treatment for B was, of course, the scarcity of resources. The court's role in this respect was perforce limited.

> I have no doubt that in a perfect world any treatment which a patient . . . sought would be provided if doctors were willing to give it, no matter how much it cost, particularly when a life was potentially at stake. It would however, in my view, be shutting one's eyes to the real world if the court were to proceed on the basis that we do live in such a world. It is common knowledge that health authorities of all kinds are constantly pressed to make ends meet. They cannot pay their nurses as much as they would like; they cannot provide all the treatments they would like; they cannot purchase all the extremely expensive medical equipment they would like; they cannot carry out all the research they would like; they cannot build all the hospitals and specialist units they would like. Difficult and agonising judgments have to be made as to how a limited budget is best allocated to the maximum advantage of the maximum number of patients. That is not a judgment which the court can make. In my judgment, it is not something that a health authority such as this authority can be fairly criticised for not advancing before the court.[3]

[1] [1995] 2 All ER 129. See also *R.* v. *Chief Constable of Sussex, ex parte International Trader's Ferry Ltd* [1995] 4 All ER 364, [1997] 2 All ER 65.

[2] *Ibid., at* 135–6.

[3] *Ibid.*, at 137.

The Master of the Rolls believed, moreover, that it was unrealistic to demand of the health authority the type of detailed financial explanation which had been required by the lower court. Our courts have made great strides in demanding reasoned decision-making from public bodies.[4] There are, however, limits to the degree of detail which can be demanded of them, particularly in this type of case. This is brought out forcefully by Sir Thomas Bingham MR in the following passage:

> I furthermore think, differing I regret from the judge, that it would be totally unrealistic to require the authority to come to the court with its accounts and seek to demonstrate that if this treatment were provided for B then there would be a patient, C, who would have to go without treatment. No major authority could run its financial affairs in a way which would permit such a demonstration.[5]

There is therefore no disagreement about the undesirability of substitution of judgment by a court engaged in judicial review. All accept that it is not for the courts to consider the relevant matter *de novo* and substitute their view on the merits on, for example, how resources should be allocated for that of the primary decision-maker. Laws J succinctly captured this point in the *First City Trading* case[6] when he stated that it was not the court's task to decide what it would have done had it been the decision-maker, since the latter has a political authority and a political responsibility which the court does not possess. There will, he said, always be a range of options which are factually open to the decision-maker, and it was not the business of the court to give effect to any preference for one possible measure over another when both lie within the proper legal limits. It should be emphasised that this is fully accepted by those systems which apply proportionality as a test of review in its own right, as duly recognised by Laws J in *First City Trading*.[7]

It must, however, also be recognised that there is no similar consensus about the proper reach of judicial review once we advance beyond this basic proposition. The literature is replete with warnings about the judiciary interfering with the "merits" of the case, and this is so even when it is clear that nothing amounting to pure substitution of judgment was in issue in the relevant case. Indeed, one of the matters which divides advocates and opponents of proportionality is whether such a concept involves too great an interference with the merits, even when it does not involve substitution of judgment. The analysis which follows will examine this matter rather more closely than hitherto. The extent to which both proportionality and unreasonableness involve some intrusion on the merits of the case, and the legitimacy of this control, will be considered in due course. Before we do so there will be an overview of the present status of proportionality within UK law.

[4] P. Craig, "The Common Law, Reasons and Administrative Justice" [1994] *CLJ* 282.

[5] [1995] 2 All ER 129, at 137H–J.

[6] *R.* v. *Ministry of Agriculture, Fisheries and Food, ex parte First City Trading* [1997] 1 CMLR 250, 278.

[7] *Ibid.*, at 279.

PROPORTIONALITY IN DOMESTIC LAW: THE CURRENT POSITION

It is well known that in the *GCHQ*[8] case Lord Diplock held out the possibility that proportionality might become an independent head of judicial review in its own right. This has not yet transpired. The leading authority on the status of proportionality is still the House of Lords' decision in *R.* v. *Secretary of State for the Home Department, ex parte Brind*.[9] The Home Secretary issued directives under the Broadcasting Act 1981 requiring the BBC and the IBA to refrain from broadcasting certain matters by persons who represented organisations which were proscribed under legislation concerning the prevention of terrorism. The ambit of this proscription was limited to direct statements made by the members of the organisations. It did not, for example, prevent the broadcasting of such persons on film, provided that there was a voice-over account paraphrasing what had been said. The applicants sought judicial review on a number of grounds, one of which was that the directives were disproportionate to the end sought to be attained. This objective was both to deny such organisations any appearance of political legitimacy, and also to prevent intimidation.

Their Lordships rejected the argument based upon proportionality. Lord Bridge held that the restrictions on freedom of speech were not unreasonable in scope, and did not believe that the applicants' case could be improved by invoking the idea of proportionality.[10] Lord Bridge did, however, agree with Lord Roskill that proportionality might at some time be incorporated within our law. Lord Roskill himself acknowledged that Lord Diplock had, in the *GCHQ* case, held this open as a possible future development, but Lord Roskill did not believe that this was an appropriate case for such a development, believing that this could lead the courts into substituting their view for that of the Home Secretary on the particular issue before the court.[11] Similar concerns are apparent in the judgments of Lord Ackner and Lord Lowry. Thus Lord Ackner[12] reasoned that if proportionality was to add something to our existing law, then it would be imposing a more intensive standard of review than traditional *Wednesbury* unreasonableness. This would mean that an "inquiry into and a decision upon the merits cannot be avoided",in the sense that the court would have to balance the pros and cons of the decision which was being challenged.[13] Lord Lowry was equally wary of overstepping the boundary between a supervisory and an appellate jurisdiction. He felt that the judges are not well equipped by training or experience to "decide the answer to an administrative problem where the scales are evenly balanced".[14] His Lordship also feared that stability would be jeopar-

[8] *R.* v. *Minister for the Civil Service, ex parte Council of Civil Service Unions* [1985] AC 374, at 410.

[9] [1991] 1 AC 696.

[10] *Ibid.*, at 748–9.

[11] *Ibid.*, at 749–50.

[12] *Ibid.*, at 762–3.

[13] *Ibid.*, at 762.

[14] *Ibid.*, at 767.

dised because "there is nearly always something to be said against any administrative decision", and that recognition of proportionality would, therefore, lead to an increase in the number of applications for judicial review, with a consequential increase in costs both for litigants and in terms of court time.[15]

The cogency of these objections will be considered in due course. Before we do so it might be helpful to provide an overview of the case law since *Brind*. These cases can most usefully be divided in the following manner.[16]

First, there are decisions concerning the application of proportionality in areas covered by EC law. It is clear as a matter of principle that national courts are bound to apply EC law principles, and they have applied proportionality in cases which have a Community law element.[17] This is exemplified by the *ITF* case.[18] The applicants were exporters of live animals across the Channel. There were serious protests against such exports at the relevant docks. The Chief Constable of Sussex deployed very significant manpower to control the protests, but then decided that, because of his limited resources, he could only provide the requisite police cover for the exporters on two days a week. ITF argued that this decision was irrational under domestic law and that it was contrary to the EC Treaty. The argument based on domestic law failed: it was for the Chief Constable to decide how to use his limited resources, and there was no way in which that decision could characterised as *Wednesbury* unreasonable. The EC claim was premised on the ground that the Chief Constable's decision constituted an export ban which was prohibited by Article 34. The House of Lords accepted that, assuming there had been a breach of Article 34, proportionality would be of relevance in deciding on the application of Article 36. This latter Article allows a defence for limitations placed on the free movement of goods where there are good reasons of, *inter alia*, public security or public health, provided that the limitation is not disproportionate. The Chief Constable's decision was held to be a proportionate response, more particularly when read in the light of the ECJ's case law concerning the extent of the state's duty to protect free movement rights against encroachment by private parties.[19] A further example of the application of proportionality in areas covered by EC law is to be found in the *International Stock Exchange* case.[20] The decision of the Stock Exchange to delist the shares of a company pursuant to powers contained in a Community directive was challenged on the grounds of proportionality. The

[15] *Ibid.*

[16] A valuable detailed discussion of this case law can be found in G. de Búrca, "Proportionality and Wednesbury Unreasonableness" in M. Andenas (ed.), *The Common Law of Europe and the Public Law of the United Kingdom* (London, Key Haven Publications, 1998), chap. 1.

[17] See, e.g., R. v. *Minister of Agriculture, Fisheries and Food, ex parte Bell Line* [1984] 2 CMLR 502; R. v. *Ministry of Agriculture, Fisheries and Food, ex parte Roberts* [1990] 1 CMLR 555; R. v. *Secretary of State for the Home Department, ex parte Adams* [1995] All ER (EC) 177; R. v. *Ministry of Agriculture, Fisheries and Food, ex parte First City Trading* [1997] 1 CMLR 250.

[18] R. v. *Chief Constable of Sussex, ex parte International Trader's Ferry Ltd*, [1999] 1 All ER 129, 157.

[19] Case C–265/95 *Commission* v. *France*, 9 Dec. 1997.

[20] R. v. *International Stock Exchange, ex parte Else* [1992] BCC 11.

court accepted that proportionality was an appropriate standard of review to apply in such a case, but found against the applicant: the relevant committee of the Stock Exchange had considered less drastic means of controlling the company short of delisting, and the court saw no reason to conclude that its findings were disproportionate. There are a number of other cases in which the courts have applied the criterion of proportionality in cases which have a Community law element.[21]

The second category concerns cases which have no Community law component, where the court either explicitly or implicitly declines to apply proportionality as an independent standard of review. Thus in the *International Stock Exchange* case[22] Popplewell J stated in the course of his judgment that it was accepted that proportionality was not a free-standing principle so far as domestic law was concerned and that it would not be proper for a judge at first instance to take steps to incorporate the concept. A similar reluctance to engage in review over and beyond that contained in the *Wednesbury* principle is also apparent in Popplewell J's decision in *Absalom*.[23] He rejected proportionality as a ground of review in an application to quash a decision of the Chief Constable which required the applicant police constable to retire from the police force. Popplewell J acknowledged that the Chief Constable had a range of penalties open to him, but felt that it would not be proper to apply a more intensive species of review than traditional irrationality. The court should not substitute its view for that of the primary decision-maker, and this was particularly so in those areas where that person had expertise.

A reluctance to stray beyond the confines of the traditional *Wednesbury* formula is equally evident in *Hargreaves*.[24] The applicants were prisoners who were serving between six and eight years in prison. When they were imprisoned in 1994 they were each told that they could apply for home leave after serving one third of their sentence. The notice made it clear that such leave was a privilege. At the same time the applicants each signed a compact with the prison authorities under which the prison promised to consider them for home leave when they became eligible and required them to be of good behaviour. In 1995 changes were made to the system whereby the applicants could only become eligible for home leave when they had completed one half of their sentence. The rationale for this change was that it would increase public confidence in the administration of justice and improve public safety. As a result the earliest date on which the applicants would be eligible for home leave was deferred for a substantial period. The applicants claimed that the changes introduced in 1995 constituted a violation of their legitimate expectations concerning home leave which had arisen both as a result of the previous policy and as a result of the

[21] See, e.g., R. v. *Secretary of State for the Home Department, ex parte Adams* [1995] All ER (EC) 177; R. v. *Ministry of Agriculture, Fisheries and Food, ex parte First City Trading* [1997] 1 CMLR 250.

[22] N. 20 above.

[23] R. v. *Chief Constable of Kent, ex parte Absalom*, 6 May 1993, unreported.

[24] R. v. *Secretary of State for the Home Department, ex parte Hargreaves* [1997] 1 All ER 397.

compact entered into between each prisoner and the prison authorities. The Home Secretary made the changes to the policy on home leave because of concern over the number of prisoners who had absconded or committed further crimes while on home leave, hence the desire to tighten up the system. There were some transitional provisions,[25] but other existing prisoners sentenced after 1992 and serving more than four years would be subject to the new criteria. The Court of Appeal held that the applicants did not have any legitimate expectations which were infringed by the change of policy, primarily because of the previous ruling of the House of Lords in *Findlay*.[26] The applicants were equally unsuccessful in their claim based on the compact with the prison authorities. It is, however, the statements by the Court of Appeal concerning the standard of review which are most relevant here. Counsel for the applicants placed reliance on the reasoning of Sedley J in *Hamble Fisheries*.[27] In that case Sedley J had held that the legitimacy of an expectation was a function of the expectations induced by the government, and the policy considerations which weighed against their fulfilment. This balance was to be struck initially by the original decision-maker. It could then be re-assessed by the court on review, and when the court performed this function the bare rationality of the decision was not the sole criterion.[28] The Court of Appeal in *Hargreaves* disagreed with this formulation.[29] It held that the authorities on which Sedley J had relied all concerned procedural rather than substantive expectations. While such a balancing role for the courts might be appropriate in such cases it was not felt to be the correct test where the matter was substantive in nature. The court accepted the argument put on behalf of the Home Secretary by Michael Beloff QC that Sedley J's balancing test was heretical, and overruled his judgment in this respect. The correct approach was, said the court, to apply the *Wednesbury* test.

The third category concerns once again purely domestic cases where the courts have, however, either explicitly applied proportionality or reasoned in a manner which is analogous thereto.[30] This current in the case law is especially noteworthy in cases dealing with penalties or fundamental rights.

There are a number of decisions where the courts have applied proportionality expressly or impliedly in the context of challenges to the penalty which has been imposed by an administrative authority, as exemplified by *Hook*[31] where

[25] There were some transitional provisions to cover those who were within 12 months of their parole eligibility and who had already successfully completed a period of home leave; and those sentenced to 4 years or more before the implementation of the Criminal Justice Act 1991 would be allowed to retain their eligibility for resettlement licence at the point at which they would become eligible for release on parole licence.

[26] *Findlay* v. *Secretary of State for the Home Department* [1985] AC 318.

[27] *R.* v. *Ministry of Agriculture, Fisheries and Food, ex parte Hamble (Offshore) Fisheries Ltd.* [1995] 2 All ER 714.

[28] *Ibid.*, at 731.

[29] [1997] 1 All ER 397, at 411–12.

[30] J. Jowell and A. Lester, "Proportionality: Neither Novel nor Dangerous" in J. Jowell and D. Oliver (eds.), *New Directions in Judicial Review* (London, Stevens, 1988), at 51–73.

[31] *R.* v. *Barnsley MBC, ex parte Hook* [1976] 1 WLR 1052, at 1057.

a stallholder had his licence revoked for urinating in the street and using offensive language. Lord Denning MR struck down the decision in part because the penalty was excessive and out of proportion to the offence.[32]

A similar trend is apparent in cases where the affected interest is a fundamental right. Lord Templeman in *Brind*[33] reasoned in a manner directly analogous to proportionality. The court was not restricted, in cases involving human rights, to asking whether the governmental action was perverse or irrational. The judge must rather inquire whether a reasonable minister could reasonably conclude that the interference with the right in question was justifiable. Any such interference must be necessary and proportionate to the damage which the restriction was designed to prevent. Lord Bridge's reasoning was similar. While his Lordship denied that proportionality could advance the applicant's claim, he none the less made it clear that the real inquiry was as to whether the reasonable minister could reasonably reach the conclusion which was now being challenged. In answering this inquiry the court was entitled to start from the premise that any restriction of the right to freedom of expression must be justified and that nothing less than an important competing public interest will suffice in this respect. The same approach is evident in *Smith*[34] where there was a challenge to the policy of prohibiting gay men and women from serving in the armed forces. Sir Thomas Bingham MR, as he then was, followed the suggestion advanced by counsel for the applicants, David Pannick QC, and held that the more substantial the interference with human rights, the more the court would require by way of justification before it would accept that the decision was reasonable.[35] In formulating the test in this manner he drew explicitly upon the dictum of Lord Bridge in *Bugdaycay*[36] and that of Lord Templeman in *Brind*.[37] There are a number of other post-*Brind* cases which adopt the same test, *Leech*[38] and *McQuillan*[39] being among the most notable examples. In *McQuillan* the applicant challenged the legality of an exclusion order imposed on him under the Prevention of Terrorism (Temporary Provisions) Act 1989, prohibiting him from entering Great Britain on the ground that he was or had been involved in acts of terrorism. He maintained that he was no longer a member of a terrorist organisation and that his life was in danger if he continued to live in Northern Ireland. The Home Secretary was not persuaded and refused to revoke the

[32] See also *R.* v. *Warwick Crown Court, ex parte Smalley* [1987] 1 WLR 237; *R.* v. *Highbury Magistrates' Court, ex parte Uchendu* (1994) 158 JP 409; *R.* v. *Secretary of State for the Environment, ex parte NALGO, The Times*, 2 Dec. 1992; *R.* v. *Manchester Metropolitan University, ex parte Nolan*, 14 July 1995, unreported.

[33] N. 9 above.

[34] *R.* v. *Ministry of Defence, ex parte Smith* [1996] 1 All ER 256.

[35] *Ibid.*, at 263.

[36] *Bugdaycay* v. *Secretary of State for the Home Department* [1987] AC 514, at 531.

[37] N. 9 above, at 748–9.

[38] *R.* v. *Secretary of State for the Home Department, ex parte Leech* [1994] QB 198.

[39] *R.* v. *Secretary of State for the Home Department, ex parte McQuillan* [1995] 4 All ER 400.

exclusion order.[40] Sedley J recognised that freedom of movement, subject only to the general law, was a fundamental value of the common law.[41] The power given to the Home Secretary to restrict this freedom, not by modifying the general law, but by depriving certain persons of the full extent of this right, was a draconian measure which could be justified only by a grave emergency. Such a power could create a form of internal exile. It was for this reason that Parliament had only sanctioned use of such a power to counter the grave threat of terrorism. It was for this reason also that the courts would scrutinise the minister's reasoning closely and "draw the boundaries of rationality tightly around his judgment".[42] This was equally true in relation to the right to life. This too was recognised and protected by the common law and "attracted the most anxious scrutiny by the courts of administrative decision-making".[43]

The fourth and final category is concerned with adjudication under the Human Rights Act 1998. Section 6 of the Act makes it unlawful for a public authority to act in a way which is incompatible with a Convention right. Many Articles of the ECHR allow for restrictions of the rights protected therein, but only on specified grounds. Thus, for example, Article 10 concerning freedom of speech and Article 11 concerning freedom of assembly and association not only require that any restriction be prescribed by law, but also that it fall within the specified list of recognised exceptions. Even if it can be argued that a restriction on speech can be linked in some way with, for example, the protection of health or morals, the ECHR specifies that any such restriction only be such as is "necessary in a democratic society" for the protection of the relevant interest. In the *Sunday Times* case[44] the European Court of Human Rights made it clear that while the word "necessary" was not synonymous with indispensable, it also did not have the flexibility of expressions such as "admissible", "useful", "reasonable" or "desirable". The word necessary implied a "pressing social need". Any interference had moreover to be proportionate to the legitimate aim being pursued, and this had to be judged not in the abstract, but by whether the interference was necessary having regard to the facts and circumstances prevailing in the case before it. The more general implications which this has for proportionality in UK law will be considered below.

[40] In refusing to revoke the order the Home Secretary merely stated that he was satisfied that M was or had been involved in acts of terrorism, and that the exclusion order appeared to be expedient to prevent further such acts. The Home Secretary also stated that it was not possible to reveal further details of why the order had been made, because this might lead to the discovery of relevant sources of information which could compromise security operations in this area.

[41] [1995] 4 All ER 400, at 421–2.

[42] *Ibid.*, at 422.

[43] *Ibid.*, at 422D.

[44] *Sunday Times* v. *UK* (1979–80) 2 EHRR 245, paras. 59, 62, 65; *Silver* v. *UK* (1983) 5 EHRR 347, para. 97; *Olsson* v. *Sweden* (1989) 11 EHRR 259.

UNREASONABLENESS: TAKING LANGUAGE SERIOUSLY

"Pure" *Wednesbury*: The Disjunction between Language and Application

It is fitting to begin with the oft-cited judgment of Lord Greene MR in the *Wednesbury Corporation*[45] case. The corporation was empowered to grant licences for Sunday entertainment subject to such conditions as it thought fit. A picture house was licensed subject to the condition that no children under 15 be admitted. It was this condition which was challenged as unreasonable and *ultra vires*. Lord Greene MR stressed that the court should not substitute its view for that of the corporation, and then proceeded to examine what the term "unreasonable" meant in this context. It is well known that there are two meanings of the term "unreasonable" contained in this judgment.

In one sense "unreasonable" was used simply as a synonym for a host of more specific grounds of attack, such as taking account of irrelevant considerations, acting for improper purposes and acting *mala fide*, which, as the Master of the Rolls accepted, tend to run into one another.

The other sense of the term unreasonable is that which has now become known as the *Wednesbury* test: a decision can be challenged if it is so unreasonable that no reasonable public body could have made it. To prove this would require something quite extreme. Lord Greene MR gave the example of a teacher being dismissed because of red hair. Lord Diplock in *GCHQ* was equally clear that this species of irrationality would only apply to a "decision which is so outrageous in its defiance of logic or of accepted moral standards that no sensible person who had applied his mind to the question could have arrived at it".[46] For Lord Greene MR, as for many later commentators, the special meaning of the term unreasonable was warranted by the constitutional position of the courts. It was to prevent them from intervening simply because they believed that a different way of exercising discretionary power would be more reasonable than that chosen by the public body. This would be to substitute a judicial view as to, for example, the most appropriate way in which to allocate aid, or to disburse licences, for that of the public body.

Defenders of this traditional approach to review contend that it enables the courts to exercise their rightful control over the administration without becoming enmeshed with the merits and without the necessity for complex balancing, both of which are said to be undesirable features of proportionality. It is true that if we take literally the language of Lord Greene's test, as overlaid by that of Lord Diplock, the courts will only interfere if the decision being challenged is absurd in the sense articulated above. If review only operated in such circumstances then it would be different from proportionality. The need for any mean-

[45] *Associated Provincial Picture Houses Ltd.* v. *Wednesbury Corporation* [1948] 1 KB 223, at 228–30.

[46] N. 8 above, at 410.

ingful balancing would be obviated by the extreme nature of the errors caught by the test: you simply do not use the colour of a person's hair as the criterion for dismissal.

There is however a difficulty with this view, which can be simply stated. If the courts really were to restrict irrationality review to such manifest absurdity then we would all be out of business, in this area at least. There would be almost no successful challenges of this kind. The reality is that the courts, while preserving the formal veneer of the *Wednesbury* test, have on some occasions interpreted and applied it to decisions which can by no stretch of the imagination be regarded as having being made in defiance of logic or of accepted moral standards. The realisation that the courts have been applying the test to catch less egregious administrative action itself casts doubt on the claim that *Wednesbury* review can be conducted without engaging in some form of balancing, and raises the question of the difference between this balancing and that which occurs within proportionality. It is clear that the claims which are being made here are in part empirical and in part conceptual, and that both aspects of the argument must be sustained.

The empirical aspect of the argument is, I believe, readily sustainable. It is hard to think of actual cases where the decisions being challenged really could be said to exemplify the type of error which Lord Greene MR or Lord Diplock had in mind. It is, by way of contrast, not difficult to point to cases where administrative action has been struck down on *Wednesbury* grounds even though it could not, without distortion of language, be said to have been so unreasonable that no reasonable public body could have taken it. In the planning sphere it has been used to invalidate conditions attached to planning permission, such as that the developer should construct an ancillary road over the frontage of the site at his own expense to which rights of passage should be given to others,[47] and that a property developer should allow those on a council housing list to occupy the houses with security of tenure for 10 years.[48] The test has also been adopted in the context of industrial relations,[49] though in this instance the decision attacked was upheld. These cases may have been correctly decided. It is, however, hard to regard the subject-matter of the actions as determinations which are so unreasonable that no reasonable authority could come to them, at least not when viewed as Lord Greene MR or Lord Diplock visualised the notion. The criterion moves closer to asking whether the courts believe that the exercise of discretion was reasonable. A similar point can be made about the formulation in *Balchin*.[50] Sedley J held that a decision would be *Wednesbury* unreasonable if it disclosed an error of reasoning which robbed the decision of

[47] *Hall & Co. Ltd.* v. *Shoreham-by-Sea Urban District Council* [1964] 1 WLR 240.

[48] R. v. *Hillingdon London Borough Council, ex parte Royco Homes Ltd.* [1974] QB 720.

[49] *UKAPE* v. *ACAS* [1981] AC 424; note, M. Elliott (1980) 43 *MLR* 580. See also R. v. *Boundary Commission for England, ex parte Foot* [1983] QB 600; R. v. *Crown Court of St. Albans, ex parte Cinnamond* [1981] QB 480.

[50] R. v. *Parliamentary Commissioner for Administration, ex parte Balchin* [1997] COD 146.

its logical integrity. If such an error could be shown then it was not necessary for the applicant to demonstrate that the decision-maker was "temporarily unhinged". The loosening of Lord Greene's test, implicit in the preceding cases, has now received explicit support from Lord Cooke in the *ITF* case.[51] He regarded the formulation used by Lord Greene as tautologous and exaggerated. It was not, said Lord Cooke, necessary to have such an extreme formulation in order to ensure that the courts remained within their proper bounds as required by the separation of powers. He advocated a simpler and less extreme test: was the decision one which a reasonable authority could reach?

The conceptual aspect of the preceding argument can also be sustained. Let it be accepted for the sake of argument that our courts have applied the *Wednesbury* test in circumstances which fall short of the absurdity postulated by Lord Greene and Lord Diplock. This is not to say that such judicial review involves substitution of judgment by the court for that of the primary decision-maker, in the sense discussed at the beginning of this paper. It is none the less difficult, as a matter of logic, to see how these judicial decisions could have been reached without some view of the merits involved, and without also some implicit balancing of the various interests which were at stake. This is even more self-evidently so once one adds in the other elements of *Wednesbury* review, which require or empower the court to intervene if the administration has taken irrelevant considerations into account. It will normally not be clear from the face of the enabling legislation which considerations should be relevant, and which irrelevant. The court will, therefore, have to make its own interpretative choices so as to reach a conclusion on such matters. When doing so it will often be making explicit or implicit value judgements about the nature of the statutory power which will have direct implications for the relative freedom of action which the administration has when deciding how to exercise its discretionary power.

"Relative" *Wednesbury*: A New Test in Old Clothing?

It is now common to acknowledge that the courts apply the principles of judicial review with varying degrees of intensity depending upon the nature of the subject-matter.[52] This is indeed clear from the earlier discussion of the case law: cases involving fundamental rights will lead to more searching judicial scrutiny than will cases involving choices of economic policy. It will suffice for these purposes to contrast the approach taken in *Brind*[53] with that in the *Hammersmith* case.[54] We have already seen the heightened scrutiny which the House of Lords

[51] R. v. *Chief Constable of Sussex, ex parte International Trader's Ferry Ltd*, [1998] 1 All ER 129, 157.

[52] P. Craig, *Administrative Law* (3rd edn., London, Sweet & Maxwell, 1994), chap. 11; Sir John Laws, "Wednesbury" in C. Forsyth and I. Hare (eds.), *The Golden Metwand and the Crooked Cord, Essays in Honour of Sir William Wade* (Oxford, Oxford University Press, 1998), at 185–202.

[53] N. 9 above.

[54] *R.* v. *Secretary of State for the Environment, ex parte Hammersmith and Fulham London Borough Council* [1991] 1 AC 521.

brought to bear in the former case. In the latter, the House of Lords reviewed charge-capping by the Secretary of State which the applicant local authorities claimed was in breach of the relevant statute. In the course of reaching his decision Lord Bridge, giving the judgment of the court, held that while the court could intervene if the Secretary of State had acted illegally (for improper purposes or on irrelevant considerations), it should, in the sphere of economic policy, be very wary of review based upon irrationality unless there was some manifest absurdity or bad faith.

The recognition that the intensity of review can vary in this manner is of relevance to the present discussion concerning reasonableness and proportionality in two ways.

First, there is little doubt that when reasonableness is intensively applied in the context of fundamental rights it approximates very closely to the type of review which would be applied under a proportionality test for the same type of case. This is unsurprising. The very recognition that certain interests are to be regarded as important rights means that any invasion of them should be kept to the minimum. Society may well accept that these rights cannot be regarded as absolute and that some limitations may be warranted in certain circumstances. Nonetheless there is a presumption that any administrative action should interfere with the right as little as possible, and no more than is merited by the occasion. In this sense the acceptance of heightened scrutiny is both a natural and logically necessary adjunct to the regard for fundamental rights. It is, therefore, natural in such cases to ask whether the interference with the right was the least restrictive possible in the circumstances. This exercise is, moreover, facilitated by the fact that the denomination of the interest as a right means that we have weighted or valued that interest, and therefore we do not have to fathom out this matter afresh on each and every occasion.

Secondly, it is questionable whether the more intensive judicial scrutiny applied by our courts in cases concerning rights can really be regarded *simply* as a modification of the traditional *Wednesbury* test. It may be more honest to recognise that this is a new test in its own right. This point requires some explanation.

A common rationalisation for heightened scrutiny in such cases is that we are simply applying the *Wednesbury* test with due regard for the nature of the subject-matter of the action. This rationale allows the courts to remain within the traditional legitimating umbrella provided by *Wednesbury*. The reasoning of Lord Greene MR was designed to ensure that substantive judicial review did not transgress the cherished boundary between review and judgment on the merits. There is little doubt that in this country the courts' reluctance to depart from *Wednesbury* has been coloured by their desire not to stray beyond their proper role in relation to the political arm of government. It has been the *Wednesbury* test itself which has served to define the bounds of judicial propriety.

The idea that heightened scrutiny in cases concerning rights can be seen simply as a variant of the original *Wednesbury* test is, however, problematic in both linguistic and conceptual terms.

In linguistic terms, they are quite simply different tests, which is readily apparent when they are juxtaposed. Lord Greene's formulation required the decision to be so unreasonable that no reasonable public body could have made it. The formula now applied in cases concerned with rights directs the court, in Lord Bridge's words,[55] to inquire whether a reasonable Secretary of State could reasonably have made the primary decision now being challenged, and the court starts from the premise that only a compelling public interest will justify the invasion of the right. Sir Thomas Bingham MR's formulation was very similar.[56] The court was to consider whether the decision was beyond the range of responses open to a reasonable decision-maker, and the greater the interference with human rights the more the court would require by way of justification. The court does not rest content with inquiring whether the decision of the minister interfering with rights was so unreasonable that no reasonable minister could have made it. We are lawyers and live by and through language. We should recognise when a concept has been changed and should not seek to deny this by hiding behind an elliptical sense of the term "reasonableness". It is true that the degree of linguistic difference between the two fades if one adopts the formulation proposed by Lord Cooke. This is of course because this latter formulation is itself a modification of Lord Greene's test.

In conceptual terms, it is equally difficult to regard judicial review in rights cases *merely* as a variant of traditional *Wednesbury*, since the premises which underlie review in the two contexts differ. The premise which underpins the classic *Wednesbury* approach, as overlaid by Lord Diplock, is that the courts should be aware of their limited role. The social and political choices which constitute administration have been assigned by Parliament to a minister or agency, and it was not for the courts to overstep their legitimate bounds when engaged in judicial review. It was this premise which shaped review in *Wednesbury* itself: the court would intervene to ensure that the agency remained within the four corners of its powers through concepts such as propriety of purpose and relevancy, but would only exercise very limited control over the rationality of the decision through *Wednesbury* unreasonableness. The premise which underlies review in rights cases is different. The courts continue to accept that they should not substitute judgment. It is also generally accepted that traditional notions of sovereignty mean that the courts cannot invalidate primary legislation on the ground that it infringes rights.[57] The courts do not, however, operate on the assumption that decisions about rights made by the political arm of government, or an agency to whom power has been delegated, must necessarily be accorded the same respect or judicial deference as, for example, allocative decisions of an economic nature. The majoritarian will is quite properly accorded less force in rights-based cases than in others. It is this

[55] Lord Bridge in *Brind*, n. 9 above, at 748–9.

[56] Sir Thomas Bingham MR in *Smith*, n. 34 above, at 262.

[57] See, however, Sir J. Laws, "Law and Democracy" [1995] *PL* 72 and "The Constitution: Morals and Rights" [1996] *PL* 622; Lord Woolf, "Droit Public-English Style" [1995] *PL* 57.

premise which serves to explain, and which is reflected in, the different meaning given to "reasonableness review". The level of unreasonableness which the applicant must prove is less extreme than in the traditional *Wednesbury* formula,[58] and the court requires more compelling justification before it is willing to accept that an invasion of rights was warranted or sanctioned.

PROPORTIONALITY AS AN INDEPENDENT GROUND OF REVIEW IN DOMESTIC LAW: THE ARGUMENTS IN FAVOUR

Whether proportionality does become an independent head of review lies with the courts. This is obvious. Whether it does ever achieve this status, or whether it is forever consigned to the wings and never takes centre stage remains to be seen. There are four principal arguments in favour of recognising it as a ground of review in its own right.

The Community and Human Rights Dimension

It would, other things being equal, be advantageous for the same test to be used to deal with claims arising under EC law, the Human Rights Act (HRA) and other non-HRA domestic law challenges. This is particularly so because it will be common to find at least two such types of claim in an application for judicial review, and it will not be uncommon to find cases where all three may be of relevance. It should, moreover, be recognised that there will be difficult borderline cases concerning the application of the HRA. The nature of the test which is to be applied should not differ radically depending on which side of the borderline a case is said to fall. It is also worth stating in this regard that not only do our courts have an obligation to apply proportionality in cases which have a Community dimension, but also they do not appear to have had any marked difficulty in doing so. We should not lose sight of this fact when considering the possible application of proportionality in cases where there is no Community law dimension.

A More Structured Analysis

Proportionality provides a more structured analysis of the kind which is often lacking under the *Wednesbury* formula. The proportionality inquiry has, as is well known, three stages: is the measure which has been adopted appropriate for attaining the desired objective; is the measure necessary for the attainment of that objective; and does it impose excessive burdens on the individual, (the

[58] This is so even taking account of the discussion in the previous section.

proportionality inquiry in its narrow sense)? This more structured analysis has a beneficial effect in that it requires the administration to justify its policy choice more specifically than under the traditional *Wednesbury* approach. The structure provided by the proportionality inquiry is also beneficial in relation to the courts themselves. It requires that the courts, when striking down a decision, do so on grounds which are more readily identifiable and ascertainable than is often the case under the *Wednesbury* test. This is of particular relevance given the arguments made in the preceding section. If it is accepted that our courts, even in cases which do not involve rights, are in reality applying *Wednesbury* more intrusively than the bare words of the test would suggest, and if it is also the case that this requires some balancing, whether explicit or implicit, then this should be as transparent as possible. The reasoning process provided by proportionality renders this more likely to occur.

A More Reasoned Analysis

Proportionality also demands a more reasoned justification from the decision-maker. This difference between proportionality and the *Wednesbury* formula was recognised by Laws J in the *First City Trading* case.[59] He acknowledged that it was not for the courts to substitute their judgment for that of the primary decision-maker, and that this was so as much in Community law as in domestic law. Laws J was surely correct to point out that one of the key differences between *Wednesbury* review and Community principles of review was that the latter required the decision-maker to provide a fully reasoned case:

> It is not enough merely to set out the problem, and assert that within his discretion the Minister chose this or that solution constrained only by the requirement that his decision must have been a reasonable one which a reasonable Minister might make. Rather the Court will test the solution arrived at, and pass it only if substantial factual considerations are put forward in its justification: considerations which are relevant, reasonable, and proportionate to the aim in view.[60]

The Normative Argument

It is generally acknowledged that proportionality can itself be applied more or less intensively, depending upon the nature of the case.[61] The UK courts have accepted that there should be heightened scrutiny in cases involving fundamental rights, and, as we have seen, such review differs little from proportionality. The central issue is therefore whether a proportionality type-test should be

[59] N. 6 above, at 278–9.

[60] *Ibid.*, at 279.

[61] P. Craig, n. 52 above, at 411–21; G. de Búrca, "The Principle of Proportionality and its Application in EC Law" (1993) 13 *YBEL* 105.

applied in cases other than fundamental rights. There is a normative justification for the use of proportionality even where this entails more intensive scrutiny than *Wednesbury*, and even where there are no fundamental rights at stake. The argument can be put in the following terms.

It can be readily accepted that the primary responsibility for making the social, economic and political choices required by modern government must be for the agency or minister to whom the task has been assigned. The primary decision-maker may, however, often have a particular desired end in view when making these choices. An agency charged with the building of a road, subject to certain cost constraints, may have a particular incentive to choose the route which will be least costly to the administration, even if this results in considerable disruption to home-owners and the general public. A public body which has to administer regulatory controls over agriculture may well seek to equalise the prices of certain products, or reduce surpluses, even where this may have severe consequences for the producer groups involved. A minister may be minded to use her regulatory powers over health and safety to impose requirements on industry which are felt by those affected not to be justified by the established scientific data, or capable of being achieved at significantly less cost in a different way. It would be quite wrong to regard the public body in these examples as biased. It would be equally misguided to believe that public decisions are always reached independently of the public body's own "agenda".

The application of proportionality in such cases does not, properly understood, sanction judicial intervention merely because the court would have balanced the relevant interest differently from that of the initial decision-maker. It does require the minister or agency to submit evidence which will be assessed by the court under the three stages of the test. Many cases are and will be decided under stage one or two. The administrator will be unable to show that the impugned measure really was suited or necessary to reach the end in view. Judicial intervention to strike down such decisions is surely justified. There is no transgression of the proper limits of the judicial role where a measure is annulled for which the public body can provide no convincing justification. If the case proceeds to stage three the court will have to apply the balancing test, but it is clear from the Community and German jurisprudence that it will be circumspect before overturning a decision on this ground. The legitimacy of overturning a decision on this ground can be defended in principle. There will be instances where, even though a measure is suited and necessary to attain the end in view, it is felt none the less that the burden on those affected is simply too great.

The present approach of our courts presupposes that the subject-matter on which review operates can be divided into cases involving fundamental rights, where the courts will review intensively, and the "rest" where the only realistic option is intervention posited on the finding of something akin to manifest unreasonableness. The subject-matter of administrative law is more varied than this. A test such as proportionality can be used to provide a more structured and searching form of review than that allowed for under *Wednesbury*, without thereby substituting judgment.

PROPORTIONALITY AS AN INDEPENDENT GROUND OF REVIEW IN DOMESTIC LAW: THE ARGUMENTS AGAINST

It would be quite wrong to pretend that there are no arguments against the recognition of proportionality as an independent head of review. Two such arguments will be analysed within this section.

Separation of Powers, Expertise and the Dilemma of Review

There is no doubt that some will be unconvinced by the arguments advanced in the previous section. They feel that any move beyond the lines laid down by the traditional *Wednesbury* principle is unacceptable and an infringement of the separation of powers. There is little that can be done to answer such objections. It is, none the less, worth reiterating the point that *Wednesbury* itself has been applied to strike down decisions which could not in any meaningful sense be regarded as absurd. The separation of powers objection should therefore be applied equally forcefully here too. It should also be remembered that the intensity with which proportionality review is applied can vary significantly.

There is, however, a more subtle version of this argument against proportionality which can be presented as follows. Courts which engage in proportionality review will normally not have expertise in the relevant area. This can be especially problematic where the subject-matter of review is highly technical. They are then faced with a choice. They can press on with a fairly intensive species of "hard look proportionality review". Claims will be made that, for example, the scientific data does not support the challenged regulatory initiative. The court will be asked to invalidate the regulation or decision on the ground that it was not suited or necessary to the end in view. If they do so they may, as in the United States, be faced with protracted trials where applicants who have failed to secure their chosen regulatory aim in the political process will seek to do so via judicial review. This form of proportionality review will undoubtedly place heavy burdens on courts in areas where they do not have expertise, and this was a factor which influenced Lord Lowry in *Brind*.[62] These problems can become more acute if the court is expected to examine in depth alternative regulatory strategies. A court may then be inclined to opt for "less intensive proportionality review", and only to overturn a decision if it was manifestly disproportionate. It is clear that the ECJ has adopted this approach in a number of areas, most notably agriculture, competition and state aid. If this

[62] [1991] 1 AC 696, at 767.

approach is taken then review will not differ greatly from traditional *Wednesbury* control, although it would be mistaken to underestimate the significance of the more structured analysis provided by the proportionality principle even in this context.

The Nature of the Subject-Matter, Justiciability and Proportionality

A second objection is that certain types of question are unsuited to a proportionality analysis. The best example of this is the inquiry demanded of the national courts by the ECJ in the Sunday Trading cases. Hoffmann J, as he then was, concluded that it would have been incorrect for the courts to substitute their view on such an issue for that of the legislature.[63] It was not, he said, the court's function to carry out a balancing exercise or form a view on whether the legislative objective could have been achieved by other means. Such matters involved compromises between competing interests which in a democratic society were to be resolved by the legislature, and the judicial function was limited to deciding whether the compromise adopted by the UK Parliament, in so far as it affected Sunday Trade could have been reached by a reasonable legislature.

This was surely correct in relation to the inquiry before the court in the instant case. Stages one and two of the proportionality inquiry were virtually meaningless in this context, while stage three required the national court to undertake an inquiry which was not in reality justiciable. Justiciability must surely impose limits on the proper reach of a proportionality test in the same way that it does in relation to other aspects of judicial review.

Whether all compromises between competing interests in a democratic society must be resolved by the legislature, and whether it is inappropriate for a court ever to ask whether an objective could have been achieved by other means, is of course, more controversial. There are, as we have seen, strong arguments to the contrary, more especially where the action being challenged is not enshrined in legislation as such, but is rather the result of ministerial or agency choice.

REASONABLENESS AND PROPORTIONALITY: THE OPTIONS

Only time will tell whether proportionality does occupy the legal stage in its own right, or whether it languishes forever in the wings. It is clear that there are three ways in which this topic could develop.

The first option would be to retain the traditional *Wednesbury* test alongside proportionality. The courts could persist with *Wednesbury* review outside those areas (the EC and the HRA) where they have to apply proportionality. Different

[63] *Stoke on Trent City Council* v. *B & Q* [1991] 1 AC 49.

grounds of challenge would be dealt with under different heads of review and *Wednesbury* would be interpreted in the traditional sense articulated by Lord Greene as overlaid by Lord Diplock: the applicant would have to show that the public body's action really was so unreasonable that no reasonable body would have made it. It would, however, be accepted that this standard of review could itself vary in intensity, as exemplified by the application of the test in cases concerned with human rights.

Those who favour this approach would argue that it thereby prevents the courts from intruding too far into the merits and obviates the need for any complex balancing, both of which are said to be undesirable features of proportionality. It is argued that the traditional approach will preserve the proper boundaries of judicial intervention. This claim is, however, undermined, in two ways.

On the one hand, it is true that if we take the language of Lord Greene literally the need for any meaningful balancing would be obviated by the extreme nature of the test: you simply do not use the colour of a person's hair as the criterion for dismissal. The reality is, as we have seen, that the courts, while preserving the formal veneer of the *Wednesbury* test, have on occasions applied it to decisions which can by no stretch of the imagination be regarded as having being made in defiance of logic or of accepted moral standards. The realisation that the courts have been applying the test to catch less egregious administrative action itself casts doubt on the claim that *Wednesbury* review can be conducted without engaging in some form of balancing, and raises the question of the difference between this balancing and that which occurs within proportionality.

On the other hand, the juridical device of varying the intensity with which the test is applied functions as a mechanism whereby the courts can exercise the degree of control which they believe to be desirable in a particular area, without thereby being accused of improper intrusion into the merits, or inappropriate balancing. The very malleability in the standard of review means, however, that it is within the courts' power to shift the line as to what is regarded as a proper or improper intrusion into the merits.

The second option would be for the courts to retain a reasonableness test for those areas not covered by the EC or the HRA, but to give it the tougher meaning ascribed by Lord Cooke: a decision would be overturned if it was one which a reasonable authority could not have made. This standard of review could also vary in intensity depending upon the subject matter of the application. Many would accept the essential premise of Lord Cooke's thesis. His Lordship argued that the proper boundaries between courts and administration could be secured by a test which was less exaggerated than the traditional *Wednesbury* formulation. To be sure the courts should not substitute their judgment on the merits for that of the administration, but this could be avoided even where the reasonableness test was formulated in the manner articulated by Lord Cooke.

This option is, however, inherently more unstable than the first. The instability of this option becomes readily apparent once we probe a little further. We should recall that the "virtue" of the traditional Lord Greene reading of the reasonableness test was that there was no need to press further. The really outrageous decision would be all too evident and indefensible. If we shift to Lord Cooke's reading of the test this no longer holds true. It would be incumbent on the judiciary to articulate in some ordered manner the rationale for finding that an administrative choice was one which could not reasonably have been made, where that choice fell short of manifest absurdity. If the courts were not obliged to explain their own findings in this manner then the new test would create unwarranted judicial discretion. It is, however, difficult to see how the articulation of the factors which would be taken into account in this regard would be very different from those used in the proportionality calculus. The courts would in some manner, shape or form want to know how necessary the measure was, and how suitable it was, for attaining the desired end. These are the first two parts of the proportionality calculus. It is also possible that under Lord Cooke's formulation a court might well, expressly or impliedly, look to see whether the challenged measure imposed excessive burdens on the applicant, the third part of the proportionality formula.

If these kinds of factors are taken into account, and some such factors will have to be, then it will be difficult to persist with the idea that this is really separate from a proportionality test. There will then be an impetus to extend proportionality from the areas where it currently already applies, the EC and the HRA, to general domestic law challenges.

The third option would be to adopt proportionality as a general criterion for review in purely domestic cases, as well as those governed by EC law or the HRA. I believe that this is the desirable solution.

The arguments in favour have been set out above. Our courts can deal with proportionality, as exemplified by judicial practice in cases which have a Community law element, where they are already obliged to apply the concept. The more structured form of analysis which proportionality brings to judicial review is to be welcomed, while the ability to vary the intensity with which the concept is applied enables the courts to be alive to differences in the nature of the subject-matter under scrutiny. The requirement of reasoned justification which forms part of the proportionality inquiry is of particular importance. Courts can exercise meaningful control over the decisions of agencies only where the latter are compelled to reveal the factual and policy foundations which guided their action. This is especially so given the normative argument adumbrated earlier.

The arguments against the recognition of proportionality as a head of review in its own right can be met. It is true that the application of proportionality will require value judgements to be made as to the intensity with which the concept is applied, particularly where the subject-matter is technical or scientifically complex. It would, however, be mistaken to assume that these choices can be avoided even under the present regime of *Wednesbury* review, and this will be all the more so if the reformulation of the reasonableness test advocated by Lord

Cooke is adopted. The other main objection to proportionality, relating to justiciability, can also be met. It should be recognised that constraints on judicial review, such as justiciability, should operate in this context, and that the courts should not be forced to balance under the guise of proportionality factors which are incommensurable.

We should, none the less, be mindful of the broader ramifications of adopting proportionality as a head of review in its own right. Legal concepts do not subsist in a vacuum. They interact with each other. The adoption of proportionality may well require us to think again about, for example, the unwillingness to accord discovery in review actions, and more generally about the way in which we regard reasons and evidence in such cases.[64] We should be more willing to acknowledge that we may well require greater scrutiny of the factual foundations of, and reasons for, agency action than has the been the case as of late. We should accept also that rendering government accountable for its actions is worth the difficulties which such an exercise might entail.

[64] See P. Craig, n. 52 above, at 417–18 and N. Green, "Proportionality and the Supremacy of Parliament in the UK", this vol.

The Influence of the European Principle of Proportionality upon UK Law

THE RT. HON. LORD HOFFMANN

The purpose of this paper is not to provide a survey of opinions but to argue a point of view. There is, however, no warranty that the author will adopt the same point of view in any other capacity.

WHAT IS PROPORTIONALITY?

Although English lawyers have met the principle of proportionality through acquaintance with the jurisprudence of the European Court of Justice and the European Court of Human Rights, it is of course derived from German law. For the purpose of identifying what we are talking about, I shall adopt the standard tripartite definition used by German writers. The principle consists of three sub-principles, namely (1) *suitability*: an administrative or legal power must be exercised in a way which is suitable to achieve the purpose intended and for which the power was conferred; (2) *necessity*: the exercise of the power must be necessary to achieve the relevant purpose and (3) *proportionality in the narrower sense*: the exercise of the power must not impose burdens or cause harm to other legitimate interests which are disproportionate to the importance of the object to be achieved.[1] Whether there is any merit in dividing the principle in this way is a point to which I shall later return. The European Court of Justice tends on the whole to use this classification although it will naturally emphasise the aspect which seems most appropriate to describe the case in hand.

THE GENERALITY OF THE PRINCIPLE

Proportionality is said to be a general principle of European law and the jurisprudence of the European Court of Human Rights. There are many specific

[1] See F.G. Jacobs, "Recent Developments in the Principle of Proportionality in European Community Law" and W. van Gerven, "The Effect of Proportionality on the Actions of Member States of the European Community: National Viewpoints from Continental Europe", both this vol.

powers, or restrictions on the use of powers, which have notions of proportionality built into them. For example, Article 10 of the European Convention on Human Rights, which confers the right to freedom of expression, provides in paragraph 2 that it may be restricted on various enumerated grounds if this is "necessary in a democratic society". The Court has interpreted this to mean that freedom of expression can be restricted only if there is a "pressing social need" and if the degree of restriction is proportionate to the importance of the social need.[2] Although a balancing exercise of this kind may be very difficult, the Article does at least identify the matters which have to be put into balance. It tells the courts that freedom of expression will trump all other interests unless they fall within a defined category, and even then can be restricted only to the minimum extent which the protection of that interest requires. This is a calculation which courts and politicians have debated since the days of the Greeks and the Romans and with which we are very familiar. So the application of the principle of proportionality can be worked out and made concrete in some detail. A body of jurisprudence can be built up as to which things count as restrictions which are necessary in a democratic society and which do not. But in this paper I am not concerned with specific applications of proportionality but with its claim to be an abstract and general principle of law. European lawyers say that proportionality is a high level principle of European law, which can and indeed must be applied to any exercise of power whatever.

ENGLISH ADMINISTRATIVE LAW

The key concept for the control of the exercise of public powers in English administrative law is that of unreasonableness or irrationality. The orthodox doctrine is that an unreasonable or irrational exercise of power is *ultra vires* because Parliament could not have intended the power to be exercised in an irrational manner. There is an infinite variety of forms of irrationality but one of them must be lack of proportionality. Lord Diplock said that the notion of proportionality meant that you must not use a steam hammer to crack a nut.[3] If a guest at a dinner party insisted, when it came to the nuts and wine, on producing a steam hammer, he could properly be described as behaving irrationally. We would regard his lack of proportionality as not being something different from irrationality but as the reason why we say he is being irrational. The same would be true of a person who adopted a solution to a problem which was unsuitable, such as trying to improve the English summer weather by banning cricket on the ground that the playing of the game was frequently observed to be accompanied by heavy downpours. If it is said that these are clear and obvi-

[2] See the *Handyside* case, Eur. Ct. HR, Series A, No. 24, 1 EHRR 737; the *Sunday Times* case, Eur. Ct. HR, Series A, No. 30, 2 EHRR 245 and *Dudgeon* v. *UK*, Eur Ct HR, Series A, No. 45 (1982) 4 EHRR 149.

[3] *R.* v. *Goldstein* [1983] 1 WLR 151, at 155B.

ous examples of lack of proportionality amounting to irrationality and that the courts are frequently concerned with more difficult and debatable ones, then of course I agree. But the main proposition to be advanced in this paper is that the solution to such hard cases is not assisted by pretending that proportionality is a freestanding principle rather than being simply a species of irrationality. The main support for the contrary view is an off-the-cuff remark of Lord Diplock in the *GCHQ* case,[4] when he said that proportionality might function as a ground for judicial review *additional* to irrationality. I think that this represents an analytical error. Irrationality is a higher level concept which includes lack of proportionality as one of its forms. The fact that English law very sensibly employs a general concept of irrationality preserves us from the necessity, which seems to afflict systems based upon nineteenth-century German administrative law, of assigning the case to one or other particular sub-species. It is of course necessary to explain precisely why the exercise of power was irrational and the most illuminating explanation may well be in terms of lack of proportionality, but English courts are not obliged to tie particular labels round the neck of each case. To go down the road of classification can lead only to metaphysical problems of distinguishing different forms of irrationality which would truly be worthy of mediaeval schoolmen and, if such distinctions are to have any practical meaning, differences in the treatment of different kinds of irrationality which could fairly be characterised as irrational.

WHO DECIDES?

The real problem about applying the principle of proportionality, or for that matter any other test of rationality, in hard cases is not whether the principle should be observed but who should decide whether it has been observed or not. No minister, accused of an irrational exercise of power, responds by denying that he is obliged to act rationally. The same is true of the subcategory of observing proportionality. The minister's answer is that in his opinion his action has been rational and proportional. The application of the principle is common to both sides: the true issue is whether the court should accept the minister's judgement that his action complies with the principle or impose its own view of the matter. This is the heart of any problem of judicial review. It is easy to give examples, like the steam hammer and the nut, where the lack of proportionality is manifest and obvious. More commonly, however, the comparison which is involved between the social importance of the object to be achieved and the burdens imposed by the means used to achieve it is a matter of social and economic judgement on which reasonable people may differ. In a democratic society, this form of judgement is entrusted to the elected representatives of the people in Parliament or the members of the Executive to whom they have

[4] *Council of Civil Service Unions* v. *Minister of State for the Civil Service* [1985] AC 374.

delegated decision-making power. So that although the power of the judges to invalidate administrative action for irrationality is expressed in general terms and there is no line drawn in the sand beyond which the court may not go, judges are constantly aware that there is such a line. Indeed, the whole art of judicial review, and I deliberately use the word art, requires a political sensitivity to the proper boundaries between the powers of the legislative, executive and judicial branches of government. In the European context the boundaries are of course somewhat differently drawn, because the ECJ is concerned not only with the division of decision-making power among the organs of the Community but also as between the Community and the Member States.

HOW DOES ONE DECIDE WHO DECIDES?

How does a court decide whether it should apply its own test of irrationality or whether it should accept the view of the decision-maker? It is commonplace to observe that in some areas of decision-making the courts are reluctant to substitute their own view of what is rational or proportional for that of the decision-maker. On the other hand, there are others, such as whether administrative action has unreasonably or disproportionately infringed basic human rights, where the courts feel on firmer ground. The current jargon of administrative law is that some kinds of decision attract a more intensive form of review from the courts than others. The distinction was noted by Lord Bridge of Harwich in *Brind*[5] when he said that "any restriction of the right to freedom of expression requires to be justified and that nothing less than an important competing public interest will be sufficient to justify it".[6] The same distinction appears in judgments of the ECJ where it is frequently said that in the area of economic decisions such as the administration of the Common Agricultural Policy, a wide margin of appreciation must be allowed to the Community organ upon which the decision-making power has been conferred.[7]

I have described the questions involved in drawing the boundaries of decision-making power as requiring political sensitivity on the part of the judges because, in the domestic context, it requires them to apply a certain view about the nature of democracy. Put shortly, democracy requires both the recognition of the decision-making power of the elected organs of the state over a large range of issues and the protection of certain fundamental rights of the individual against infringement even by majority decision. There are no hard and fast rules to tell judges how these two elements of a democracy are to be reconciled and they have to tread a delicate line which avoids the extremes of populism on the one hand and judicial over-activism on the other. In the case of the ECJ,

[5] R. v. *Secretary of State for the Home Department, ex parte Brind* [1991] 1 AC 696.

[6] *Ibid.*, at 748–9.

[7] See, e.g., Case C–331/88 R. v. *Minister for Agriculture, Fisheries and Food, ex parte Fedesa* [1990] ECR I–4023.

there are in addition the standard problems of a federal state in reconciling the objects of the Community with the sovereignty of the Member States.

WHAT HAS THIS TO DO WITH PROPORTIONALITY?

The reason I have dwelt at some length and in a general kind of way about the basic problems of judicial review is to show that the matters which we take into account in applying the principles of judicial review can have nothing to do with whether the administrative action in question is said to have lacked proportionality or to have been irrational in some other way. The intensity of the review, the division of decision-making power between courts, legislature and executive depends upon the nature of the decision—whether it is a question of social or economic policy, whether it affects human rights and so forth—and not upon the way in which the decision-maker is alleged to have got it wrong. I can illustrate the point by reference to what is said to be another general principle of European Community law, namely that of non-discrimination or, looked at from the other end, the principle of equal treatment. Here again, as in the case of proportionality, one finds the notion of equal treatment built into specific rules, which prohibit certain grounds of discrimination, such as sex or nationality, unless there is what is called objective justification.[8] The ECJ and the courts of the Member States have developed an extensive jurisprudence as to what counts as objective justification and, although there are difficult cases, the question whether such justification exists is recognised to be a matter for the court. But there is also said to be a general principle of non-discrimination; that everyone should be treated alike unless there is a good reason for treating them differently. At this level, the principle of non-discrimination seems to me no more than an axiom of rational behaviour: that one should treat like cases alike and different cases differently. The word to describe a person who, without reason, treats similar cases differently is whimsical. He is not behaving rationally. As a general principle, therefore, equal treatment is nothing more than another aspect of rationality. No decision-maker would lay claim to a right to be whimsical. The problem arises when the decision-maker considers that he had good reason for treating people differently and the people affected think that he did not. Who should decide whether the principle has been observed? What counts as a good reason for treating some people differently from others? Some grounds, such as race or sex, are now, at the end of the twentieth century, so generally regarded as unacceptable in a European state that the courts would have little difficulty, even in the absence of specific legislation, of characterising discrimination on such grounds as irrational. But what about age, or ownership of property, or relative wealth, or citizenship of a country outside the European

[8] See also E. Ellis, "The Concept of Proportionality in European Community Sex Discrimination Law", this vol.

Union? Whether discrimination on such grounds should be acceptable is usually regarded as a matter to be decided by a majority in Parliament. So, as in other forms of alleged irrational decision-making, the problem is not the principle by which one decides whether a decision was rational or not but the question of who should make that decision.

BRIND

The theory of proportionality which had casually been trailed by Lord Diplock in *GCHQ*[9] was given a full airing by Lord Lester of Herne Hill QC and Mr David Pannick in *Brind*.[10] It was emphatically rejected by the two judges who gave the matter extended consideration, namely Lord Ackner and Lord Lowry. Both judges fastened upon the important point: did the fact that the excess of power alleged against the Minister happened to take the form of lack of proportionality mean that the court should draw the boundary between accepting his opinion and substituting its own at a different point? Both said that this obviously could not be the case: the considerations which influence the court in deciding where to draw that boundary are altogether different. So if the European principle of proportionality did have such an effect, it could not be part of English law.

Does this mean that Lord Ackner and Lord Lowry actually rejected the European concept of proportionality? This is more a question for a European lawyer than for me. But I do not think that they did. Indeed, I find it conceptually very difficult to see how in European Community law or any other system of law the important question in *Brind*, which was whether the Home Secretary or the House of Lords should decide whether it thought that preventing the IRA from appearing on television was necessary in the interests of national security, could be affected by the particular way in which his decision was said to be unreasonable. The grounds upon which the ECJ has allowed a margin of appreciation in these matters to a Community organ or a Member State seem to me in substance, and allowing for the special problems of federalism, no different from those upon which an English court would do so.

I think, if I may be so bold as to say so, that part of the reason for the widely-held view that our approach differs from that of Europe on this question has been the way in which academic writers have presented the principle of proportionality. They have seemed much more interested in dissecting the principle itself and allocating cases to the various categories of suitability, necessity and *Verhältnismäßigkeit im engeren Sinn* than in discussing what seems to me the all-important question of the extent of the margin of appreciation and the grounds upon which it is allowed. Compared with this, the former exercise

[9] *Council of Civil Service Unions* v. *Minister of State for the Civil Service* [1985] AC 374.
[10] *R.* v. *Secretary of State for the Home Department, ex parte Brind* [1991] 1 AC 749.

seems to me no better than train spotting. English judges do not go in for this kind of analysis because they are able to deploy a general principle of irrationality. I am not sure that we are any worse off on that account. But that does not mean that the effect of what we actually do is any different.

SUNDAY TRADING

What I have said so far should explain the dismay and incredulity shown by the English courts when asked by the ECJ in *Torfaen Borough Council* v. *B & Q plc*[11] to apply the principle of proportionality in the Sunday trading cases. If ever there was a case in which it should have been obvious to the ECJ that the question was one for decision by the democratically elected organs of state, this was it. It is true that the case might be said to have raised a federal question: the ECJ itself may have said (although it would not have been wise to do so) that the cause of the Single Market and allowing the maximum number of Dutch bulbs to be exported to England outweighed any social advantages which the Parliament of the UK might see in keeping shops closed on Sundays. That would have meant that none of organs of government of the Member State, whether legislative, executive or judicial, was entitled to decide in favour of a prohibition on Sunday trading. But the notion of remitting this question to a national court and asking it to decide whether the effect on Dutch bulb imports was disproportionate to the advantages secured by prohibiting Sunday trade was so far from being justiciable as to be bizarre. Once the ECJ had decided that the decision-making power lay with the Member State at all, that should have been the end of the matter. It was in my view quite wrong to try to allocate that decision-making power to the judiciary of the Member State rather than its legislature. And this was in effect what the Court of Justice recognised in its subsequent decision in *Stoke on Trent City Council* v. *B & Q plc*.[12]

THE *TESCO* CASE

Tesco Ltd. v. *Secretary of State for the Environment*[13] was an interesting case on proportionality because it vividly emphasised the importance of the decision-making power. Local planning authorities have power to enter into agreements with developers about various things which the developer must do to avoid or mitigate adverse effects of the development. For example, a developer who wants to build a supermarket may be willing to finance various measures to avoid the traffic congestion which the customers may cause in surrounding streets. Authorities often insisted upon such agreements as a condition of

11 Case 145/88 [1989] ECR 3851.
12 Joined Cases C–306/88, C–304/90, and C–169/91 [1992] ECR I–6457.
13 [1995] 2 All ER 636.

granting planning permission. But there was widespread concern that some authorities were abusing these agreements by accepting benefits entirely unrelated to the development as the price of granting permission. Particularly where two rival developers wanted a permission, the authority appeared to be conducting an auction in which the developer which offered the best package of benefits for the town got the permission. To keep these practices under control, the Department of the Environment issued a circular which laid down a policy, to which the planning authorities had to have regard, that the benefits provided by a developer should be limited to what was considered necessary to mitigate any planning detriments likely to be caused by the development. In other words, planning authorities were to observe proportionality in the benefits which they exacted. To enforce this policy, the Department said that it would allow appeals from developers who had been asked to provide disproportionate benefits and order the planning authority to pay the costs.

In the *Tesco* case, Sainsburys had been granted planning permission for a supermarket at Witney in return for an agreement to provide a very large sum towards the construction of a by-pass. This annoyed Tesco, which had also applied for permission but had not been willing to pay so much. It complained that the benefit accepted was disproportionate because, although Witney needed a by-pass, the extra supermarket traffic would not have made things much worse. But Tesco could not appeal to the Secretary of State because only a developer who has been refused permission can appeal. Another landowner cannot appeal against planning permission being granted. Tesco therefore applied for judicial review, claiming that the grant of permission was unlawful because of its lack of proportionality.

The House of Lords decided that the decision-making power as to whether proportionality existed between planning detriments and benefits provided by the developer lay with the planning authority or, on appeal from the authority, the Secretary of State. It did not lie with the courts. The reason was the nature of the decision. To say that benefits were disproportionate to planning detriments involved forming a view on the extent of those detriments, and this would require the court to get involved in the planning merits of the application. This the House of Lords was unwilling to do. It followed that, although no one disputed that the principle of proportionality applied and the Secretary of State had insisted as a matter of policy that it should be applied, the case turned entirely upon who had the power to decide whether it had been applied or not.

FUTURE DEVELOPMENTS

I see little future for proportionality in this country as a freestanding principle. The influence of the European approach to these matters is that in some cases it may help the courts to explain why they think that the decision-maker behaved irrationally, although I find it hard to think how this would differ from the explanation they would have given if they had never heard of the principle of proportionality. This can be seen from the collections which are sometimes made of old cases in which English judges are said unwittingly to have applied the principle of proportionality in the same way as the *bourgeois gentilhomme* spoke prose.[14] I see no harm in calling these cases an application of the principle of proportionality as long as one does not thereby distract the court from more serious matters.

[14] M. Jourdain in Molière, *Le Bourgeois Gentilhomme*, Act 2, Scene 4: "il y a plus que quarante ans que je dis de la prose sans que j'en susse rien".

Proportionality and the Human Rights Act 1998

DAVID FELDMAN

The Human Rights Act 1998,[1] when it comes into force, will make a range of "Convention rights" part of municipal law in the United Kingdom. These rights, based on those contained in the European Convention on Human Rights (ECHR), should produce huge changes in the way our public authorities, including courts and tribunals, approach all aspects of the law. Nevertheless, at present it is difficult to predict either the overall effect of the Act or the role which related concepts and doctrines, such as proportionality, will play. Sydney Kentridge QC has predicted that "the most difficult and important problem facing British courts will be to develop (or, rather, invent) a coherent and defensible doctrine of proportionality".[2] This would be essential, he said, to take account of the fact that the doctrine of the margin of appreciation, used increasingly by the European Court of Human Rights to avoid the need for difficult decisions on the proper scope of justifications for interfering with rights, will not be available in domestic law. Courts will have to decide what rights are really to be regarded as absolute, and apply the proportionality doctrine in a principled way to the others. The way in which proportionality operates will be critical if everyone, including every person and organisation with unpopular views or unattractive antecedents and characteristics, is to enjoy the protection of effective remedies for violations of their Convention rights by public authorities.

This paper considers how proportionality might work in relation to the Act. To do so, it develops two main themes relating to the way in which the Act is based round the formulation of rights in the ECHR and the place of proportionality within that scheme. The first theme is that the relationship between the Act and the ECHR will give rise to a number of tensions, and that the legal

[1] Here and throughout the paper I assume that the Human Rights Bill, currently awaiting its Report stage in the House of Commons having earlier passed through the House of Lords (which will in due course reconsider it in the light of Commons amendments), will become an Act in more or less its present form. I therefore write of it as an Act rather than a Bill, since it will be as an Act that it is likely to be held to have imported principles of proportionality, and I refer to sections rather than clauses. It should be borne in mind that section and Schedule numbers *etc.* may change if further amendments are made.

[2] Sydney Kentridge QC, "The Incorporation of the European Convention on Human Rights" in the University of Cambridge Centre for Public Law, *Constitutional Reform in the United Kingdom* (Oxford, Hart Publishing, 1998), chap. 7, at 70.

culture[3] of the jurisdictions in which the Act will apply[4] will strongly influence the background values in the light of which courts and tribunals will approach the task of resolving them. Doctrines like proportionality will be tools to be used to resolve tensions between individual freedoms and community interests. The legal culture will affect the way in which proportionality is conceptualised and deployed in municipal law, although it is equally true that the Act is likely to alter the culture itself. The second theme concerns the relationship between proportionality, which provides judges with a framework within which to evaluate the justifications advanced by public authorities for interfering with rights, and other doctrines which limit the reviewing powers of the judges. Such doctrines include (in the Strasbourg case law) the margin of appreciation, and (in municipal law) the ideas of justiciability and of deference to the reasoning and conclusions of specially qualified decision-makers. The way in which these ideas are applied to cases arising under the Act will affect the effectiveness of the Act. It will also tell us something about the way in which our legal culture is developing. The challenge is to adapt to a culture of rights without losing the current beneficial concern for the interests of society as a whole and groups within it. We in the UK are about to embark on a cultural adventure in which public lawyers will play a leading part. Proportionality is likely to be one of the instruments which we will use. An understanding of its potentiality and limitations as an instrument will be valuable.

As a starting point in the quest, the first section of this paper outlines the relationship between the Act and the jurisprudence developed under the European Convention on Human Rights. Section II considers the relationship between a number of concepts which may interact: proportionality, irrationality, the margin of appreciation, justiciability and the deference due to public decision-makers. Section III speculates about how the doctrine of proportionality may have different effects in relation to the various kinds of legal proceedings available under the Act. Some tentative conclusions are drawn in Section IV.

I. THE HUMAN RIGHTS ACT 1998 AND THE STRASBOURG CASE LAW

The Human Rights Act 1998 and the European Convention on Human Rights

The Human Rights Act 1998 seeks to protect rights while upholding the legislative supremacy of Parliament. Public authorities other than Parliament will

[3] I will not attempt to define "legal culture" here. Professor Roger Cotterrell, *The Sociology of Law: An Introduction*, (2nd ed., London, Butterworths, 1992), at 23, writes: "Lawrence Friedman has used the term legal culture to suggest the whole range of ideas which exists in particular societies—and varies from one society to another—about law and its place in the social order. . . . These ideas inform legal practices. . . . Variations in legal culture may thus explain much about differences in the ways in which seemingly similar legal provisions or institutions may function in different societies." For my present purposes, I treat the principle of proportionality as one such institution.

[4] I will concentrate on England and Wales, but similar points can be made about Scotland and Northern Ireland.

normally act unlawfully if they act in ways which violate a "Convention right", except so far as their acts are compelled by primary legislation which cannot be interpreted so as to be compatible with the right in question.[5] Convention rights are set out in Schedules 1 and 3 to the Act in the terms used in the English version of the relevant parts of the ECHR. Legislation must be interpreted as far as possible so as to be compatible with Convention rights. In order to minimise the tension between protection of fundamental human rights and the maintenance of the legislative supremacy of Parliament, the drafters refused to try to entrench the Act or to confer on judges a power to disapply primary legislation which is inconsistent with the Convention rights recognised in the Act, but created the novel remedy of a declaration of incompatibility where a superior court holds legislation to be incompatible with Convention rights.[6] Yet there is another tension which the Act seeks to resolve and which has received little attention. The Human Rights Act 1998 will encapsulate a subtle and dynamic approach to the problem of reconciling the dualism of domestic and international law which is part of our constitutional orthodoxy with the desire to ensure that people in the UK have an effective remedy in the UK for violations of their Convention rights by public authorities, as required by Article 13 ECHR. This is achieved by way of the provisions concerned with interpretation of the Convention rights.

Under section 2(1) of the Act, Convention rights will have to be interpreted *taking into account* relevant decisions, reports, judgments and opinions of the Strasbourg organs. This appears to make such decisions, etc., a source of law to which anyone interpreting the Convention rights in the UK must have regard. However, the decisions, reports, judgments and opinions will not *bind* domestic courts and tribunals in interpreting Convention rights for domestic legal purposes. It follows that courts and tribunals will be free to depart from interpretations adopted by the Strasbourg organs where there seems a good reason to do so, having taken them into account. This makes it clear that the Convention rights as applied in the UK will be ECHR rights in terms of their phraseology, but not necessarily in their content. Convention rights in domestic law will derive their authority from Parliament, and will be inspired by, but not validated by, the ECHR. The rights in English law need not be identical in their effects to those achieved when the Strasbourg organs interpret the relevant Articles of the ECHR. There should be an implication that the Convention rights in domestic law will be at least as extensive and as difficult to interfere with as under Strasbourg interpretations of the ECHR. Were this not so, the Act would not help the UK to meet its obligation under Article 13 of the ECHR to provide an effective remedy before a national authority for violations of the rights.[7]

[5] See Human Rights Act 1998, ss. 3, 6.

[6] See Human Rights Act 1998, s. 4.

[7] See D. Feldman, "Remedies for Violations of Convention Rights under the Human Rights Act" [1998] *European Human Rights Law Review* 691.

Yet for good reasons there will be divergences between the outcomes of similar cases under the Act and in Strasbourg. First, the Convention rights which are to apply in the UK are Anglophone versions of polyglot originals. The Strasbourg organs have to deal with the official versions of the rights in the ECHR in both French and English. They must refer to both when resolving ambiguities in either, and must ensure that the two texts are interpreted consistently with each other. Because the Convention rights as set out in Schedules 1 and 3 to the Bill are in English only, our courts and tribunals will not be bound by the French version. It will presumably be permissible for our judges to examine the French text of the Convention rights, but it will be necessary to do so only if the Strasbourg organs have referred to the French text in the course of report, decision, judgment or opinion which the English court must consider under section 2(1). The effect will rarely be significant, but it continues to be the case that the Convention rights which can be enforced in domestic courts and tribunals in the UK will be analytically different in terms of the source of their authority, and so, potentially, in terms of their scope, from those which apply in public international law. This does not entirely compromise the claim to be incorporating the ECHR into domestic law. The process of transformation always entails adjustment. In the case of the ECHR as currently administered there are good reasons why it should be so. One would be justified in thinking that sometimes it would lead to unsatisfactory results were our public authorities to treat an authoritative opinion or decision of the Strasbourg organs on the interpretation of a provision in the Convention as decisive for the purposes of domestic law, for three reasons.[8]

First, there are signs that the Court is becoming increasingly inclined to moral conservatism. Restrictive interpretations are being given to certain rights. Even where a right is held to exist, the Court is increasingly ready to hold that interferences are permitted, giving expansive readings to provisions permitting interference. It is at least arguable that what our domestic courts and tribunals should do in some cases is protect our rights against erosion by the Strasbourg organs. Secondly, the Court has relied increasingly on the "margin of appreciation", allowing States a wide discretion when assessing the appropriate extent of interferences with rights in response to a perceived threat. As will be explained below, the margin of appreciation is a doctrine of questionable value even in public international law, but it has absolutely no place in domestic law. If judges in UK courts ignore that doctrine as they should, it will almost automatically lead them to reach a different result from that which the Court reached in similar cases, even if the Court's interpretation of the scope of the relevant Convention right is accepted. Thirdly, the dynamic character of the Convention provides a further reason for sometimes limiting the precedential value of Strasbourg case law. It is open to the Court to develop over time the

[8] For a fuller assessment, see J. McBride, "Proportionality and the European Convention on Human Rights", this vol.

approach it takes to the interpretation of particular provisions. If there is reason to think that the Court would not now follow one of its own previous decisions, that would be a good reason for domestic courts and tribunals to interpret a provision in the way in which they consider that the Court would now be most likely to interpret it. It will therefore be entirely proper for our courts and tribunals to adopt a flexible approach to interpreting the rights, not in order to interpret rights in ways which make them more limited or allow greater interference with them in the UK than would be allowed in Strasbourg, but to allow them to be faithful to the dynamic character of the Convention and to save litigants time and money by rendering recourse to Strasbourg unnecessary.

Nevertheless, this poses certain problems for anyone speculating about the impact of the doctrine of proportionality in interpreting and applying Convention rights. Under the Convention, proportionality is a case law development. It is a concept used by the Commission and Court to provide practical standards which can be used when deciding what is, as the Convention puts it in several articles, "necessary in a democratic society" for one of the purposes for which interference with a particular right is expressly permitted. It also operates in relation to implied limitations on other Convention rights, and the respect of exercise of a state's power to derogate from Convention rights under Article 15. Under section 2(1) of the Act, our courts and tribunals must have regard to Strasbourg case law concerning proportionality, but are not bound to employ it. If our courts and tribunals do use proportionality, they need not necessarily adopt the same model of it as has been developed by the Court and Commission. Our courts and tribunals are unlikely to discard proportionality as an instrument in the UK for understanding the scope of limitations on Convention rights. Throwing over proportionality entirely would lead to too wide a rift between the interpretation of Convention rights in the UK and their interpretation under the ECHR, and would undermine the main purpose of the Bill. However, it is more likely than not that the courts and tribunals which use the idea will bring to its elucidation ideas different from those which most strongly influenced the Strasbourg organs.

What will these ideas be? Initially, there is likely to be some cross-fertilisation from the way in which the doctrine of proportionality is used in the European Court of Justice.[9] Next, the common-law aversion to, and version of, proportionality is likely to have some effect. Lord Diplock suggested the possibility that English law might develop proportionality as a ground of judicial review,[10] but in *R.* v. *Secretary of State for the Home Department ex parte Brind*[11] the

[9] See F. Jacobs "Recent Developments in the Principle of Proportionality in European Community Law" and T. Tridimas, "Proportionality in Community Law: Searching for the Appropriate Standard of Scrutiny", both this vol.

[10] *R.* v. *Minister for the Civil Service, ex parte Council of Civil Service Unions* [1985] AC 374 (HL), at 410.

[11] [1991] 1 AC 696. Lord Bridge (at 749) and Lord Roskill (at 750) left open the possibility that proportionality might develop as an independent ground of review at some future time. Lord Templeman (at 751) was clearly prepared to contemplate the use of proportionality in human rights

House of Lords decided that proportionality did not yet form part of English law, save in so far as it was an aspect of the doctrine or the ground for judicial review of executive action variously described as unreasonableness or irrationality. This decision will no longer be binding after the Act comes into force, altering the position fundamentally by requiring a rights-based approach which takes account of the Strasbourg case law. It will be open to any court or tribunal to depart from the view of the House of Lords in *Brind's Case*. In any case, some at least of the Law Lords who decided *Brind* gave a clear indication that the common law might itself be on the road towards developing its own doctrine of proportionality, the question being when courts would arrive at it rather than whether it was permissible for them to attempt to do so. More of a problem might be posed by the tendency of some judges to project proportionality as an alternative formulation of the *Wednesbury* principle (whatever that might be these days).[12] If this notion were to take hold, reducing proportionality in relation to the Convention rights to a version of *Wednesbury* unreasonableness, it would be far too easy for public authorities to justify extensive interferences with rights. It would too often undermine the enforceability of Convention rights under the Act, and would defeat the purpose of the legislation. What is needed, then, is a version of proportionality which respects the central importance of the Convention rights to the citizen and to the outsider, to the democratic polity and to the freedom to think and do as we like in our own homes, to the dignity of humanity and to the functioning of society.

If this is to be achieved we must first clearly understand the place which proportionality can have in legal reasoning under the Human Rights Act 1998. The structure of analysis in cases under the 1998 Act can be represented in a series of stages as follows:

1. *Analyse the act, rule or decision which is said to violate a Convention right* to establish what interest of the victim is detrimentally affected.
2. *Decide whether the act, rule or decision actually interferes with a Convention right.* To do this, we will need to decide whether the interest affected corresponds to or falls within any of the Convention rights. At this stage the Convention rights must be interpreted taking account of their interpretation by the Strasbourg organs.
3. *If a Convention right is implicated, assess whether, and if so how, the act, rule or decision in question interferes with the right.* This is a stage at which both law and fact must be considered: both the legal and practical impact of the act, rule or decision must be elucidated.
4. *If the act, rule or decision interferes with a Convention right, evaluate any justification which the public authority offers for the interference in terms*

contexts. Lord Ackner and Lord Lowry were decidedly opposed to proportionality (see 762–3 and 766–7). See also P. Craig, "Unreasonableness and Proportionality in UK Law", this vol.

[12] A similar view is taken by Lord Hoffmann in "The Influence of the European Principle of Proportionality Upon English Law", this vol.; cf. the assessment by P. Craig in his paper, n. 11 above.

of the permitted justifications under the terms of Schedule 1 to the Act and any other relevant provisions of the Act. What justifications are permitted under the relevant Article, read in the light of any special exceptions in the body of the Act? At this point proportionality may become an issue in relation to those Convention rights which expressly or impliedly permit interferences which require to be justified by showing that the interferences are directed to achieving a legitimate purpose, upholding rather than denying the Convention rights in question, and are not disproportionate to that purpose. For example, in *Fayed* v. *United Kingdom*[13] the Court held that providing a public interest privilege against liability in defamation for Board of Trade inspectors was a legitimate interference with a person's right of access to court to uphold his reputation-related rights, given the state interest in overseeing the operation of companies, as long as the extent of the privilege was not disproportionate to the aim pursued.

5. *Only if the justification advanced by the state for the interference satisfies any prior conditions for justifiability (for example, that it be prescribed by or in accordance with the law, and that there be some evidence that the particular interference was necessary in order to achieve a legitimate purpose) do we reach the proportionality test.* Proportionality, as Harris, O'Boyle and Warbrick remind us,[14] "is the final factor the Strasbourg authorities take into account in determining whether an interference with a right is necessary". The question is whether the interference is disproportionate to the legitimate aim pursued. If it is not proportionate, it is not necessary, and the justification fails.

Thus both the content and the significance of the principle of proportionality is restricted in the case law of the Strasbourg organs.[15] The principle is relevant only at a very late stage in the analysis of a case, when the court has decided that a Convention right has been interfered with, and that the justification offered by the State has a basis in domestic law and was or may have been for a legitimate purpose. It allows the Court to balance a number of factors. Was the interference of a kind likely to be effective in achieving its objective?[16] Was the interference sufficiently narrowly drawn and accurately aimed to affect only cases falling within the legitimate purposes for an interference, avoiding other cases,

[13] (1997) 18 EHRR 393.

[14] D.J. Harris, M. O'Boyle and C. Warbrick, *Law of the European Convention on Human Rights* (London, Butterworths, 1995), at 300.

[15] See J. McBride, n. 8 above, and also M.-A. Eissen, "The Principle of Proportionality in the Case law of the European Convention on Human Rights" in R. St. J. Macdonald, F. Matscher and H. Petzold (eds.), *The European System for the Protection of Human Rights* (Dordrecht, Martinus Nijhoff, 1993), chap. 7; Harris *et al.*, n. 14 above, at 11–12, and 300–1.

[16] *Weber* v. *Switzerland*, Eur. Ct. HR, Series A, No. 177 (1990) at para. 51 of the Judgment; *Observer and Guardian* v. *United Kingdom*, Eur. Ct. HR, Series A, No. 216 (1991) at para. 68. But compare the approach of the Commission in *Purcell* v. *Ireland*, Eur. Comm. HR, App No. 15404/89, 70 DR 262 (1991) and *Brind and McLaughlin* v. *United Kingdom*, Eur. Comm. HR, App. Nos. 18714/91 and 18759/91, 77–A DR 42 (1992).

or was it more extensive than necessary?[17] Is there evidence that the victim in the particular case fell within the legitimate scope of the exception to the right?[18] At the end of the process of reasoning, where there is doubt about the justifiability of an established infringement of a Convention right, the principle allows the Court to balance the reasons for and against regarding the infringement as justifiable, reviewing the conclusion of the political, administrative or judicial authorities of the state concerned. However, that review is not unfettered. The Court often limits its role to a form of secondary review, asking not whether the national authority reached the right answer but whether the answer which was given was within the State's "margin of appreciation". This brings us to the relationship between the doctrines of proportionality and margin of appreciation.

Proportionality and the Margin of Appreciation

The Court's review of state action must be conducted with some delicacy. States do not like to have their considered judgements on the balance of public interests reviewed by outsiders. The Commission and Court have therefore developed another doctrine which, in the case law, diminishes (sometimes to a worrying degree) the practical significance of the proportionality principle. This is the "margin of appreciation" which is allowed to States in deciding what is justifiable in response to a pressing social need.[19] There are three possible forms of the margin of appreciation doctrine. All of them are questionable, because, despite assertions of ultimate control by the Court, they reduce the capacity of the Court to review decisions within States as to the propriety or proportionality of interferences with rights.[20] Of the three approaches, the Court has generally adopted the second of those which are arranged here in ascending order of expansiveness.

[17] *Sunday Times* v. *United Kingdom*, Eur. Ct. HR, Series A, No. 30 (1979) at para. 67 of the Judgment; *Campbell* v. *United Kingdom*, Eur. Ct. HR, Series A, No. 233 (1992).

[18] *Kokkinakis* v. *Greece*, Eur. Ct. HR, Series A, No. 260–A (1993) at para. 49 of the Judgment.

[19] See R. Higgins, "Derogations under Human Rights Treaties" (1976–77) 48 *British Year Book of International Law* 281–320, at 296–315; R. St. J. Macdonald, "The Margin of Appreciation" in Macdonald *et al.*, *European System for the Protection of Human Rights* (Dordrecht, London, M. Nijhoff, 1993), chap. 6; P. Mahoney, "Judicial Activism and Judicial Restraint in the European Court of Human Rights: Two Sides of the Same Coin" (1990) 11 *Human Rights Law Journal* 57–88, at 78–85; J.G. Merrills, *The Development of International Law by the European Court of Human Rights* (2nd edn., Manchester, Manchester University Press, 1993), chap. 7; Harris *et al.*, *Law of the European Convention on Human Rights*, n. 14 above, at 12–14.

[20] See R. St. J. Macdonald, "The Margin of Appreciation" in Macdonald *et al.*, n. 15 above, chap. 6; H. Petzold, "The Convention and the Principle of Subsidiarity" in Macdonald *et al.*, n. 15 above, at 41–62; P. Mahoney, n. 19 above, at 57–88; D. Feldman, "Human Rights Treaties, Nation States and Conflicting Moralities" (1995) 1 *Contemporary Issues in Law* 61–85; T.H. Jones, "The Devaluation of Human Rights under the European Convention" [1995] *PL* 430–49; P. Mahoney, "Universality versus Subsidiarity in the Strasbourg Case Law on Free Speech: Explaining Some Recent Judgments" [1997] *European Human Rights Law Review* 364–79; Lord Lester of Herne Hill QC, "Universality versus Subsidiarity: A Reply" [1998] *European Human Rights Law Review* 73–81; N. Lavender, "The Problem of the Margin of Appreciation" [1997] *European Human Rights Law Review* 380–90.

The first form is the least extensive and so the least objectionable, but has not been used by the Court. Where a pressing social need has been objectively established to interfere with a right, the state would have a degree of discretion in deciding the appropriate extent of any interference. This would limit the discretion to the stage at which a judgment must be made about the propriety of a specific interference in order to achieve a legitimate objective recognised under the Convention in response to a pressing social need accepted as such by the Court.

The second form of the margin of appreciation is that developed by the Court in *Handyside* v. *United Kingdom*,[21] a case concerned with the forfeiture in England of copies of *The Little Red Schoolbook*, containing information for school-children about *inter alia* sex, which had circulated freely elsewhere in Europe but had been held to be obscene in England. The majority of the Court held that the UK was entitled to form its own view on moral issues, and then to enforce it where it considered that there was a pressing social need to do so. The majority wrote in their judgment[22]:

> By reason of their direct and continuous contact with the vital forces of their countries, state authorities are in principle in a better position than the international judge to give an opinion on the exact content of those requirements as well as on the "necessity" of a "restriction" or "penalty" intended to meet them . . .

In other words, the State is allowed a good deal of flexibility (the extent of the leeway depending on the context) *both* in deciding whether there is a pressing social need to interfere with rights, *and* in deciding how great an interference is justified to deal with that need. Although the Court went on to assert a power "to give a final ruling on whether a 'restriction' or 'penalty' is reconcilable with freedom of expression as protected by Article 10",[23] that supervisory jurisdiction seems to apply only in respect of the extent of the interference, not the soundness of the reason for it.

A third possible form of the margin of appreciation would be even more extensive, involving deference to decisions of the State as to the scope of rights or the application of other principles justifying restrictions on rights. Fortunately, these extensions are largely precluded by the doctrine of the autonomous meaning of Convention terms, without which there would be no objective, supra-national standards for interpreting a State's human rights obligations in international law.[24]

In so far as the doctrine of proportionality as applied by the Strasbourg organs is limited by the margin of appreciation, proportionality will not be directly transferable to the UK under the Human Rights Act 1998. The reason for this lies in the nature and purpose of the concept of a margin of appreciation.

[21] Eur. Ct. HR, Series A, No. 24 (1976).

[22] Series A, No. 24 (1976) at para. 48 of the Judgment.

[23] *Ibid.*, at para. 49.

[24] F. Matscher, "Methods of Interpretation of the Convention" in Macdonald *et al.*, n. 15 above, chap. 5, at 70–3; Harris *et al.*, n. 14 above, at 16–17.

It is less what has been called "a lubricant at the interface between individual rights and public interest"[25] than a lubricant at the interface between international and national authorities. As the quotation above from the judgment in the *Handyside* case makes clear, it dictates deference on the part of international organs to the judgments of public authorities which are in "direct and continuous contact with the vital forces of their countries" and are therefore "in a better position than the international judge to give an opinion" on what is required locally for such purposes as protecting morality or coping with a state of emergency. The international judge's lack of familiarity with local conditions cannot be used by a judge in a domestic jurisdiction as an excuse for limiting his or her supervision of public authorities' compliance with human-rights requirements within that jurisdiction.[26]

I am not suggesting that judges in our courts will not use the *term* "margin of appreciation". Indeed, they are already doing so. A *Lexis* search[27] revealed between 20 and 30 such uses per year between the beginning of 1995 and the middle of 1998. Some of these were entirely legitimate references to the case law of the Strasbourg organs (often to distinguish it). Others were marginally less appropriate, albeit maintaining a link with public international law: the term was used to describe the way in which States parties to international conventions (especially concerned with refugees and political asylum) may adopt different interpretations of their obligations under those treaties where there is no means of obtaining a single authoritative interpretation. Some usages of the term were very odd indeed, for example justifying the refusal of the Employment Appeal Tribunal to review findings of fact by industrial tribunals, or to grant leave to appeal to the Court of Appeal, where the industrial tribunal's decision was said to be within the "margin of appreciation" allowed to a fact-finding body which has seen the evidence.[28] In other cases again the term has been used mistakenly as a synonym for the distinct idea of deference to an expert decision-maker, considered further below[29]; as a reformulation of a principle of judicial restraint when operating review for *Wednesbury* unreasonableness[30]; or, entirely perversely, to give some colour of respectability to a decision to defer to the view of a wholly inexpert inferior tribunal on a question of its *vires*.[31] I

[25] Harris *et al.*, n. 14 above, at 14–15.

[26] It is reassuring to see that this has already been accepted by at least one member of the High Court bench: Sir John Laws, "The Limitations of Human Rights" [1998] *PL* 254–65, at 254. See also Kentridge, n. 2 above, at 70.

[27] The search term was "margin w/3 appreciation and date aft 1994".

[28] See, e.g., *Kapadiya* v. *New India Assurance Co. Ltd*, unreported, EAT/25/97, transcript from *Lexis*.

[29] See, e.g., *R.* v. *Medicines Control Agency, ex parte Pharma Nord Ltd., The Times*, 29 July 1997 (DC), transcript available from *Lexis*.

[30] See, e.g., the formulation by David Pannick QC which the Court of Appeal adopted in the much-cited passage in *R.* v. *Ministry of Defence, ex parte Smith* [1996] QB 517.

[31] See, e.g., *R.* v. *Radio Authority, ex parte Bull* [1998] QB 294, criticised by J. Stevens and D. Feldman, "Broadcasting Advertisements by Bodies with Political Objectives, Judicial Review, and the Influence of Charities Law" [1997] *PL* 615–22.

merely suggest that when the term is used in municipal law it cannot have the same meaning, or the same rationale, as it has in the case law of the Strasbourg organs.

Of course, the fact that one possible source of restriction on proportionality-based reasoning will not be justifiable in relation to the Human Rights Act 1998 does not mean that there will not be other restrictive doctrines. For instance, Advocate General Jacobs has described how the margin of appreciation doctrine was itself adapted from principles operating within national systems of administrative law to govern the extent of judicial intervention in the decisions of other state organs and to keep such intervention within constitutionally proper bounds.[32] It is to these other limitations, which have a proper place within domestic systems of public law and which will undoubtedly have a role to play in the development and application of a doctrine of proportionality under the Human Rights Act 1998, that we turn in the next section of this paper.

II. PROPORTIONALITY IN THE UK AND THE LIMITS ON IT

The Relationship between Proportionality and Irrationality

As mentioned earlier, English judges have sometimes expressed the view that proportionality is simply an aspect of the principle of judicial review sometimes known as irrationality or *Wednesbury* unreasonableness. This view is advanced by Lord Hoffmann in his chapter of this book.[33] There is certainly a relationship between the doctrines. Both of them are designed to allow a court to review the balance struck by a public authority between competing interests, while placing limits on the scope of such review. However, when one passes beyond the most general and abstract level of analysis there are more differences than similarities between the concepts.[34] For present purposes, therefore, it is only necessary to observe that the balance of English authority does not favour the view that proportionality is merely an aspect of irrationality, although in many cases they may yield similar results.[35]

There are three ways in which the principles of rationality and proportionality may diverge. First, the doctrine of proportionality requires the reviewing court to assess the fairness of the balance which the national authority has struck, not merely its reasonableness. Very often in the Strasbourg case law the

[32] F.G. Jacobs, *The European Convention on Human Rights* (Oxford, Clarendon Press, 1985), at 201.

[33] Lord Hoffmann, "The Influence of the European Principle of Proportionality upon UK Law", this vol.

[34] These are discussed in detail by P. Craig in "Unreasonableness and Proportionality in UK Law", this vol.

[35] See *Brind* [1991] AC 696 (HL); *R.* v. *Chief Constable of Sussex, ex parte International Trader's Ferry Ltd* [1997] 2 All ER 65 at 80 *per* Kennedy LJ (under appeal to the House of Lords at the time of writing).

margin of appreciation allowed to States obscures the significance of this difference. Nevertheless, the difference is real. For example, in *X, Y and Z* v. *United Kingdom*[36] children complained that the UK authorities, by not recognising a female-to-male transsexual as their father when he was performing the role of father in the family, had infringed their right to respect for their private or family lives under Article 8 of the Convention. The Court considered that, despite the margin of appreciation, it had to assess whether the State had fairly balanced all the interests, taking account of the interests of the State (for example, that in being able to define matters relating to the civil status of its nationals) and of the legal and practical disadvantages which non-recognition of the *de facto* relationship inflicted on the children. The Court by a majority held that the State had shown that the way in which it had balanced the interests had not been unfair. This is a different test from asking the question which an English court would currently ask in judicial review proceedings: is the balance struck by the authority so wholly irrational that no reasonable authority, properly understanding its legal responsibilities and the facts, could have reached it?

Secondly, the proportionality test may go slightly further than the other related tests under *Wednesbury*, based on a failure to take account of relevant considerations, taking account of irrelevant considerations, or using a power for an improper purpose. An unfair balance may be struck even after all the relevant interests have been considered, irrelevant ones ignored, and the proper purpose for the power borne clearly in mind. The proportionality doctrine directs attention not only to the interests or considerations weighed against each other, but also to the relative weights which the primary decision-maker attached to the various interests or considerations. These are matters which our courts are reluctant to scrutinise, feeling that they lie within the special competence of the primary decision-maker.[37] So far as they are used at all, these aspects of the *Wednesbury* test have been said to relate to the legality of a decision or *vires* of a decision-maker, not to its irrationality or reasonableness.[38] A decision-maker who takes account of an irrelevant consideration is likely to be held to have acted outside his powers, not to have erred in exercising a power he or she had.

Finally, the principles and approaches of judicial review developed in cases which pre-date the Human Rights Act 1998 (including *Associated Provincial*

[36] Eur. Ct. HR, 1997–II R & J 619, (1997) 24 EHRR 143.

[37] See the Court of Appeal's strictures on any reasoning by judges in judicial review proceedings which take the courts close to reviewing the substantive merits of decisions, in *R.* v. *Criminal Injuries Compensation Board, ex parte Cook* [1996] 2 All ER 144, and *R.* v. *Secretary of State for the Home Department, ex parte Hargreaves* [1997] 1 All ER 397. Contrast the following footnote from Sir John Laws, "Wednesbury" in C. Forsyth and I. Hare, *The Golden Metwand and the Crooked Cord: Essays on Public Law in Honour of Sir William Wade* (Oxford, Clarendon Press, 1998), 185 at 197, n. 34: "[i]n 'The Ghost in the Machine: Principle in Public Law' [1989] *PL* 27 I argued that a true case of perversity was itself a procedural challenge, because 'a [*Wednesbury*] failure is as much a piece of unfairness as a failure to give a person a proper hearing'. But I put it the wrong way round. A failure to to be fair is unreasonable."

[38] See *In re Lonrho plc* [1990] 2 AC 154 (HL).

Picture Houses Ltd v. *Wednesbury Corporation*[39] itself) are not self-evidently appropriate to protection of human rights. They offer too restricted and discretionary a set of remedies to be adequate for that purpose. When, as will often happen, issues under the Human Rights Act 1998 arise in proceedings in criminal law, tort, restitution or company law (to mention but a few likely contexts) the courts may feel entitled to be more interventionist than would be the case in judicial review proceedings.[40] Even in judicial review proceedings, when Convention rights under the Act are in issue the scope of the rights and of any permitted interference with them should not be seen as a matter of irrationality, or error within jurisdiction. The Act itself provides in section 3(1) that subordinate legislation is to be interpreted whenever possible to be compatible with Convention rights. If this proves impossible, section 3(2)(c) impliedly requires all incompatible subordinate legislation to be treated as invalid or ineffective, unless primary legislation (which would have to be interpreted as narrowly as possible: see section 3(1)) made it impossible for the subordinate legislation to be made in a way compatible with the Convention. Administrative acts by public authorities are unlawful to the extent of any incompatibility unless mandated by primary legislation: see section 6(1). The scope of rights, including permitted interferences with them, is thus a matter of *vires* or legality, not irrationality. With the greatest respect to Lord Hoffmann's view, it seems unlikely that proportionality and irrationality will share the same role or content in relation to review under the Human Rights Act 1998. It is unlikely to be helpful to treat proportionality analytically as a brand of irrationality or version of unreasonableness in cases brought under the Human Rights Act 1998, even if the distinction will sometimes make little difference to the outcome.

Justiciability

In order to embark on a judicial inquiry into an issue, the issue and the context in which it arises must be justiciable. In English public law there is generally a presumption in favour of justiciability. A party who argues that an issue is non-justiciable must show good reasons for asking the court to decline to exercise its jurisdiction. Such reasons usually relate to one of three factors.

The first factor relates to the capacity of the judicial process to take cognizance of the issue, for example where the cause of action is said to arise from public international law which is not part of domestic law under existing constitutional arrangements. Claims based on international human rights law used to be non-justiciable in this sense within the UK, but to the extent that the right in question is part of one of the Convention rights protected under the Human

39 [1948] 1 KB 223.

40 See, e.g., the emergence of a particularly anxious standard of scrutiny in fundamental human rights cases in *Bugdaycay* v. *Secretary of State for the Home Department* [1987] AC 514 (HL), and *R.* v. *Ministry of Defence, ex parte Smith* [1996] QB 517 (CA).

Rights Act 1998 this will no longer be the case. Secondly, the nature of the problem which is posed may make it unsuitable for judicial decision if it does not require a dispositive, right-or-wrong answer. Courts will rarely be prepared to adjudicate on the merits of issues in relation to which another person or body has a lawful discretion which is not rule-bound, such as the exercise of a policy-based prerogative or the making of a charitable gift.[41]

The third factor is the suitability of the judicial process for establishing the facts which are needed in order to decide the issue. If the rules of evidence or one party's claim to protect information on the ground of public interest immunity would make it impossible for the facts to be established, the judicial process is clearly an unsuitable forum for resolving the issue. This is not an absolute bar to justiciability, however. Different courts or tribunals may have procedures and evidential rules more or less well adapted to the resolution of a particular type of issue. This form of justiciability therefore relates to particular tribunals rather than to adversarial or inquisitorial processes as a whole. For example, as Advocate General Jacobs and Professor van Gerven suggest in their papers in this volume,[42] the criminal courts might be less appropriate fora for dealing with matters of public health policy in cases concerning pharmaceutical law; but other courts (such as the Divisional Court) may be well able (and indeed required by Community law) to inquire into and assess government policy on fishing quotas, as in the *Factortame* cases.

To see how the second and third of these aspects of justiciability might affect the operation of proportionality under the 1998 Act, we can usefully consider how *Brind*[43] might be decided. The applicants challenged a ban on broadcasting the voices of terrorist sympathisers. The ban clearly interfered with the speakers' and broadcasters' rights to freedom of expression under Article 10(1) ECHR. As no primary legislation required the Secretary of State to impose the ban, the question would be whether it was justified under Article 10(2). The ban was prescribed by law within the meaning of the Convention. Was it necessary in a democratic society for the purpose of protecting national security or preventing crime? Assuming that it was introduced in good faith for those purposes, and not to stifle a political point of view in a way entirely incompatible with a democratic society, the remaining questions are (a) whether there was a pressing social need for action, and (b) whether the ban as introduced was a proportionate response to that need.

The existence of a pressing social need can hardly be denied where national security is threatened by a public emergency threatening the life of the nation,

[41] See P. Craig, "Prerogative, Precedent and Power" in C. Forsyth and I. Hare (eds.), *The Golden Metwand and the Crooked Cord: Essays on Public Law in Honour of Sir William Wade* (Oxford, Clarendon Press, 1998), 65; *R.* v. *Criminal Injuries Compensation Board, ex parte P* [1995] 1 All ER 870 (CA), at 880–2 (Neill LJ), 885–6 (Evans LJ), 887–9 (Peter Gibson LJ).

[42] F.G. Jacobs, "Recent Developments in the Principle of Proportionality in European Community Law" and W. van Gerven, "The Effect of Proportionality on the Actions of Member States of the EC: National Viewpoints from Continental Europe", both this vol.

[43] [1991] 1 AC 696 (HL).

within the meaning of Article 15. How does one decide whether such an emergency exists? The European Commission and Court of Human Rights have claimed to make their own assessments, but in reality have accepted the judgment of the State affected by the emergency wherever there is any evidence to support it.[44] As Harris *et al.* comment, "[t]his degree of scrutiny is hardly different from accepting the parties' own view of the situation . . . [I]t cannot be asserted that the margin of appreciation allowed to a state on the question of the existence of the emergency is anything but wide".[45] The margin of appreciation being inapplicable to domestic proceedings, would the English courts be any more demanding when evaluating the government's claim that there was a pressing social need by reason of a threat to national security or a public emergency endangering the life of the nation?

The answer will sometimes be "No". This answer is dictated not by the margin of appreciation but by the well-established principle of justiciability, which is deeply rooted in our judicial culture. Our courts have historically been reluctant to embark on their own assessments of national security issues. Instead, they have tended to defer in such matters to the Executive, which is thought to be in a better position to obtain and evaluate relevant information.[46] The origin of this reluctance, and of the notion of "national security" itself, is obscure. It has been traced by Professor Laurence Lustgarten and Professor Ian Leigh to an extension from the prerogatives relating to war, defence of the realm and maritime prizes in time of war.[47] As Dr Christopher Forsyth has pointed out, this was broadened in the *GCHQ* case[48] into a trump card which could be used in any context and any proceedings.[49] Once it had been invented in World War I, a claim by the Executive to be acting to protect national security has rarely been subjected by courts to systematic, let alone rigorous, analysis. Indeed, it is one of the curiosities of the notion of national security that it is regularly deployed for forensic purposes without being defined or analysed. This has deprived judges and commentators of the tools which would be needed in order to delimit the legal scope and incidents of national security.[50] Where courts have brushed up against national security matters, it has been common for them to accept the Executive's assessment of its demands whenever there is any evidence to support it, and sometimes even when there is none. For example, in the *GCHQ* case[51]

[44] See e.g. *Ireland* v. *United Kingdom*, Eur. Ct. HR, Series A, No. 25 (1978) at para. 207 of the Judgment; *Brannigan and McBride* v. *United Kingdom*, Eur. Ct. HR, Series A, No. 258–B (1993) at para. 45 of the Judgment.

[45] N. 14 above, at 493.

[46] See D. Feldman, "Public Law Values in the House of Lords" (1990) 106 *LQR* 246.

[47] L. Lustgarten and I. Leigh, *In from the Cold: National Security and Parliamentary Democracy* (Oxford, Clarendon Press, 1994), at 323–30.

[48] *R.* v. *Minister for the Civil Service, ex parte Council of Civil Service Unions* [1985] AC 3374 (HL).

[49] C. Forsyth, "Judicial Review, the Royal Prerogative and National Security" (1985) 36 *NILQ* 25.

[50] See L. Lustgarten and I. Leigh, n. 47 above, at 321–3 for a taxonomy of the legal forms and contexts in which national security has been relevant.

[51] N. 48 above.

the unions challenged a decision, taken without consultation, to ban unions at GCHQ. The House of Lords held that the failure to consult the unions had breached a legitimate expectation of consultation. Nevertheless, their Lordships demanded no evidence to support the government's assertion that giving notice of its intention to introduce the ban would have endangered national security, so that it had been justifiable to disregard the unions' expectation. The government argued, and the House accepted, that the security implications of giving notice were either self-evident, and so needed no evidence, or had to be taken on trust because of the sensitive nature of the evidence which would have been needed to prove them. In reality, these matters are never self-evident, because of the pall of secrecy which surrounds them and which it is in the interests of the Executive to maintain. Hence Lustgarten and Leigh argue persuasively that the pretence of self-evidence is a convenient ruse enabling judges to conceal what they call "abdication of the judicial role to the executive".[52]

A similar reticence on the part of the judges can be seen in relation to deportation decisions[53] and the closely analogous use of exclusion orders in relation to terrorism related to the affairs of Northern Ireland.[54] In effect, national security issues are non-justiciable. In the context of *Brind*, therefore, the prevailing legal culture suggests that the courts would be unlikely to embark on any very robust review of the existence of a pressing social need to maintain national security in the face of a terrorist threat, or of the appropriateness of the steps which the executive took to deal with the danger. Nothing in the Human Rights Act 1998 compels a different approach from that adopted formerly. Although the margin of appreciation, properly so called, does not apply in domestic proceedings, the principle of justiciability operates just as effectively in its stead. However, there is likely to be a presumption in favour of justiciability, such as was applied to the exercise of prerogative powers in the *GCHQ* case. For reasons which will be developed below, greater attention may be paid to the specific kind of national security consideration being asserted by a public authority. Furthermore, even if in at least some cases the courts accept that the judgment of pressing social need in national security cases cannot be effectively challenged, the 1998 Act may enable or encourage them to be more assertive in reviewing the appropriateness of the measures taken in response to that need, bringing proportionality into play, subtly altering the prevailing legal culture.

In the *GCHQ* case, Lord Diplock foreshadowed the development of a ground of judicial review based on proportionality. The case law of the Strasbourg organs makes this the very context in which one might expect proportionality

[52] N. 47 above, at 330 ff.

[53] See e.g. *R.* v. *Secretary of State for the Home Department, ex parte Hosenball* [1977] 1 WLR 766 (CA); *R.* v. *Secretary of State for the Home Department, ex parte Cheblak* [1991] 2 All ER 319 (CA); *R.* v. *Secretary of State for the Home Department, ex parte Chahal* [1995] 1 All ER 658 (CA).

[54] *R.* v. *Secretary of State for the Home Department, ex parte Stitt*, *The Times*, 3 Feb. 1987; *R.* v. *Secretary of State for the Home Department, ex parte Adams* [1995] All ER (EC) 177; *R.* v. *Secretary of State for the Home Department, ex parte Gallagher*, *The Times*, 16 Feb. 1994; *R.* v. *Secretary of State for the Home Department, ex parte McQuillan* [1995] 4 All ER 400.

to play a part under the Human Rights Act 1998, particularly as the margin of appreciation is inapplicable. It ought usually to be possible for the proponent of an interference with a fundamental freedom to show how the interference will contribute to averting a threat to national security. If that cannot be done, the courts should not usually countenance an assertion that a public authority is protected by national security considerations, either with regard to the straightforward justiciability of an issue or in relation to an evidential claim for public interest immunity. If this were not the case, the significance of the reasoning of the House of Lords in *R.* v. *Secretary of State for the Home Department, ex parte Bugdaycay*,[55] to the effect that decisions affecting fundamental rights such as the right to life attract the most anxious judicial scrutiny, would be devoid of real effect.

Another factor makes it possible, even in national security cases, that the courts may be prepared to treat some claims to national security protection or public interest immunity more critically than others, once the 1998 Act has made Convention rights weightier elements in domestic law. Not all national security considerations operate at the same level of gravity or urgency, and some are more readily counterbalanced by other considerations (including rights) than others, as Hutton LCJ pointed out in the context of Northern Ireland terrorism in *Doherty* v. *Ministry of Defence*[56] and *R* v. *H.M. Coroner for Greater Belfast, ex parte Ministry of Defence; Same* v. *Same, ex parte McNeil*.[57] Once this is recognised, the evaluation of such claims in the context of the Act will involve a balancing process, taking account of the significance of the right affected and the weight of the national security considerations. Once the significance of Convention standards is accepted in domestic law, as Sedley J said in *R* v. *Secretary of State for the Home Department, ex parte McQuillan*:

> the legal standards by which the decisions of public bodies are supervised can and should differentiate between those rights which are recognised as fundamental and those which, while known to the law, do not enjoy such a pre-eminent status. Once this point is reached, the standard of justification of infringements of rights and freedoms by executive decision must vary in proportion to the significance of the right which is at issue . . . Whether this in itself is a doctrine of proportionality I do not now pause to ask; if it is, the House of Lords has long since contemplated its arrival with equanimity . . . [Lord Hutton's] careful analysis of the differential character of issues for which the shield of national security may be claimed fortifies me in suggesting that the grounds given in the present case, if they do not fall altogether outside the ambit of national security, at the very least lie on a point on the scale which a court, with proper safeguards, can assess against the importance of the other rights involved.[58]

In *Ex parte McQuillan* Sedley J felt bound by authority to hold that, as a matter of English (although not Northern Ireland) law that course was not yet open

[55] [1987] AC 514.
[56] [1991] NIJB (No. 1) 68, (NI CA), at 86.
[57] 1994, NI CA, transcript 2439–41.
[58] [1995] 4 All ER 400, at 422–4.

to him. He felt bound to accept assertions of national security which appeared questionable. The Court of Appeal reached a similar conclusion in respect of a decision by the Home Secretary to return a militant Sikh separatist to India, from which he had fled fearing torture and death from the police and security forces in the Punjab. The Home Secretary decided that the asylum-seeker represented a threat to security in the UK which outweighed the risk to him of being returned to India. In *R* v. *Secretary of State for the Home Department, ex parte Chahal*[59] the Court of Appeal held that in national security cases it could only ask whether the way in which the Home Secretary had struck that balance could be stigmatised as *Wednesbury* unreasonable, and concluded that it had no evidence to form the basis of such an assessment. The position within the UK ought to be different in the new age which the Human Rights Act 1998 will usher in. The unsuccessful applicant in *Chahal's Case* successfully petitioned the Strasbourg organs under the ECHR. In *Chahal* v. *United Kingdom*[60] the European Court of Human Rights examined the evidence, and decided that returning Chahal to India would subject him to such a risk of torture or inhuman treatment as to constitute a violation of Article 3 of the ECHR. As Article 3 rights are absolute, there could be no room for striking a balance between the risk of torture and the threat which Chahal might pose. It followed that, in cases involving Article 3 and national security, judicial review and habeas corpus did not offer an effective remedy as required by Article 13 for violations of rights where judges were permitted to balance security risks against the risk of torture, or could allow the Home Secretary to do so.

In some cases, then, no balancing of rights against security will be permitted. Even where non-absolute rights are in issue, the careful balancing required by a doctrine of proportionality should become a major check on the acceptability of claims to the shield of national security, both in relation to the existence of threats to national security and their significance in relation to the interference with rights in the particular case. There will be some cases in which the national security considerations are so sensitive and important that the courts will still decline to intervene, but the doctrine of proportionality should be able to operate (giving appropriate but not unquestioning weight to national security) whenever the court is not satisfied that it ought to treat the particular type of national security consideration as being of such overriding sensivity and importance as to make the decision in respect of it essentially non-justiciable.

The recent decision of the European Court of Human Rights in *Tinnelly & Sons Ltd and others and McElduff and others* v. *United Kingdom*[61] makes it clear that this is the approach which should be applied to weighing non-absolute rights against national security considerations under the ECHR. The applicants in the *Tinelly* case were Catholics in Northern Ireland who were aggrieved by the refusal of two undertakings to enter into contracts with them for the provi-

[59] [1995] 1 All ER 658.

[60] Judgment of 15 Nov. 1996, especially at paras. 151 ff.

[61] Case no. 62/1997/846/1052–1053, Judgment of 10 July 1998.

sion of services to the undertakings. They lodged complaints with the Fair Employment Agency ("FEA") under the Fair Employment (Northern Ireland) Act 1976. The Secretary of State for Northern Ireland issued certificates under section 42 of the Act stating that the refusal to offer contracts was "an act done for the purpose of safeguarding national security or the protection of public safety or order". By virtue of section 42(2) those certificates were conclusive evidence of the facts asserted. In proceedings for judicial review of the certificates, applications for discovery were met with a public interest immunity certificate. The court upheld the claim to public interest immunity in respect of most of the documents, and dismissed the application for judicial review. Although the judge suspected that the real reasons for refusing to contract had nothing to do with national security, he held that the issue of the section 42 certificate had to be accepted as conclusive because its issue had been neither an abuse of process nor fraudulent. As a result, the FEA was unable to investigate the complaints further. In the *McElduff* case the petitioners had complained to the Fair Employment Tribunal (the statutory successor to the FEA) under the same legislation about discrimination, and had been met by a section 42 certificate with the result that they withdrew their claim.

The petitioners alleged that there had been a violation of their right to a fair hearing by an independent and impartial tribunal under Article 6(1) of the ECHR in the determination of their civil rights. This was accepted unanimously by both the Commission and the Court. The Court held that the right under the 1976 Act not to be discriminated against in the award of contracts was a civil right.[62] The right to institute proceedings before a court in civil matters is an aspect of the "right to a court" under Article 6(1). It is subject to implied limitations, in respect of which the State has a margin of appreciation, "although the final decision as to the observance of the Convention's requirements rests with the Court", which:

> must be satisfied that the limitations applied do not restrict or reduce the access left to the individual in such a way or to such an extent that the very essence of the right is impaired. Furthermore, a limitation will not be compatible with Article 6(1) if it does not pursue a legitimate aim and if there is not a reasonable relationship of proportionality between the means employed and the aim sought to be achieved.[63]

The Court accepted that national security gave rise to special considerations in Northern Ireland. Nevertheless, there was no opportunity for either the FEA, the Tribunal, or (because of the public interest immunity claim) the High Court in judicial review proceedings to assess the justification for issuing the section 42 certificate, which in turn entirely precluded the petitioners' opportunity to enforce their civil rights. This was disproportionate in the light of the absence of effective judicial scrutiny of the grounds on which the certificate was issued. The onus lay on the government to persuade the Court that there were good

[62] Para. 61 of the Judgment.
[63] *Ibid.*, at para. 72.

reasons for interfering with the petitioners' rights under Article 6(1) to that extent, and the government had failed to discharge that burden either before the Northern Ireland High Court (which however was powerless to do anything about it) or before the Strasbourg organs.[64]

Under the Human Rights Act 1998, therefore, our courts and tribunals, taking account of this unanimous decision of both the Court and the Commission, will have difficulty in maintaining the traditional view that national-security claims by government are effectively non-justiciable, at least in respect of litigation about civil rights and obligations within the meaning of Article 6(1). At the very least, courts and tribunals will have to be satisfied that there are good grounds for making national-security claims. Public authorities will also have to satisfy the courts that the impact of public interest immunity certificates, or certificates such as those under section 42 of the 1976 Act, does not deprive people of the essence of the Article 6(1) right, and is not disproportionate to the aim pursued. When not precluded by primary legislation, new procedures will have to be developed to allow this sort of investigation to be conducted while preserving national security. When primary legislation applies, it will have to be interpreted so far as possible in a way compatible with the Article 6 rights. When that is impossible, superior courts will be able to grant a declaration of incompatibility. The importation of proportionality should significantly alter the legal culture concerning the relationship between the judiciary and the executive in national security and public interest matters which affect human rights, even where those rights are not absolute.

"The Deference due to a Man of Pedigree"[65]

Conceptually separate from questions of national security and the margin of appreciation, although often confused with them, is the very proper deference displayed to expert or otherwise specially qualified decision-makers or decision-making procedures, to which Lord Hoffmann refers in his paper in this book.[66] This is, of course, different from an uncritical deference paid to all decision-makers, however inexpert, which sometimes distorts judicial review.[67] Proper deference requires the court to assess a decision-maker's qualifications for making the type of decision in question. The better the qualifications, the greater the deference. When deciding on the proper extent of deference to the judgment of other decision-makers, judges must consider the identity of the decision-maker

[64] Case no. 62/1997/846/1052–1053, Judgment of 10 July 1998 at para. 73–79.

[65] The reference is to Pooh-Bah, the self-important nobleman holding the combined office of Lord High Everything Else in W.S. Gilbert's *The Mikado*.

[66] Lord Hoffmann, n. 33 above.

[67] For such a case see *R.* v. *Radio Authority, ex parte Bull* [1997] 2 All ER 561 (CA), discussed by J. Stevens and D. Feldman, "Broadcasting Advertisements by Bodies with Political Objects, Judicial Review, and the Influence of Charities Law" [1997] *PL* 615.

and the way in which his, her or its qualifications are particularly suited to making sensible or legitimate decisions about the particular issue.

A decision-maker may be qualified in a number of different ways, all of which are regularly taken into account by judges in deciding on the proper scope of judicial intervention. Technical expertise may be desirable where technical issues are under consideration. Democratic accountability may be desirable where the issues concern public policy, affecting many people. A procedure which makes it likely that the decision-maker will have been in possession of all the facts and arguments is likely to improve the quality of decision-making and generate judicial deference towards the decision, irrespective of the personal qualifications of the decision-maker. What is important is that the judge should think carefully about the types of qualification relevant to the particular decision, taking account of the constitutional position and accountability of the decision-maker, and should give appropriate weight to them when deciding what to do if the decision does not coincide with the judge's own assessment of the rights and wrongs of the case. This has been encapsulated in a number of important decisions in administrative law in England[68] and Canada.[69]

In relation to proportionality, this means that a judge balancing the various competing interests and rights should give additional weight to the informed view taken by a properly qualified primary decision-maker in the light of an appropriate pre-decision procedure.

III. THE LIKELY IMPACT OF THE DOCTRINE OF PROPORTIONALITY ON THE OPERATION OF THE HUMAN RIGHTS ACT 1998 IN ENGLAND AND WALES

In so far as it is likely to be shaped by the general approach of the Strasbourg organs, one can say that the doctrine of proportionality will probably be applied in different ways depending on three major factors. The first is the nature of the right which is being interfered with; the second is the ground which the public authority advances for interfering with it; the third is the source and form of that interference. In relation to the first of these, the Strasbourg organs consider that it is easier to justify interfering with some rights than with others. Rights have different weights. The weight of the right is set against the legitimate interests of other people or of the State when judging the justifiability of an interference

[68] See, e.g., *Nottinghamshire County Council* v. *Secretary of State for the Environment* [1986] AC 240 (HL); *Hammersmith and Fulham LBC* v. *Secretary of State for the Environment* [1991] 1 AC 521 (HL); *R.* v. *Criminal Injuries Compensation Board, ex parte P* [1995] 1 All ER 870 (CA), at 881–2, *per* Neill LJ; *Tesco Stores Ltd.* v. *Secretary of State for the Environment* [1995] 2 All ER 636 (HL); *R.* v. *Criminal Injuries Compensation Board, ex parte Cook* [1996] 2 All ER 144 (CA); D. Dyzenhaus, "The Politics of Deference: Judicial Review and Democracy" in M. Taggart (ed.), *The Province of Administrative Law* (Oxford, Hart Publishing, 1997), chap. 13.

[69] See *Canadian Union of Public Employees Local 963* v. *New Brunswick Liquor Corporation* [1979] 2 SCR 227 (SC Can.); Madame Justice Claire L'Heureux-Dubé, "The 'Ebb' and 'Flow' of Administrative Law on the 'General Question of Law' " in M. Taggart, n. 68 above, chap. 14.

with the right. The weight which is attached to the interests of the right-holder as against those of the community is greatest when the right is most significant to the life, dignity or political participation of the right-holder or to the ideal of the rule of law which the Convention embodies. It is thus particularly difficult to justify interfering with Articles 2 and 3 and to some extent with Articles 6 and 10. Within Article 10, political expression is given greater weight, and so more extensive protection against governmental interference, than other forms of expression.[70] Community interests and standards have greater weight in relation to rights which impose a cost on the community, such as that to education under Article 2 of Protocol 1, and rights which rely on national institutions to make them effective, such as a right to marry under Article 12.

The second factor is the ground on which the public authority asserts that it is justified in interfering with the right. The grounds on which interference with rights may be justified give rise to rather more complex issues than the weight of the right itself. In Strasbourg, States are likely to be most easily able to invoke the public interest in security of the State and *ordre public*, in relation to which the Strasbourg organs tend to regard the judgment of state authorities as having particular significance. It is after all the essence of a State's sovereignty to be able to protect itself and its citizens against violence and subversion. As tribunals of international law, the European Commission and Court of Human Rights are bound to give this factor great weight. Another area in which the assessment is slanted in favour of the State is where a right is restricted to protect morality in a field where there is no pan-European consensus as to the moral standard which should be applied. In such cases, extensive interference may be seen as proportionate. To a great extent this is because the margin of appreciation is here at its widest. As Professor Don Greig has written, "[a] tension still exists, even at the end of the twentieth century, between an internationalist perspective of law and a State sovereignty view of the world. Although the balance has been shifting from the latter towards the former, the war is still being waged on a number of fronts, of which reservations law is one".[71] Another is the proportionality of limitations on accepted rights in the light of the margin of appreciation. The position in our municipal law under the Human Rights Act 1998 may turn out to be different, because the practice of deference to national authority (founded on the principle of subsidiarity) does not apply. However, as argued above, although the margin of appreciation properly so called is not applicable in municipal proceedings, judicial restraint may nevertheless be encouraged by other doctrines, including justiciability and the deference due to expert decision-makers.

The third factor is the source and form of the interference. Is the victim aggrieved by a legislative or common-law rule of general application, a decision affecting only a single person or a few people, or an isolated act in the exercise

[70] See J. McBride, n. 8 above.

[71] D.W. Greig, "Reservations: Equity as a Balancing Factor?" (1995) 16 *Australian Year Book of International Law* 21, at 164.

of a general power or implementing a more general policy or decision? In principle, the more people are affected by the behaviour of a public authority the more difficult it should be to justify the interference. On this basis the general rule which is incompatible with Convention rights should be subjected to the most stringent scrutiny, although the intensity of the harm inflicted or threatened to the victim of a violation of Convention rights will also have to be placed in the balance. A slight harm suffered as a result of a legislative rule—for example, the inability to broadcast the voice of a terrorist sympathiser, as in *Brind*—may be easier for the State to justify on a proportionality test than a disastrous harm resulting from an individual decision, such as a compulsory purchase order which deprives one of one's home. As Advocate General Jacobs demonstrates in his paper in this volume, there is a parallel here with Community law, in which the Court of Justice observes a similar analysis. Nevertheless, if the purpose of proportionality is to require a fair balance to be struck between the various competing interests, a legislative rule of general application imposing a given restriction of a right should be harder to justify than a single administrative or judicial act imposing the same restriction on only a few people. This perhaps explains why Professor van Gerven, in his chapter in this book,[72] observes a greater willingness on the part of national courts to use proportionality in constitutional law than in administrative law. Is it in practice likely that the proportionality principle will be applied in this way under the Human Rights Act 1998? Sensible as this would be in terms of public law and human rights principles, I suspect that it will not immediately generally appeal to municipal courts in the UK, at least in relation to primary legislation, for the following reasons.

Parliamentary Legislation and Declarations of Incompatibility

The habit of deference to Parliament's wide legislative competence is a significant, if not fundamental, element in our current legal culture, related to respect for democratic accountability in legislation. It is likely to skew the way in which the principle of proportionality is applied to Parliamentary legislation. Although superior courts are empowered by the Human Rights Act 1998, section 4, to grant a "declaration of incompatibility" when they decide that it is impossible to interpret primary legislation[73] in a way which is compatible with Convention rights, the ingrained deference to the legislative authority of Parliament and the parliamentary accountability of the relevant minister is likely to inhibit judges from holding that a legislative rule is disproportionate

[72] W. van Gerven, "The Effect of Proportionality on the Actions of Member States of the EC: National Viewpoints from Continental Europe", this vol.

[73] A declaration of incompatibility may also be made where subordinate legislation is incompatible with Convention rights and cannot be quashed because the incompatibility is mandated by primary legislation.

once it has been shown to be a considered response to a pressing social need. This should not be the case. The declaration of incompatibility leaves the legislation effective, and merely opens up the possibility of amending the law by a fast-track procedure known as a "remedial order" (see section 10 and Schedule 2). A minister has no obligation to make such an order or to introduce corrective primary legislation. Failure to do so is not itself unlawful or a violation of a Convention right, even after a declaration of incompatibility (section 6(6)). It is therefore possible to view the declaration as a means by which the courts can ask government and Parliament to think again, returning the matter for them to reconsider the proportionality of the interference with rights in the light of the court's judgment. Such a reference-back procedure hardly threatens the separation of powers between Parliament, Executive and Legislature: if anything it is an expression of it. Similarly the democratic imperative which the legislative supremacy of Parliament tries to advance is bolstered, not challenged, by the procedure. That is the genius of the solution adopted in the Act to the constructive tension between the supremacy of Parliament and the protection of citizens' rights. In principle it should follow that, other things being equal, the courts ought to be willing to apply the proportionality test more rigorously and critically to Acts of Parliament, which affect many people and which remain in force after a declaration of incompatibility, while the executive and legislative arms contemplate their response, than to subordinate legislation which may affect many people but which, if quashed for unlawfulness due to incompatibility, ceases to have any effect.

Judicial Review and Other Proceedings Involving Human Rights Act 1998 Questions

In applications for judicial review of administrative action, the Act will require the courts to develop substantive grounds of review consistent with the Convention. In effect, incompatibility with Convention rights will be an element of illegality, reversing the effect of *Brind*. When invited to hold that individual decisions or official acts which affect relatively few people are incompatible with Convention rights because they are disproportionate to a pressing social need, courts should be cautious. Fewer interests are adversely affected by such decisions and acts than by legislation, and the damage to the public interest caused by quashing or granting other remedies may be considerable. Yet there will be cases where the damage to the victim will be so serious as to outweigh public interests in regulation of a field of activity. Sometimes, as in *Laker Airways* v. *Department of Trade*[74] and *R* v. *Chief Constable of Sussex, ex parte International Trader's Ferry Ltd*,[75] the harm to the victim will amount to

[74] [1977] QB 643 (CA).
[75] [1997] 2 All ER 65 (CA), under appeal to the House of Lords at the time of writing.

bankruptcy or the denial of the freedom to pursue one's career. In such cases, the courts should not be slow to apply a rigorous proportionality test to the reasons advanced by a public authority to justify interfering with Convention rights.

This approach would lead courts to assess proportionality against the background of all the values which underpin the UK's constitution and the Human Rights Act 1998. In doing so, proper weight should be given to the importance of providing effective remedies where a violation is found is of primary importance. Despite the failure to include Article 13 of the Convention (the right to an effective remedy before a national authority for violations of Convention rights) among the Convention rights, it is clear, from the parliamentary record of debates on the Human Rights Bill and from the White Paper which explained the government's policy in relation to it, that a primary purpose of the Bill was to ensure compliance with Article 13.[76] Apart from the declaration of incompatibility, section 8(1) of the Act will provide for a court or tribunal to grant "such relief or remedy, or make such order, within its powers as it considers just and appropriate". This may allow new kinds of remedy to be developed, although it gives a power to award damages for violations of the Convention only if the court or tribunal already has "power to award damages, or to order the payment of compensation, in civil proceedings" (section 8(2)).

This could lead to the victim needing to fight multiple proceedings in order to obtain an effective remedy or just satisfaction. The risk is heightened by the number of different courts and tribunals which will have jurisdiction to decide Convention-related arguments, although it has been reduced by amendments introduced during the Committee stage in the House of Commons allowing ministers to make rules allowing new types of remedies to be available in tribunals for which they are responsible.[77] They may be relevant to the exercise of a judicial discretion to exclude evidence in criminal proceedings, to questions of procedure in civil actions, and to the substantive issues to be decided by Social Security Appeal Tribunals. The impact of interference and the balance between the interests involved may well turn out to be different in each of those contexts, leading to different judgments about proportionality for different purposes. This would be inconvenient. The courts will have to decide the level of concreteness or abstraction at which they will make proportionality decisions: that of the individual case, the area of public administration as a whole, or the applicable legislation or rule. This will not be easy.

[76] *Rights Brought Home: The Human Rights Bill*, Cm 3782 (London, The Stationery Office, 1997), paras. 1.18–1.19; House of Lords *Official Report*, 18 Nov. 1997, vol. 583, col. 475, Lord Irvine of Lairg LC.

[77] For an overview of the remedial provisions, see D. Feldman, "Remedies for Violations of Convention Rights under the Human Rights Act" [1998] *European Human Rights Law Review* 691.

In Non-Human Rights Act Matters

How will all this affect proportionality as it operates, or may come to operate, in proceedings which do not directly involve the Human Rights Act 1998 and the Convention rights? At present, courts are usually reluctant to use proportionality as a basis for quashing official decisions, although occasionally a decision is made which seems to be explicable only on the basis that a proportionality principle is being used but not identified as such.[78] It seems to me to be likely that the growing frequency with which courts will have to grapple with issues of proportionality will lead them to be more open about using proportionality-based reasoning in other circumstances. This would be in line with reassurances offered in print by distinguished academics and practitioners to the effect that proportionality does not pose a threat of violent revolution.[79] Administrators of all kinds are already familiar with the notion of proportionality, and use it to guide their own decisions. Agencies habitually assess alternative courses of action by reference to the advantages and costs, to themselves and others, which they involve. That is a form of proportionality. So is the balance of convenience test for the granting of interim injunctions. What a rights-based proportionality test adds is a foundation of fundamental rights, which should carry far greater weight than most other interests in the calculation most of the time. As Professor van Gerven suggests in his paper in this volume,[80] it might perhaps represent the start of a move from French-style review on the basis of strict legality to a more Germanic, rights-based review for disproportionality.

IV. THE WAY FORWARD?

This has been a piece of crystal-ball-gazing of the worst sort: it offers only doubtful guidance as to what is likely to happen, and little prescriptive advice as to what we ought to do about it. I have suggested that the way in which proportionality will operate in the context of the Human Rights Act 1998 should not necessarily be dictated by the way it has so far worked in Strasbourg. The structure of the Act does not require that Strasbourg case law should be adopted wholesale, and there are good reasons for our courts and tribunals to take a fresh, albeit respectful, look at the Strasbourg jurisprudence on proportionality.

[78] See, e.g., *R.* v. *Secretary of State for the Home Department, ex parte Leech* [1993] 4 All ER 539 (CA).

[79] See, e.g., J. Jowell and A. Lester, "Beyond *Wednesbury*: Substantive Principles of Administrative Law" [1987] *PL* 369; J. Jowell and A. Lester, "Proportionality: Neither Novel nor Dangerous" in J. Jowell and D. Oliver (eds.), *New Directions in Judicial Review* (London, Stevens, 1988); S.A. de Smith, Lord Woolf and J. Jowell, *Judicial Review of Administrative Action* (5th edn., London, Sweet & Maxwell, 1995), at 605; M. Hunt, *Using Human Rights Law in English Courts* (Oxford, Hart Publishing, 1997), at 216–21; Lord Steyn, "The Weakest and Least Dangerous Department of Government" [1997] *PL* 84, at 94.

[80] W. van Gerven, n. 42 above.

The approach of the Strasbourg organs has been seriously affected by their deference to nation States, manifested in the doctrine of the margin of appreciation. As many commentators have noted with regret, the Commission and Court have not adequately explained or justified the factors which influence the breadth of the margin of appreciation which they allow in different contexts. Even when mitigated by a search for common European standards this:

> perpetuates the pragamatism of the Court's approach and prevents the emergence of a coherent vision of the Court's function. . . . As a supranational institution, the Court faces a genuine difficulty over its proper role. The whole enterprise of rights protection on this scale requires the striking of a delicate balance between national sovereignty and international obligation.[81]

The margin of appreciation is thus inappropriate for use within domestic jurisdictions, but moreover, because it limits in an unpredictable way the capacity of the Court and Commission to review the judgments of national authorities on the basis of proportionality, domestic courts and tribunals may find the jurisprudence of the Court of little help in guiding the development of a principle of proportionality for domestic legal purposes.

Confronted by this difficulty, our administrators, legislators and judges will inevitably be influenced by the background of public law principles operating in our domestic law. Notions of justiciability and judicial restraint in the face of decisions of expert or democratically accountable bodies form part of that background. They will be relied on, and it is right that they should be. Part of the job of judges and other public bodies is to secure a combination of continuity, guaranteeing stability and the maintenance of authority, and change where necessary. The pursuit of legitimacy demands that judges and tribunals are conscious of their limited role in the process of securing rights, and that the grounds for justifying interferences with rights are authoritatively delimited by statute, rather than being set entirely by the judges themselves. At the same time, if a structure of reasoning for establishing a fair balance between competing interests is needed, proportionality can provide it, but only if public authorities accept that the passage of the Human Rights Act 1998 has subtly altered the established boundaries of judicial competence. The old doctrines will remain in place, carefully conserved by the Act, but should operate in a legal landscape which the Act will itself have altered. The legal and constitutional culture of the UK will continue to influence developments, but will in turn be influenced by them. Judges will still owe deference to established authority, but will also owe more deference than previously to people's rights. New judicial techniques will have to be developed to shape reasoning to support judicial decisions in a changing constitutional landscape. One such technique will almost certainly be a domesticated version of the principle of proportionality which already operates in EC law, in the Strasbourg case law under the ECHR, and under many municipal constitutional systems. Over time, the new culture of which this will be part

[81] Macdonald, in Macdonald, n. 15 above, at 124.

is likely to change the face of our public, and perhaps our private, law. It will undoubtedly lead to a flood of litigation, and (as Professor Tridimas says in his chapter in this book[82]) will increase transaction costs substantially, at least until settled case law begins to develop. On the other hand, it ought to contribute to introducing a more principled quality into public and political life and public administration, to the general benefit of society. That is the ultimate objective of public lawyers. It will introduce a refreshingly normative new element to the constitution. We can look forward to a constitutional era as exciting perhaps as any since 1689. To quote once more from Sydney Kentridge QC's address in Cambridge (this time adapting Wordsworth), "Bliss was it in that dawn to be a public lawyer, but to be young . . ."[83]

[82] T. Tridimas, "Proportionality in European Community Law: Searching for the Appropriate Standard of Scrutiny" this vol.

[83] Kentridge, op. cit., n. 2, at 71.

Proportionality and the Supremacy of Parliament in the UK

NICHOLAS GREEN

It is not my function to carry out the balancing exercise or to form my own view on whether the legislative objective could be achieved by other means. These questions involve compromises between competing interests which in a democratic society must be resolved by the legislator. The duty of the Court is only to enquire whether the compromise adopted by the United Kingdom Parliament, so far as it affects Community trade, is one which a reasonable legislator could have reached. The function of the Court is to review the acts of the legislatures but not to substitute its own policies or values.[1]

Some public comments on the decision of the European Court of Justice, affirming the jurisdiction of the courts of Member States to override national legislation if necessary to enable interim relief to be granted in protection of rights under Community law, have suggested that this was a novel and dangerous invasion by a Community institution of the sovereignty of the United Kingdom Parliament. But such comments are based on a misconception. If the supremacy within the European Community of Community law over the national law of Member States was not always inherent in the EC Treaty . . . it was certainly well established in the jurisprudence of the European Court of Justice long before the United Kingdom joined the Community. Thus, whatever limitation of its sovereignty Parliament accepted when it enacted the European Communities Act 1972 was entirely voluntary. Under the terms of the Act of 1972 it has always been clear that it was the duty of the United Kingdom Court, when delivering final Judgment, to override any rule of national law found to be in conflict with any directly enforceable rule of Community law. Similarly, when decisions of the European Court of Justice exposed areas of United Kingdom statute law which failed to implement Council Directives, Parliament has always loyally accepted the obligation to make appropriate and prompt amendments. Thus there is nothing in any way novel in according supremacy to rules of Community law in those areas to which they apply and to insist that, in the protection of rights under Community law, national courts must not be inhibited by rules of national law from granting interim relief in appropriate cases is no more than a logical recognition of that supremacy.[2]

[1] *Per* Hoffmann J, as he then was, in *Stoke on Trent City Council* v. *B & Q* [1990] 3 CMLR 31, at para. 47.

[2] *Per* Lord Bridge in *R.* v. *Secretary of State for Transport, ex parte Factortame and Others* (No. 2) [1991] 1 AC 603, at 658G–659C.

INTRODUCTION

It is no easy task to persuade a judge that he should impose his judgment over that of a democratically elected parliament exercising, through the legislative process, a common will reflected, at some prior date, in an election manifesto. Nonetheless, Community law requires the courts to do just that and intervene in the exercise of legislative discretion in accordance with the duty under Article 5 of the Treaty to uphold the supremacy of Community law. The purpose of this paper is to examine the issues which arise when a court is required to review legislation on grounds of proportionality.

PROPORTIONALITY

The starting point must therefore be with the definition of proportionality. The case law of the Court of Justice has, regrettably, lacked a certain definitional precision. Views differ as to whether proportionality contains two or three constituents.[3] Usually the Court of Justice identifies only two stages to the analysis namely, whether the means employed by the legislature to achieve the objective in question correspond to the importance of that objective, and whether the means are "necessary" for the achievement of that objective.[4] Where the Court adopts the three part test it is almost certainly echoing a more precise German definition which requires: that the disputed measure be appropriate and necessary in order to attain the objective legitimately pursued by the legislation in question; that where there exists a choice between different means of achieving that objective recourse is to be had to the least *dirigiste* or interventionist of those measures; and, finally, it requires, more broadly, that the disadvantages caused must not be disproportionate to the aims pursued.[5] When seeking to encapsulate the doctrine English judges have tended to be more pithy and have referred to using sledge hammers to crack a nut when a nutcracker will do.

[3] See F.G.Jacobs, "Recent Developments in the Principle of Proportionality in European Community Law", this vol.

[4] See, e.g., Case 66/82 *Fromançais SA* v. *FORMA* [1983] ECR 395, at para. 8. See also Van Gerven AG in Case C–159/90 *Society for the Protection of Unborn Children Ireland Ltd* v. *Stephen Grogan* [1991] ECR I–4685, at para. 27 of the Opinion.

[5] J. Schwarze, *European Administrative Law* (London, Sweet & Maxwell, 1992) states at 689 that, in German law, three factors can be distinguished which govern the application of the proportionality principle:

> "1. First, the State measures concerned must be *suitable* for the purpose of facilitating or achieving the pursuit objective.
>
> 2. Secondly, the suitable measure must also be *necessary*, in the sense that the authority concerned has no other mechanism at its disposal which is less restrictive of freedom. . . . It is not the method used which has to be necessary, but the excessive restriction of freedom involved in the choice of method.
>
> 3. Finally, the measure concerned may not be *disproportionate* to the restrictions which it involves. . . ."

A NEW ROLE FOR THE JUDICIARY

This paper focuses upon the test of proportionality as a curb on the powers of legislatures and parliaments to legislate without hindrance from the courts. That general principles of Community law (and indeed of course the provisions of the Treaty) may be used as a sword (or shield) against legislation has been a characteristic of the development of Community administrative law from the outset of the Community. However, the fact that the Community has seen fit to permit its legislature to be made subservient to superior rules of law applied in the hands of the Court of Justice has not led national legislatures or parliaments, or domestic courts, to view with equanimity the prospect of the judiciary intervening in the domestic legislative process. In the United Kingdom the judiciary has historically viewed itself as subservient to the will of Parliament. Traditionally, the courts have accepted, as an article of faith, the unimpeachability of Parliament, and for many centuries have viewed the will of Parliament as the exercise of the purest form of democracy into which an unelected judiciary should not trespass. The courts uphold but do not usurp the will of Parliament. Naturally, it is different where the courts are asked to review administrative acts because, for example, those administrative acts may diverge from the will of Parliament and for that reason be *ultra vires*. Community law, as Lord Bridge pointed out in the House of Lords in *Factortame* (*No. 2*) in the quotation in the preface to this paper, has eaten away at these tenets of faith. Parliament, since the United Kingdom joined the Community, is no longer sovereign. The judge must now respect and reflect this new "federal" relationship between domestic and supra-national authority. Community law (and the Community legislative process) takes precedence and therefore Parliament cannot, *in principle*, be immune from challenge.

Where Community law has travelled the common law may follow. For instance once the courts accepted, in *Factortame*, that injunctive relief was available against the Crown in cases involving Community law, English law soon followed suit.[6] Once Community law recognised a right of restitution against the State for sums overpaid, English law soon followed suit.[7] Now that Community law requires Parliaments and legislatures to be responsible monetarily for certain of their defaults English law might follow suit. In *Factortame* (*No. 3*)[8] (the damages action) the Court of Appeal stated :

> We note that there is nothing in Community law which prevents national courts from imposing liability on their own Government in other circumstances . . . None of the Respondents has asked this court to go further than it is obliged as a matter of Community law to go. So we leave for consideration on another occasion the

[6] *M* v. *Home Office* [1994] 1 AC 327.

[7] *Woolwich Equitable Building Society* v. *IRC* [1993] AC 70 (HL).

[8] *R.* v. *Secretary of State for Transport, ex parte Factortame and Others*, Lord Woolf MR, Schiemann LJ and Robert Walker LJ (not yet reported, 7 Apr. 1998).

> circumstances, if any, in which, quite apart from any requirement of Community law, our law will give a remedy for damage caused by legislation enacted in breach of a superior legal rule. Traditionally this remedy has not been available in our law. Now that it is undoubtedly available in circumstances which contain a Community law element it may be right on some future occasion to re-examine that tradition.

In this respect at least the English judges have shown themselves receptive to new sources of guidance and inspiration. The *Factortame* litigation is, of course, a recent example of the willingness of the English courts to embrace their new role as guardians of a supreme law, even in the face of the will of Parliament. Once this approach is accepted as commonplace a series of secondary, or subsidiary, legal and practical questions arise. For example, what remedies must be made available by the courts to curb the excesses of the legislature? What documentary and other evidence must be made available by government so that the courts can effectively and accurately perform the task of review? Are different tests to be applied to the grant (or refusal) of different types of relief, for example injunction, declaration or damages? Some of the most acute of these secondary problems have arisen, most recently, in claims arising in the English courts for damages against the state on the basis of the *Francovich/Factortame*[9] principles. These cases have included claims based on allegations of disproportionate legislative and administrative acts.

The emergence of a new role for the courts in reviewing legislative acts has created unease amongst many of the judiciary. Contrast, for example, the two quotations set out at the beginning of this paper. It is one thing for courts to rule in a way allowing English law to evolve by reference to developments in Community law; it is entirely another matter for judges to strike at domestic legislation simply because it is said to offend some elusive general principle of Community law. Such unease is understandable when what is being required of judges is a far more intrusive exercise than has hitherto been required of the courts. Application of the doctrine of proportionality to legislation can only exacerbate such feelings. The judge, in applying such a test, must effectively stand in the very shoes of both the policymaker and the legislature and decide whether the objective sought was legitimate, whether the means adopted were commensurate and whether, even if commensurate, they were the least intrusive to achieve the legitimate goal in end. This necessarily inserts, or catapults, the judge into the epicentre of democratic decision-making. Judges may feel ill-equipped to resolve the extremely complex issues arising. The judge moreover risks being the subject of ill-educated criticism from arch-democrats and opponents of judicial intervention into politics. It is felt, with justification, that even ill-founded criticism can undermine the integrity of the judicial process. There is a further fear that an intrusive form of judicial review will deter the adoption of otherwise beneficial (if controversial) legislation. This so-called "chill factor" has been recognised by the Court of Justice as a proper reason justifying judicial

[9] Case C–9/90 *Francovich* v. *Italy* [1991] ECR I–5357.

caution, though not as a reason for denying monetary claims altogether.[10] It is these fears which have led the UK judiciary to express the view that with the incorporation of the European Convention on Human Rights (ECHR) into domestic law they prefer the solution of not empowering themselves to overturn legislation but rather confining their jurisdiction to the grant of declarations which, in turn, trigger certain obligations on Parliament to remedy the defect in question. Where, however, Community law (which includes the principles of the ECHR in their capacity as general principles of law) is concerned, the judge is unable to shrink from the task of delving deeply into the legislative process. This does not mean the judge is usurping the will of Parliament or subverting democracy. On the contrary, the function of judicial review remains the same, namely to ensure that Parliament remains within the ambit of its proper powers. The judge is in, Community cases, doing no more than ensuring respect for the "federal" division of powers between national and community authority.

THE INTENSIVE SCRUTINY REQUIRED IN A COMMUNITY JUDICIAL REVIEW

The dictum of Lord Bridge in *Factortame* (*No. 3*) set out at the beginning of this paper, to the effect that a corollary of joining the Community was to confer upon the courts the power to regulate the conduct of Parliament, was designed to dispel the commentary, conveyed mainly in the press, at the time of the judgment of the Court of Justice in *Factortame* (*No. 1*) (establishing the right to interlocutory relief against the Crown), that the *Grundnorm* of the constitution had shifted by virtue of that judgment. That "shift" occurred when the European Communities Act 1972 was passed, not when the Court of Justice applied the doctrines of supremacy and effective protection of rights to a particular fact situation. Indeed, in the decade prior to that dictum in the House of Lords, the High Court had embarked upon its own voyage of discovery in a series of cases in which the courts were required by applicants to review the decisions of public bodies said to be contrary to Community law. In these cases the applicants submitted that the traditional *Wednesbury* criterion of review was inapposite and, indeed, unlawful as the lodestar against which the impugned decision was to be measured. Instead the courts should simply apply the rule invoked to the measure impugned and decide whether the latter infringes the former. On its proper construction the rule invoked may or may not confer a discretion on the decision-maker. In many cases the text of the measure does not on its face confer a discretion on the decision-maker (for example, "the product shall be authorised if . . .", or, the "service provider will be entitled to registration if . . ."). On a review the courts will, in such circumstances, decide whether the decision was right or wrong. If the text of the measure confers a discretion

[10] The ECJ recognised in *Factortame* (*No. 3*) [1996] ECR I–1029, at 1147, para. 45, that the chill factor was a reason for limiting the availability of damages to only those cases where a legislature had committed a sufficiently serious breach of the law as opposed to a mere breach.

expressly or impliedly (for example, "the competent authority may" or "if the competent authority is satisfied"), then on a review the courts will respect the discretion but apply a Community standard of review, that is to say, ask whether the discretion was exercised in a manner breaching a general principle of Community law or whether it was otherwise manifestly wrong.

In *R.* v. *MAFF, ex parte Bell Lines*[11] the High Court was concerned with national regulations restricting the import of certain products to specified ports of entry; in particular, it had to decide whether such regulations constituted an infringement of Article 30 and, if so, whether they were justified under Article 36 on grounds of protection of health. The respondent Ministry submitted that the legality under Community law of the disputed regulations was to be assessed by reference to the *Wednesbury* unreasonableness or irrationality test. Forbes J concluded that were the question to be one of "ordinary *Wednesbury* principles" he would then have had difficulty in acceding to the application. However, he concluded that it was not necessary to apply this test since Community law required that he decide the matter *on the merits* even though this entailed fact finding. In rejecting the *Wednesbury* unreasonableness approach the judge stated:

> I do not believe that this country should be left in a situation where, if it were plain that a decision of a Minister was one which was contrary to Community law, or that part of the Community law which becomes part of this country's domestic law, those persons with rights arising under Community law should be denied any means of enforcing them. In my view that would be wrong . . .[12]

The test laid down by Forbes J in *Bell Lines* was endorsed by the High Court in *R.* v. *Secretary of State for Social Security, ex parte Schering Chemicals Ltd.*[13] The Court stated:

> [In *Bell Lines* the Court] held that there was a breach of Article 30, not saved by the application of Article 36 upon health control grounds. Argument was advanced as to the court's approach, and whether or not the powers of the court were limited to our courts' traditional approach to [judicial review] cases. Forbes J did not feel that he was bound by such restraints, and said that the English court was being drawn ineluctably into the business of fact finding, particularly in cases concerning whether or not measures of control are capable of constituting an impermissible restriction and breach of Community law. He did not shrink from his task, and found a breach of Article 30 both on the basis of the rules in *Wednesbury* and upon the basis that the court was in a case of that kind unfettered in its approach to whether or not the circumstances showed that there was upon the facts a breach of Community law.
>
> This court is, in my judgment, in accordance with the guidance of Forbes J, not to be restricted by a reluctance to evaluate evidence, and if it finds a breach of Community law it must take steps to see that the breach does not continue. This approach and principle were again followed by Taylor J and by the Court of Appeal

[11] [1984] 2 CMLR 502.
[12] *Ibid.*, at 511.
[13] [1987] 1 CMLR 277.

in the case of *Bomore* [[1986] 1 CMLR 228]. The test is not in such cases solely the traditional *Wednesbury* test.[14]

On the facts of the case the Court concluded that the regulations infringed Article 30 and were not justified by any public health considerations. In so finding the court accepted that it had to review the facts in relation to public health. In *R.* v. *MAFF, ex parte Roberts*[15] the High Court had to review the compatibility of a domestic rule prohibiting the export of sheep with Articles 34 and 36 EC. The court summarised the submission made to it by the applicants as the correct test to be applied:

> In deciding whether the Minister was correct to take the view that in the light of the factual position he might well be in breach of EEC law if he imposed a total ban, the applicants submit that I must approach the matter not by way of judicial review but on whether the Minister's view of the law was correct. That is to say, not whether he was reasonable to take his view of the law (given for instance, though not conceded, that the matter might be unclear) but that I should rule by way of original jurisdiction whether the Minister was entitled to take that view even if I thought it were reasonable of him so to do. As [counsel] put it succinctly, if the Minister gets the law wrong the court should say so. It is not for the court to say in effect that it was not unreasonable for him to get the law wrong.
>
> Thus what is submitted by the applicants is that I should try this as if it were a civil action. Find the facts (which are not substantially in dispute) and then decide, given those facts, whether the Minister was right as a matter of law not to impose a ban or, putting it the other way, whether he was wrong in law to take the view that in the light of those facts it would have been illegal to impose a ban.[16]

The court accepted the applicants' submission on this point and the prior ruling of the court in *Ex parte Bell Lines Ltd.*[17]

In *Stoke on Trent City Council* v. *B & Q*, Hoffmann J (as he then was) was required to review the Sunday trading legislation with the Community rules on the free movement of goods and, being a constituent part of those rules, the principle of proportionality. It was in this context that the learned judge expressed the reservations set out in the quotation at the beginning of this paper. However, upon reference to the Court of Justice, Advocate General van Gerven stated, of the conclusion reached by Hoffmann J:

> In my view the national court may not automatically accept the view of the national legislature or limit itself to deciding whether the national legislature, in the light of the proportionality requirement, could reasonably have adopted the legislative provisions in question.[18]

[14] *Ibid.*, at 286 paras. 58 and 59. See also *R.* v. *Secretary of State for Social Services, ex parte Bomore Medical Supplies Ltd* [1986] 1 CMLR 228 where the Court of Appeal, applying a full merits review, decided on the facts that a reimbursement scheme operated by the Department of Health and Social Security infringed Art. 30 and was not justified under Art. 36.

[15] [1991] 1 CMLR 555.

[16] *Ibid.*, at 576–7, paras. 79 and 80.

[17] Cf. 579, para. 85.

[18] [1993] 1 CMLR 426, at 457, para. 27 and n. 55.

Advocate General van Gerven cited in support of his conclusion *Miro*[19] which established that any national rule which, in its effect, precluded a national court from reviewing the merits of an impugned decision or measure amounted to an unlawful repudiation of review. The case concerned the illegality of the Dutch law on the appellation of imported drinks as "Genever". Advocate General Slynn (as he then was) stated of the task confronting the national court:

> What is necessary to protect the consumer in any given case where proceedings are before a national court is in my view for the national court to decide, *in the light of all the facts*, subject to the judgment of this Court as to what is a matter of law incapable of falling within such a jurisdiction.[20]

The Court ruled as follows:

> The German Government further submits on this point that the question whether a ban on using the appellation "Genever" is necessary for products which do not satisfy requirements depends on the commercial view prevailing in the country concerned. *Since the national authorities are in the best position to judge such facts, it is for those authorities and not the Court to reach a decision on them. When the national legislature, which is competent to take such a decision, has settled the matter, the national court is bound in its assessment.*
>
> As regards the latter argument, it must be stated that neither Article 30 of the Treaty nor indeed Article 36 reserves certain matters to the exclusive jurisdiction of the Member States. When in order to satisfy mandatory requirements recognised by Community law national legislation creates obstacles for the fundamental principle of the free movement of goods, it must observe the limits laid down by Community law. It is for the Court, which interprets Community law in the final instance, and for the national courts, which reached their decision on the basis of that interpretation to ensure that those limits are observed. *In the final analysis the German government's argument amounts to repudiation of review by the Court and therefore runs counter to the uniformity and effectiveness of Community law. It must therefore be rejected.*[21]

These cases have led academic commentators to conclude that :

> Where Community rights are in issue, the discretion of the administration will be limited and the *Wednesbury* case law has no application; and the English Court must if necessary make its own findings of fact in deciding whether the measures are challenged lawful. The Court may be required to find that a measure is unlawful even though it would not be invalidated on the *Wednesbury* approach.[22]

This recognition has already been applied to the doctrine of proportionality. Thus the House of Lords in *R.* v. *Home Secretary, ex parte Brind*[23] ruled that proportionality played no part in English administrative law though it was

[19] Case 128/84 [1985] ECR 3731.

[20] *Ibid.*, at 3736 (emphasis supplied).

[21] *Ibid.*, at 3744 (emphasis supplied).

[22] *Per* Lord Woolf and J. Jowell, in S.A. De Smith, H. Woolf and J. Jowell (eds.), *Judicial Review of Administrative Action* (5th edn., London, Sweet & Maxwell, 1995), in chapter 21 "EC Law in English Administrative Law" at para. 21.119.

[23] [1991] 1 AC 696.

accepted that it was a more exacting test for judicial review than that permitted under traditional English law. Professor Wade has stated of the distinction between reasonableness and proportionality:

> In the law of a number of European countries there is a principle of proportionality which ordains that administrative measures must not be more drastic than is necessary for attaining the desired result. This doctrine has been adopted by the European Court of Justice in Luxembourg and may well infiltrate British law through the decisions of that Court, since British law must conform to Community law. Lord Diplock took judicial notice of this prospect when he set out the categories of judicial review in 1985, but he spoke if only as a possibility for the future. Encouraged by these *dicta* claimants have invoked proportionality in a number of cases but so far without success.
>
> Where attempts have been made to rely upon proportionality judges have tended to equate with reasonableness. But the House of Lords have detected a difference in that proportionality requires the court to judge the necessity of the action taken as well as whether it was within the range of courses of action that could reasonably be followed. Proportionality is therefore a more exacting test in some situations and is then to be rejected as requiring the court to substitute its own judgment for that of the proper authority. While leaving the door open for future developments by way of Community law, the House has closed it to proportionality in domestic law for the time being.[24]

There is thus "daylight" between English standards of judicial review and a standard of review predicated upon proportionality. Equally, for that matter, in relation to the principle of legitimate expectations a substantial degree of daylight has been found to exist between the doctrine in English and Community law. In *Ex parte Hamble Fisheries*[25] Sedley J ruled that the principle of legitimate expectations was a matter of both substance and procedure and should have the same scope and effect in English law as it did in Community law. In *Ex parte Hargreaves*,[26] the Court of Appeal criticised the ruling in *Hamble Fisheries*. It rejected the proposition advanced by Sedley J as heresy and ruled that legitimate expectations did not apply in the substantive context but only, and to a limited degree, in a procedural context.

The most recent formulation of the test to be applied in an English judicial review of a decision said to be contrary to Community law is to be found in the judgment of Laws J in *R.* v. *MAFF, ex parte First City Trading Ltd.*[27] In that case the court was asked to review the refusal of the respondent to grant monetary aid to beef exporters on grounds that the refusal was contrary to the Community law principle of equal treatment, and its mirror image, non-discrimination. The judge accepted that proportionality was an integral part of the doctrine of non-discrimination since, even if a court found that the different treatment of similar categories of person was warranted, it still had to assess

[24] H.W.R. Wade, *Administrative Law* (7th edn., Oxford, Clarendon Press, 1994), at 403.
[25] [1995] 2 All ER 714.
[26] [1997] 1 All ER 397.
[27] [1997] 1 CMLR 250.

whether the conduct of the decision-maker with regard to both categories of person was objectively justified at which point in the analysis proportionality played a significant part. He thus accepted a submission made on behalf of the applicant that:

> The fact that proportionality is an integral part of the principle of equality also serves to curtail any otherwise broad discretion, since the measure in dispute must itself be finely attuned (proportionate) to the objective justification advanced for it.[28]

Laws J made a number of pertinent observations about the process of evaluation in a Community law case. First, in relation to a case of alleged discrimination under both English domestic and Community law the judge would examine whether apparently identical cases were treated differently. A finding to that effect would give rise to *prima facie* irrationality even in English law. The court would also, under both domestic and Community law, look for an explanation of the difference but under the domestic law review the explanation would be rejected only on grounds of perversity or irrationality. There, concluded the judge, "marks the divide".[29] Under the Community law review the decision-maker was bound to demonstrate a substantive justification for a discriminatory decision.[30] Secondly, he observed that whilst there plainly was a discretion accorded the decision-maker under domestic law there was also a "margin of appreciation" accorded the decision-maker under Community law though it was a "nice question" how far that margin of appreciation went. The judge was clear of one thing: it was a narrower discretion than arose under English law. Thirdly, he observed that in cases involving fundamental principles of Community law the ECJ has proceeded on the footing that the facts have to be examined by the reviewing court and a view reached whether the decision taken measures up to the substantive standards which the Court requires of it. This represents a diversion from the traditional process of judicial review in the UK which eschews the detailed evaluation of the underlying evidence.

For present purposes the primary relevance of the judge's remarks lay in his analysis of what margin of appreciation was to be accorded a decision maker (which necessarily includes a legislature or Parliament):

> There must, however, remain a difference between the approach of the court in arriving at a judicial decision on the question whether a measure is objectively justified and that of the primary decision-maker himself in deciding upon the measure in the first place. Within the diverse contexts in which the principle of equality may be called in question, there will no doubt always be a range of options *factually* open to the decision-maker. It is not the court's task to decide what it would have done had it been the decision-maker, who (certainly in the case of elected government) enjoys a political authority, and carries a political responsibility, with which the court is not endowed.

[28] [1997] 1 CMLR 250, at 278.

[29] *Ibid.*, also at 279.

[30] See also E.Ellis, "The Concept of Proportionality in European Community Sex Discrimination Law", this vol.

> The court's task is to decide whether the measure in fact adopted falls within the range of options *legally* open to the decision-maker. In the nature of things it is highly unlikely that only one of the choices available to him will pass the test of objective justification: and the Court has no business to give effect to any preference for one possible measure over another when both lie within proper legal limits. In this sense it may be said that the decision-maker indeed enjoys a margin of appreciation.
>
> The difference between *Wednesbury* and European review is that in the former case the legal limits lie further back. I think there are two factors. First, the limits of domestic review are not, as the law presently stands, constrained by the doctrine of proportionality. Secondly, at least as regards a requirement such as that of objective justification in an equal treatment case, the European rule requires the decision-maker to provide a fully reasoned case. It is not enough merely to set out the problem, and assert that within his discretion the Minister chose this or that solution, constrained only by the requirement that his decision must have been one which a reasonable Minister might make. Rather the court will test the solution arrived at, and pass it only if substantial factual considerations are put forward in its justification: considerations which are relevant, reasonable and proportionate to the aim in view. But as I understand the jurisprudence the court is not concerned to agree or disagree with the decision: that would be to travel beyond the boundaries of proper judicial authority, and usurp the primary decision-maker's function. Thus *Wednesbury* and European review are different models—one looser, one tighter—of the same juridical concept, which is the imposition of compulsory standards on decision-makers so as to require the repudiation of arbitrary power.[31]

The courts have thus accepted that a more intensive scrutiny may be required in appropriate types of case involving EC law than is traditional in non-EC cases. This is not to say that in every EC judicial review the national court must delve deeply into the decision making process since there may be some types of issue where under Community law decision-makers and legislatures are accorded a very wide margin of appreciation, such that, provided they act within the confines of that margin, the grounds of review will still be relatively limited.

FAULT?

A ruling by a court that an Act of Parliament is disproportionate and therefore unlawful as being contrary to Community law suggests, at least at one level, fault on the part of the legislature. The issue whether some measure of culpability is a requirement of liability is one which surfaced before the Court of Justice in *Factortame (No. 3)*.[32] In that case a number of points arose. The first was whether an obligation on the part of an applicant for relief to prove fault would serve, in practice, to make it impossible or extremely difficult for him to obtain effective reparation for loss or damage resulting from a breach of

[31] [1997] ICMLR 250, at 278–9, paras. 67–9.

[32] Joined Cases C–46 & 48/93 [1996] ECR I–1029.

Community law where the breach was attributable to the national legislature. The second was whether, if fault was relevant, it was to be defined by reference to a single set of criteria which would be applicable in all Member States or whether it was to be determined by reference to national notions of fault in domestic tort law. Thirdly, was fault relevant at all?

So far as the first question was concerned the ECJ observed that proof of fault was likely, in many cases, to render the right to reparation illusory. In this regard the Court condemned the condition imposed by English law which required proof of misfeasance in public office. The Court made the obvious point that "such an abuse of power [is] inconceivable in the case of the legislature".[33] Consequently, to require proof of misfeasance would in practice make the right to reparation impossible or extremely difficult to attain. As such it would be required to be set aside where an infringement of Community law was attributable to the national legislature. The Court is plainly correct in this regard. How does one attribute misfeasance to a democratically elected parliament implementing, in good faith, the contents of an election manifesto? As for the question whether fault could have a universal and uniform content, the Court addressed this in the context of a question from the Bundesgerichtshof which had sought to establish whether a national court was entitled to make reparation conditional upon the existence of fault, whether intentional or negligent, on the part of the organ of the State to which infringement was attributable. The Court tersely replied that "the concept of fault does not have the same content in the various legal systems".[34] The Court continued to observe that a Member State, acting in a field in which it enjoyed a wide discretion to make legislative choices was liable only if the breach was "sufficiently serious". In determining whether a breach was "sufficiently serious" to warrant an award of damages the national court would necessarily take into account the factors identified by the Court of Justice as relevant which themselves could be categorised as entailing a degree of objective and subjective fault. Nonetheless, the Court emphasised that the obligation to pay damages could not depend upon any condition based upon a notion of fault going beyond that of a "sufficiently serious" breach of Community law. The real obstacle to incorporating fault into any review of the acts of a legislature was expressed effectively by Advocate General Tesauro in his Opinion. He emphasised that fault was an essentially subjective or "mental or psychological" factor. To add, as a condition of recovery, an element of fault to the fact of infringement necessarily meant that this subjective or mental or psychological factor had to be measured or quantified. He stated:

> Seeking fault in the subjective sense—and, a fortiori, wrongful intent—as regards legislative activity raises some considerable difficulties even at the conceptual level, especially since fault as a condition of state liability has always been the subject of profound reflection and conflicting assessments. In particular, attention has been

[33] Joined Cases C–46 & 48/93 [1996] ECR I–1029, at 1154, para. 73.
[34] *Ibid*., at 1155, para. 76.

> drawn to the difficulties of identifying conduct displaying fault on the part of the public authorities on the basis of the same criteria used for the purposes of civil law, especially since the mechanisms devised for explaining the actions of legal persons by attributing to them the same manner of acting as natural persons are said to prove completely useless or at least inadequate from this point of view. Indeed, even viewed in the abstract, it appears difficult to identify conduct involving fault in the rule-making activity of the legislator or even to conceive of its possibly being aware of the breach. In contrast, it cannot be presumed that the legislator pursues a general interest invariably and in any event.[35]

The position of the Advocate General and of the Court reveals a healthy disapproval of any presumption about the innate goodness of parliaments. The Court of Justice has seemingly preferred the parliamentary lobby correspondents' view of the legislative process as one which (if one draws on the experience of Westminster) takes advantage of absences from the House due to late night sittings and the wheeling in of semi-invalid MPs to swell the lobbies in order to see legislation passed. Nonetheless, and despite this scepticism, the Court recognises the inherent difficulties of incorporating fault into the review process.

The analysis of fault in *Factortame* (*No. 3*) was to see whether it played a part in the test for the award of damages in respect of an already established breach of the law. As for fault in the context of proportionality there is no reason to suppose that it plays any formal part whatsoever. Proportionality is, at root, a somewhat mechanical test. Courts approach the question in stages. There is little room in this process of analysis for a court to conclude that a legislative measure is disproportionate upon the basis of an unacceptable subjective, mental or psychological element attributable to Parliament. Conceivably, a *Pepper* v. *Hart* statement, on the part of a relevant minister, which revealed deep cynicism and an absence of good faith, could underscore a judge's conclusion about the disproportionality of a particular measure. It could provide support for a conclusion that the measure was not needed for the pursuit of some legitimate object, or it could even throw doubt on the legitimacy of the object itself. However, in such a case the court would simply be taking account of admissible evidence in order to apply the proportionality test. The judge would not be deciding whether there was, or was not, fault in any legal sense. Fault *per se* is not a condition precedent for establishing that a legislative measure is disproportionate.

PROPORTIONALITY AND EVIDENCE: THE *MODUS OPERANDI* OF REVIEW

In a judicial review, predicated upon domestic law alone, the procedure governing the application is laid down in RSC Order 53. The applicant lodges Form 86A which sets out, though not necessarily in exhaustive detail, the basic

[35] *Ibid.*, at 1111, para. 85.

propositions of fact and law which are relied upon, and the applicant may exhibit (alternatively include in an affidavit) such additional factual material upon which it seeks to rely in order to obtain leave. This documentation is the raw material upon which the leave judge makes his decision. If leave is granted, the applicant must serve an originating motion, the Form 86A and supporting affidavit on all directly affected parties. The respondent has 56 days from the service of the notice of motion in which to file an affidavit in reply. RSC Order 53 does not require the respondent to serve evidence and it is not uncommon for respondent decision-makers to serve relatively short evidence. This is the practice notwithstanding that a public authority has a duty to conduct its case with "all the cards face upwards on the table".[36] There is no general right to discovery of relevant documents in judicial review proceedings and orders for discovery are unusual. Discovery will only be ordered if necessary for disposing fairly of the cause or matter or for saving costs.[37] In a judicial review these principles are construed relatively sparingly. In practice discovery is infrequently sought by the applicant. Discovery will normally be granted if a party's evidence is incomplete or there is evidence demonstrating that it is inaccurate or there is a dispute over material facts evident on the face of the affidavits. It is not generally possible to obtain discovery to check the accuracy of an affidavit.[38]

Applications for leave to cross-examine deponents on their affidavits are extremely rare. Lord Diplock stated that cross-examination should be allowed "whenever the justice of the particular case so requires".[39] However, judges in the Divisional Court rarely conclude that cross-examination is necessary to ensure justice. Where there is a dispute as to the facts and no cross-examination, the court will proceed on the basis of the affidavit evidence of the person who does not bear the onus of proof, that is to say, the respondent.[40]

Many applicants in domestic judicial review proceedings have complained that the procedure adopted places them at an inherent advantage, at least when compared with an equivalent action commenced by way of writ. In addition, the justification for a bifurcated procedural approach has been much reduced as the courts have whittled away at the distinction between public and private law.[41]

[36] *R.* v. *Lancashire CC, ex parte Huddlestone* [1986] 2 All ER 941.

[37] RSC Ord. 24, r. 8.

[38] See *R.* v. *Secretary of State for the Environment, ex parte London Lesbian & Gay Centre* 19 July 1991, *The Independent*, 6 Sept. 1991.

[39] *O'Reilly* v. *Mackman* [1983] 2 AC 237, at 283.

[40] See *R.* v. *Reigate Justices, ex parte Curl* [1991] COD 66.

[41] See, e.g., *Mercury Communications Ltd* v. *Director General of Telecommunications* [1996] 1 WLR 48, *per* Lord Slynn at 57: in an action for a declaration against the Director General of Telecommunications, begun by way of originating summons, the Director General applied to strike out the summons on the basis that the matter was governed by public law; the House of Lords disagreed and held that in circumstances where a public law respondent was made a defendant then the courts had an inherent power to regulate the procedures (for example, as to discovery and cross-examination) so as to ensure justice. See also *Trustees of the Dennis Rye Pension Fund* v. *Sheffield City Council* (1998) 10 Admin. LR 112 (CA).

In a Community law case the position has become quite different. As the decisions referred to above demonstrate, when an applicant challenges a legislative measure on the basis of proportionality the English courts have accepted that they must roll their sleeves up and review the facts. This necessarily calls for a different approach to evidence. The most extreme example of this has been in the recent action for damages brought by the 97 Factortame applicants against the government for the introduction and implementation of the Merchant Shipping Act 1988.[42] It is often overlooked that the claim for damages for breach of Community law was introduced at a very early stage into the proceedings, which were commenced in 1987. Following the judgment of the Court of Justice concluding that the Merchant Shipping Act 1988 infringed Articles 52 and 221 EC, the applicants proceeded with their claim for damages against the Secretary of State for Transport.

In order to explain the way in which the claim for damages proceeded it is necessary to say something about the applicants in question. In the popular press there is only one category of applicants, namely the Spanish. In reality there were a number of other nationalities whose interests were prejudicially affected by the introduction of the Merchant Shipping Act 1988. The 1st–83rd applicants were Spanish fishermen; however, the 84th applicant was an English company—Rawlings Trawlings Ltd.—owned by a Spaniard who was resident outside Spain, in fact in the UK; the 85th–97th applicants represented the interests of Mr and Mrs O'Connor who were Irish and Belgian nationals respectively. The O'Connors had been resident in the UK approximately since 1977; they had operated as a major part of the UK fishing fleet since 1978, long before quotas under the Common Fisheries Policy (CFP) were introduced in 1983; they acquired quota from the United Kingdom authorities and were on no analysis "quota hoppers"; they crewed with British fleets and landed their catch in English ports where the fish were sold. They were—in short—integral and substantial parts of the domestic UK fleet. Section 14 of the Merchant Shipping Act 1988 included, as is well known, nationality, domicile and residence conditions for being able to register a vessel and, therefore, fish against British quota. The O'Connors were accepted as having been resident and domiciled in the UK but their nationality was plainly an obstacle and was relied upon to prevent registration of their vessels. Section 14(4) of the 1988 Act provided a dispensation procedure from the otherwise onerous and strict provisions of the legislation. It provided that in certain cases of persons who were otherwise domiciled and resident in the UK the nationality condition could be waived. The criterion for such waiver was essentially long residence.

After *Factortame (No. 2)*,[43] the Divisional Court directed that the claim for damages against the government should proceed effectively by way of a trial. Pleadings were then exchanged. The respondent Ministry pleaded that the

[42] *R.* v. *Secretary of State for Transport, ex parte Factortame Ltd and Others* [1998] Eur. LR 475 (DC; [1998] 3 CMLR 192 (CA).

[43] [1996] ECR I–3905.

criterion it adopted to determine whether an applicant for dispensation under section 14(4) should be granted that dispensation was residence in the UK between 1973 and 1978 and participation in the British fishing industry during that period. The logic of this criterion was said to be the fact that it was catches during this period which were taken into account in 1983 when quotas were allocated to the Member States. This was, thus, the respondents' pleaded position, which was supported by affidavit evidence from the respondents. The 85th–97th appellants contended that the section 14(4) criteria were applied in a wholly disproportionate manner and that even if *ex hypothesi* there was a justification for excluding the Spanish, such justification could not extend to them. Had the matter proceeded by way of domestic judicial review it is by no means certain that the accuracy or otherwise of the respondents' position would have been tested. However, in October 1996 the Divisional Court ordered discovery, not just from the Department of Transport, but from the government as a whole. This order was made pursuant an application for wide discovery which, when the hearing of the application occurred, the respondents did not oppose. The government was perhaps mindful of the statement of the Court of Justice in *Factortame* (*No. 3*)[44] that for purposes of determining liability parliaments were simply constituent parts of the Member States as a whole upon which the liability fell. Member States were in effect indivisible for the purpose of complying with Community law, and hence it would have been difficult to contend that discovery should be confined to only one department of state even though many other departments were involved with the Merchant Shipping Act 1988. The government might also have been conscious of the developing approach to governmental disclosure in criminal cases.[45] Discovery took the government many months and, initially, gave rise to in excess of 600 lever-arch files of documents. Subsequently a mere 35 plus files of documents were produced for the trial in July 1997. The documents included material from every relevant government department, including from the Cabinet itself and from the UK Permanent Representative's office. The Divisional Court also made a request to the Community for disclosure of all the Community's relevant documents. This engendered discovery from the Commission and (on the very last day of the trial in the Divisional Court in July 1997) from the Council of Ministers.

Discovery demonstrated that the respondents' assertion that the dispensation criteria were predicated upon residence and operation within the fleet during the period 1973–8 was unsupportable. The Divisional Court was scathing in its criticism of the respondent and the manner in which it operated the dispensation provisions. The Court stated:

> It appears that the Registrar General of Shipping refused the dispensation in pursuance of a policy which the respondent says evolved between 1988–1990 and which it is pleaded by the respondent required involvement in the British fishing industry for

[44] [1996] ECR I–1029, at 1148, para. 46.

[45] R. v. *Blackledge and Others* (1996) 8 Admin. LR 361, 372.

a period covering at the very least the years 1973–1978. This policy never seems to have been stated clearly in documents at the time; those documents reveal uncertainty and confusion as to the criteria to be adopted when considering dispensation. Nor was the policy applied with consistency, since discovery has revealed that there were a number of exceptions, which included one who was a school boy in 1973 and a New Zealander who had fished only since 1980.[46]

The Court of Appeal was equally, and possibly even more, critical of the respondents' conduct in the exercise of its discretion under section 14(4) of the Act. It reiterated the concern expressed by the Divisional Court and added that if there was any doubt about the seriousness of the breach committed by the Secretary of State then the way in which these particular applicants were treated "would undoubtedly increase the seriousness of the breach". The Court stated:

> Section 14(4) gave the Secretary of State a wide discretion to mitigate the effect of the nationality condition. The way that these applicants were treated illustrates that that discretion was not as a matter of policy operated in a way which concentrated its impact on those against whom the nationality condition should have been aimed, namely those engaged in quota hopping. While it could not be expected that general provisions of the 1988 Act should never affect the interests of individuals who did not deserve to be targeted, those individuals could at least expect that the Secretary of State would try and achieve a result which minimised the impact on them. Regrettably this does not appear to have happened. Instead what appears to have occurred is that those who had the responsibility for operating section 14(4) lost sight of what had been the whole purpose of the sanction.[47]

The moral of this tale is that in the absence of effective means of testing evidence judicial review is necessarily a process which risks being slanted in favour of the respondent. The fact that the case involved Community law enabled the applicants to obtain extensive pre-hearing discovery and to prepare witness statements,[48] and enabled the Court to embark upon detailed review unfettered by traditional English judicial review shackles. Had discovery not been ordered then it is by no means certain that the applicants would have succeeded. In the Community law context the disadvantages of domestic judicial review are capable of being swept away.

So far as proportionality is concerned, it is plain that a court will often not be in a position effectively to conduct a judicial review without proper disclosure of evidence from the respondent. It is evident from the very definition of the doctrine of proportionality and its constituents that there are many factual and legal matters which a court will necessarily require to be evaluated in coming to a conclusion. Whilst, at first blush, an issue such as the object to be attained by

[46] [1997] Eur. LR 475, at 501c.

[47] *Ibid.*, transcript, 24. On 6 July the Court of Appeal granted the government leave to appeal to the House of Lords.

[48] In the event at the trial the respondents chose not to challenge the contents of these statements which therefore stood uncontroverted as evidence. The deponents were not called to be cross-examined.

legislation may appear to be apparent, that will not always be the case. Again, the *Factortame* litigation demonstrates the problems which identifying the objectives of legislation may pose. The discovery provided in that litigation highlighted that, over a period of time from 1987 onwards, the government pursued a series of related, though different, objectives. Two separate pieces of correspondence rarely articulated the objective in identical language. Different Ministers had different views of what was sought to be achieved. Sometimes differences were subtle and at other times more profound. The debates in Parliament were invariably ill-informed and confusing. Variously the objectives of the Merchant Shipping Act 1988 were described as: to curb the abuse of quota hopping; to protect the objectives of the CFP; to protect the attribution of quotas to a sovereign State; to protect the attribution of quotas to a fishing community; to protect the attribution of quotas to different regions of a Member State; and to uphold the flagging and vessel registration policy of a Member State. Identification with precision of the objective of the Merchant Shipping Act became important for many applicants. Much of the strength for example of the claims of the 85th–97th applicants turned upon the fact that, on analysis, their continued participation in the British fleet would not cause prejudice to *any* one or more of the myriad objectives allegedly sought by the enactment of the Act. In the *Factortame* litigation the objectives of the legislation in question were found in documents as diverse as: instructions to Parliamentary Counsel; interdepartmental minutes and notes; internal briefing notes for ministers; advice from Law Officers to the Cabinet and to ministers; instructions to the diplomatic representation in the UK Permanent Representative's office; correspondence between various governmental bodies and the European Commission; letters from MPs to constituents; and correspondence between Cabinet ministers.

Furthermore, no authoritative source of guidance exists to explain what the objectives of an Act are. *Pepper* v. *Hart* statements made by ministers in Parliament may very well reflect not so much the underlying truth but a carefully constructed justification for public consumption uttered at a particular point in time in the course of an evolving political debate. Even if accurate, *Pepper* v. *Hart* statements may be too broad to be constructive or simply not relevant to the provision being challenged.

Identifying the objectives of legislation will not be the only matter requiring detailed scrutiny of documents. When it comes to determining whether the measures adopted were commensurate with the objectives in question and whether less intrusive methods could, *in fact*, have been used to achieve those objectives, not only will internal discovery be relevant to the exercise but the Court may also have to listen to expert evidence. This may particularly be the case when a court is asked to review the proportionality of legislation in complex technical or economic areas. It will almost inevitably be an argument posed by an applicant alleging that the government adopted "a sledge hammer to crack a nut", that in the light of evidence from some sophisticated and refined economist or scientist a model of intervention could have been adopted to achieve the same end with fewer adverse effects for the applicant. Cross-examination of these experts may well be inevitable and essential if the court is to be properly educated as to the proportionality of the actual measures adopted.

A recent example of Divisional Court judges being required, in the course of a Community judicial review, to decide between two sets of competing evidence was provided by *R.* v. *Customs & Excise, ex parte Lunn Poly*.[49] There, the applicant alleged that variations to insurance premium tax (IPT) which had the effect of increasing the tax to 17½ per cent for travel agents but only 4 per cent for other insurance brokers, who were in competition with travel agents for the provision of holiday insurance, constituted an unlawful state aid contrary to Article 92 EC. One of the issues upon which the Divisional Court was required to adjudicate was whether the alleged aid distorted competition. It was confronted with two sets of affidavits, one suggesting that there was a distortion (the applicants'), the other suggesting that no such effect existed (the respondents'). Kay J, giving the judgment of the court, observed that it was most unsatisfactory that the court should be required to choose between two competing economic propositions in the absence of oral evidence and cross-examination. Cross-examination had been sought by neither applicant nor respondent. (There was no question of the respondents' evidence being preferred as a matter of principle.[50]) Nonetheless, the court accepted implicitly that it had to decide the factual issue and in the circumstances of the case it preferred the applicants' evidence, namely that the differential rates of tax distorted and threatened to distort competition by favouring those to whom the lower rate applied. The court accordingly concluded in that case that the tax in question constituted a state aid, that it distorted competition and affected trade between the Member States of the EU, that it had not been notified to the European Commission in accordance with the provisions of Article 93, and that, in the premises, it was unlawful.

CONCLUSIONS

The doctrine of supremacy coupled with the principle of effective protection of rights necessarily means, and has meant since the UK joined the Community, that Parliament is no longer supreme and that its processes may be subjected to judicial scrutiny and criticism upon application of the principle of proportionality. There is nothing intrinsically remarkable or novel in this proposition. Judges are not usurping any democratic function. That is not to say that the results of judicial scrutiny will not be viewed with deep suspicion by politicians and cause considerable unease amongst the judiciary. The *Factortame* litigation

[49] *Per* Kay J and Kennedy LJ, unreported decision of 2 Apr. 1998.
[50] See n. 40 above.

has however demonstrated that, when embarked upon in a proper spirit of objectivity the courts can exercise effective judicial protection. It is to be expected that with the advent of the ECHR as a set of justiciable rules and principles judges (and the public) will become more familiar with closer judicial scrutiny of Acts of Parliament. It is the personal view of this author that, with Community law and the ECHR requiring judges to roll their sleeves further up the judicial arm than before, in time *Wednesbury* will wither as judges recognise the artificiality of maintaining a different judicial tool kit for a residual category of cases which have no Community or ECHR element to them.

The Concept of Proportionality in European Community Sex Discrimination Law

EVELYN ELLIS*

Several contributors to this work have examined the theoretical and practical differences between the operation of the *Wednesbury* test and that of the principle of proportionality in the field of administrative law.[1] A number of interesting insights have been revealed by this examination, but two in particular might be said to be especially notable in the present context. These are, first, that the strict line which is traditionally drawn between review for legality and review of merits is over-simplistic[2] and, secondly, that the proportionality principle permits considerably more intrusive judicial scrutiny than does a test of pure unreasonableness.[3]

The object of the present paper is to test these hypotheses against the background of a substantive field of EC law, namely sex discrimination. In addition, the case law on sex discrimination provides practical evidence of the way in which the EC principle of proportionality is absorbed into, and enforced through, the law of a Member State; it also provides an opportunity to investigate whether the operation of proportionality in a substantive and predominantly private law context yields any further understanding of its potential and limitations as a tool for the review of administrative action.

THE ROLE OF PROPORTIONALITY IN DISCRIMINATION LAW

The first question must be to ask what part the principle of proportionality plays in sex discrimination law. The answer is that its chief role has been to condition

* I am grateful to my colleagues, Professors Tony Arnull and David Feldman, who both read earlier drafts of this paper and made useful comments. The usual disclaimer of course applies.

[1] See in particular P. Craig, "Unreasonableness and Proportionality in UK Law" and N. Green "Proportionality and the Supremacy of Parliament in the UK", both this vol.

[2] See also D. Oliver, "Is the Ultra Vires Rule the Basis of Judicial Review?" [1987] *PL* 543; Lord Woolf, "Droit Public—English Style" [1995] *PL* 57; Sir John Laws, "Law and Democracy" [1995] *PL* 72; and Lord Irvine, "Judges and Decision-Makers: The Theory and Practice of *Wednesbury* Review" [1996] *PL* 59; cf. C. Forsyth, "Of Fig Leaves and Fairy Tales: The Ultra Vires Doctrine, the Sovereignty of Parliament and Judicial Review" (1996) 55 *CLJ* 122.

[3] Cf. Lord Hoffmann, "The Influence of the European Principle of Proportionality upon UK Law", this vol.

and limit in terms of principle the circumstances in which an allegation of unlawful discrimination can be refuted; superficially at least, this seems to be analogous to the role it plays in administrative law in providing a yardstick and a mechanism for the supervision of the legality of decision-making. Since the right not to be discriminated against on the ground of sex is explicitly recognised by the ECJ as a fundamental human right,[4] the application of the principle of proportionality in discrimination law might also be seen as an aspect of the more general principle by which the ECJ requires a restrictive interpretation to be placed on any erosions into or curtailments of fundamental human rights[5]; once again, this has resonances in the field of administrative law, in particular in relation to the ECHR.

There are two somewhat different situations in which an allegation of discrimination may be refuted. The first is where there has undoubtedly been discrimination on the ground of sex but a specific legislative exception or defence is invoked. As will be seen below, EC law demands that such a defence is only permissible where its use is proportionate to the end to be served.

The second is in relation to proof of the essential elements of indirect discrimination. Sophisticated systems of law recognise that discrimination, a statutory tort, is not restricted to situations in which there is a deliberate or straightforward disadvantaging of one person or group of people over another, but that it also extends on occasion to cases in which an apparently innocuous practice produces such a result. This second subspecies of discrimination is known as "indirect discrimination" and is a necessary part of the legal armoury if longstanding patterns of behaviour which damage particular groups are to be eliminated.

Bilka-Kaufhaus GmbH v. *Weber von Hartz*[6] concerned one such hitherto-accepted practice, namely the less favourable treatment of part-time workers as compared to their full-time colleagues. A department store belonging to a large chain entitled its employees to a supplementary retirement pension provided that they had worked for the company for at least 20 years, 15 of which had to be full-time. Ms Weber von Hartz, who had mainly worked part-time for the company, could not satisfy these conditions and was therefore refused a pension. This, she claimed, amounted to indirect sex discrimination against her since the effect of the pension scheme rules was to disadvantage part-timers, the great majority of whom in this instance (as in many others) were female. Had this been the only question before the courts, the matter would have been simple to resolve. However, in accordance with the normal principles of causation in tort, it was also necessary to demonstrate that the disadvantage suffered by part-timers was caused by their sex. This is a much harder task to accomplish in cases of indirect discrimination than in cases of direct discrimination, because in the latter category the two sexes receive different treatment. Where indirect

[4] See Case 149/77 *Defrenne* v. *Sabena* [1978] ECR 1365.

[5] See, e.g., Joined Cases C–74 and 129/95 *Criminal Proceedings Against* X [1996] ECR I–6609.

[6] Case 170/84 [1986] ECR 1607.

discrimination is alleged, a court is really required to arrive at its conclusion by a process of elimination: if the adverse impact being experienced by one group cannot be explained away as referable to a cause other than sex, the anti-discrimination legislation obliges the court to conclude that sex is the root or cause of that adverse impact. The establishment of a cause other than the difference of sex is referred to in both domestic and EC law as the "justification" of alleged indirect discrimination.[7] Thus, for example, Article 2 of Directive 97/80[8] provides that indirect discrimination is negated where it "can be justified by objective factors unrelated to sex".[9]

In the *Bilka* case, the ECJ explained that the principle of proportionality plays a crucial role in the establishment of such justification. Unconvinced by the more conservative submissions of its Advocate General, it laid down that:

> It is for the national court, which has sole jurisdiction to make findings of fact, to determine whether and to what extent the grounds put forward by an employer to explain the adoption of a pay practice which applies independently of a worker's sex but in fact affects more women than men may be regarded as objectively justified economic grounds. If the national court finds that the measures chosen by Bilka correspond to a real need on the part of the undertaking, are appropriate with a view to achieving the objectives pursued and are necessary to that end, the fact that the measures affect a far greater number of women than men is not sufficient to show that they constitute an infringement of Article 119.[10]

In other words, it is only where the disadvantageous practice is proportionate to the acceptable end which it purports to serve that the employer will have a defence to an allegation of indirect discrimination. Thus a disproportionate response by an employer even to a perceived need will, in these sorts of circumstances, fail to constitute justification.

PROPORTIONALITY IN RELATION TO DEFENCES TO DISCRIMINATION

It is clearly vital to the robustness of a prohibition on sex discrimination that any exceptions which are permitted to it be given as limited an interpretation as is consistent with their objectives. EC sex discrimination law in fact contains few exceptions. As it was originally drafted, none were articulated in Article 119

7 See further E. Ellis, "Gender Discrimination Law in the European Community" in J. Dine and B. Watt (eds.), *Discrimination Law: Concepts, Limitations, and Justifications* (London, Longman, 1996).

8 [1998] OJ L14/6.

9 See also the Sex Discrimination Act 1975, s. 1(1)b)(ii).

10 [1986] ECR 1607, at 1628. It is to be noted that this is an example of what W. van Gerven refers to as the ECJ's "two-pronged approach", as distinct from the "three-pronged approach", to the definition of proportionality: see "The Effect of Proportionality on the Actions of Member States of the European Community: National Viewpoints From Continental Europe", this vol. See also F.G. Jacobs, "Recent Developments in the Principle of Proportionality in European Community Law", this vol.

of the Treaty which mandates equal pay, and at the most only three seem to be permitted by the Equal Treatment Directive.[11] Article 2(2) of this Directive allows Member States to exclude "those occupational activities and, where appropriate, the training leading thereto, for which, by reason of their nature or the context in which they are carried out, the sex of the worker constitutes a determining factor". Article 2(3) allows provisions for the protection of women "particularly as regards pregnancy and maternity", and Article 2(4) appears to permit certain forms of positive action:

> This Directive shall be without prejudice to measures to promote equal opportunities for men and women, in particular by removing existing inequalities which affect women's opportunities in the areas referred to in Article 1(1) [access to employment, vocational training, working conditions and some aspects of social security].

The Treaty of Amsterdam of 1997 up-dated the wording of Article 119 of the Treaty of Rome and added to it, *inter alia*, a new paragraph 4 dealing with positive action.[12] This states:

> With a view to ensuring full equality in practice between men and women in working life, the principle of equal treatment shall not prevent any Member State from maintaining or adopting measures providing for specific advantages in order to make it easier for the under-represented sex to pursue a vocational activity or to prevent or compensate for disadvantages in professional careers.

Whether or not this new provision represents a true exception to the equality principle remains to be decided by the ECJ. The extent to which the pre-Amsterdam legislation permitted positive discrimination was not clear from the Court's case law,[13] and it is at least arguable that the new provision does no more than codify the existing jurisprudence.[14]

The applicability of the principle of proportionality to all such exceptions was asserted by the ECJ in *Johnston* v. *Chief Constable of the RUC*,[15] in which the Chief Constable sought to rely on Article 2(2) of the Equal Treatment Directive to defend himself against the allegation that, by refusing to arm female officers and thereafter not renewing their contracts of employment with the police service, he had discriminated unlawfully against them. The ECJ held that:

> [I]n determining the scope of any derogation from an individual right such as the equal treatment of men and women provided for by the Directive, the principle of proportionality, one of the general principles of law underlying the Community legal order, must be observed. That principle requires that derogations remain within the limits of what is appropriate and necessary for achieving the aim in view and requires the prin-

[11] Dir. 76/207 [1976] OJ L39/40.

[12] The new formulation had its origin in the Agreement on Social Policy annexed at Maastricht in 1993 to the EC Treaty but from which the UK was excluded.

[13] See in particular Case C–450/93 *Kalanke* v. *Freie und Hansestadt Bremen* [1995] ECR I–3051 and Case C–409/95 *Marschall* v. *Nordrhein Westfalen* [1997] All ER (EC) 865.

[14] See further E. Ellis, *EC Sex Equality Law* (2nd edn., Oxford, Clarendon Press, 1998), at 244–60.

[15] Case 222/84 [1986] ECR 1651.

ciple of equal treatment to be reconciled as far as possible with the requirements of public safety which constitute the decisive factor as regards the context of the activity in question.[16]

Since this was an Article 177 reference, it concluded that it was for the national court:

to say whether the reasons on which the Chief Constable based his decision are in fact well founded and justify the specific measure taken in Mrs Johnston's case. It is also for the national court to ensure that the principle of proportionality is observed and to determine whether the refusal to renew Mrs Johnston's contract could not be avoided by allocating to women duties which, without jeopardising the aims pursued, can be performed without firearms.[17]

The same principles apply where it is not merely an employer trying to defend an apparently discriminatory activity but also where national legislation sanctions discrimination. This emerged from *Commission* v. *UK*,[18] an Article 169 enforcement action in respect *inter alia* of exceptions contained in the UK's Sex Discrimination Act of 1975 for employment in private households and in small businesses. Both exceptions were rejected by the ECJ, effectively on the ground that they were disproportionate to the aims they sought to further:

It must be recognised that the provision of the 1975 Act in question is intended, in so far as it refers to employment in a private household, to reconcile the principle of equality of treatment with the principle of respect for private life, which is also fundamental. Reconciliation of that kind is one of the factors which must be taken into consideration in determining the scope of the exception provided for in Article 2(2) of the Directive. Whilst it is undeniable that, for certain kinds of employment in private households, that consideration may be decisive, that is not the case for all the kinds of employment in question.

As regards small undertakings with not more than five employees, the UK has not put forward any argument to show that in any undertaking of that size the sex of the worker would be a determining factor by reason of the nature of his activities or the context in which they are carried out.

Consequently, by reason of its generality, the exclusion provided for in the contested provision of the 1975 Act goes beyond the objective which may be lawfully pursued within the framework of Article 2(2) of the Directive.[19]

The same process of reasoning applies in the field of social security where sex equality is demanded by Directive 79/7[20] but subject to certain exceptions, the most important of which is contained in Article 7(1)(a). This excludes from the equality principle:

[16] *Ibid.*, at 1687.
[17] *Ibid.*, at 1687.
[18] Case 165/82 [1983] ECR 3431.
[19] *Ibid.*, at 3448. Cf. Case C–189/91 *Kirsammer-Hack* v. *Sidal* [1993] ECR I–6185, discussed below.
[20] [1979] OJ L6/24.

the determination of pensionable age for the purposes of granting old-age and retirement pensions and the possible consequences thereof for other benefits.

In *Secretary of State for Social Security* v. *Thomas*,[21] the ECJ held that discrimination occurring in relation to benefits other than old-age and retirement pensions can be excused under this provision only if such discrimination is "objectively necessary in order to avoid disrupting the complex financial equilibrium of the social security system or to ensure consistency between retirement pension schemes and other benefit schemes".[22]

It is therefore evident that the doctrine of proportionality contains the potential, both in theory and in practice, to enable the ECJ to maintain effective and meaningful supervision over the use put by both employers and the Member States to the exceptions permitted to the equality principle. There can be little doubt that it represents a more powerful weapon in this context than would a power to reject merely on the ground of unreasonableness.

PROPORTIONALITY AND THE JUSTIFICATION OF INDIRECT DISCRIMINATION

There is a pleasing analogy in this context with the differential rigours of the *Wednesbury* test and that of proportionality in public law. Before the articulation of the *Bilka* criteria for determining the existence of objective justification, UK courts had to rely on their own resources to interpret the meaning of justification for the purposes of the domestic anti-discrimination legislation.[23] After some disagreement in the Employment Appeal Tribunal over the standard to be adopted,[24] the Court of Appeal settled for a test of reasonableness in *Ojutiku* v. *Manpower Services Commission*.[25] Two men of African origin had failed to obtain sponsorship for a management studies course from the Manpower Services Commission. The Commission imposed certain requirements for the grant of sponsorship, first that applicants be experienced in a post of commercial, administrative, professional or industrial responsibility and, secondly, that they should have either a degree or higher national diploma or membership of a professional body. The applicants could satisfy this second requirement but not the first. It was accepted by the Court of Appeal that the first requirement had an adverse impact on persons of the applicants' racial origins, and the only issue therefore was whether its imposition was justifiable. All three members of the Court of Appeal attempted to put flesh on the bones of the statutory test. Eveleigh LJ said:

[21] Case C–328/91 [1993] ECR I–1247.

[22] *Ibid.*, at 1273. See also Case C–154/92 *Van Cant* v. *Rijksdienst voor Pensioenen* [1993] ECR I–3811 and Joined Cases C–377–384/96 *De Vriendt* v. *Rijksdienst voor Pensioenen*, not yet reported.

[23] S. 1(1)(b)(ii) of the Race Relations Act 1976 uses the same terminology for the definition of indirect discrimination as does the Sex Discrimination Act 1975.

[24] See *Steel* v. *Union of Post Office Workers* [1978] ICR 181 and *Singh* v. *Rowntree Mackintosh Ltd.* [1979] ICR 554.

[25] [1982] ICR 661.

> For myself, it would be enough simply to ask: is it justifiable? But if I have to give some explanation of my understanding of that word, I would turn to a dictionary definition which says "to adduce adequate grounds for"; and it seems to me that if a person produces reasons for doing something, which would be acceptable to right-thinking people as sound and tolerable reasons for so doing, then he has justified his conduct.[26]

Kerr LJ considered that "justifiable" was "a perfectly easily understandable ordinary word" and that, particularly significantly in the present context, it "clearly applies a lower standard than the word 'necessary' ".[27] Stephenson LJ rejected "justification by convenience" and said that the party applying the discriminatory condition must prove it to be justifiable "in all the circumstances on balancing its discriminatory effect against the discriminator's need for it. But that need is what is reasonably needed by the party who applies the condition".[28]

The Court of Appeal was unanimous in holding that the Commission had justified its position. An employee of the Commission had given evidence to the industrial tribunal to the effect that it was essential not to support candidates for courses if there was no real likelihood of their eventually getting a job and that, if the Commission were to support such candidates, this would have an adverse effect on the reputation of the sponsorship scheme which would in the long run operate to the detriment of all those selected for such courses. In the words of Eveleigh LJ:

> [T]his was not a mere expression of opinion by the Commission. [Its employee] gave reasons for his views; he spoke of actual inquiries made by him and he spoke of his own experience in the field. He was cross-examined on the matter; his evidence was accepted and for myself I cannot see any rule of law which requires an employer to call evidence from outside.[29]

There can be little doubt that the Commission's conduct was here subjected to a far lower standard of scrutiny than would have been the case had a test of proportionality been applied. As seen above, the criterion of necessity for the conduct challenged was expressly rejected by the Court of Appeal and, moreover, although a test of reasonableness was adopted it was clear that it was quite easily satisfied and required no objective or outside corroboration. The risk of perpetuating discrimination where judges need look no further than the views of "right-thinking people" is a palpable one.

It is therefore of particular interest and importance to notice the change wrought by the switch to proportionality as the standard by which justification is to be established in the decision of the House of Lords a decade later in *R.* v. *Secretary of State for Employment, ex parte EOC*.[30] The Equal Opportunities

26 *Ibid.*, at 668.
27 *Ibid.*, at 670.
28 *Ibid.*, at 674.
29 *Ibid.*, at 666.
30 [1994] 2 WLR 409.

Commission (EOC) sought in judicial review proceedings to establish the discriminatory, and therefore unlawful, nature of the threshold provisions of the Employment Protection (Consolidation) Act 1978; it alleged in particular that the requirement to have worked for at least two years in full-time employment or five years in part-time employment in order to be eligible for the employment protection conferred by the statute contravened EC anti-discrimination law.[31] The Secretary of State had argued that the threshold provisions favoured the creation of part-time work. Whilst the House of Lords agreed that the bringing about of an increase in the availability of part-time work might constitute a proper aim of social policy and could therefore justify any resulting alleged indirect discrimination against women, the Secretary of State had failed to prove this contention. The threshold provisions had not been shown to result in the creation of more part-time jobs and therefore could not be said to be appropriate and necessary to achieving the aim asserted. It is worth quoting the words of Lord Keith of Kinkel, whose views in this respect were echoed by all the other members of the House:

> The question is whether the threshold provisions of the Act of 1978 have been shown, by reference to objective factors, to be suitable and requisite [for the purpose of increasing the availability of part-time work]. As regards suitability for achieving the aim in question, it is to be noted that the purpose of the thresholds is said to be to reduce the costs to employers of employing part-time workers. The same result, however, would follow from a situation where the basic rate of pay for part-time workers was less than the basic rate for full-time workers. . . . Legislation which permitted a differential of that kind nationwide . . . would surely constitute a gross breach of the principle of equal pay and could not possibly be regarded as a suitable means of achieving an increase in part-time employment. Similar considerations apply to legislation which reduces the indirect cost of employing part-time labour. Then as to the threshold provisions being requisite to achieve the stated aim, the question is whether on the evidence before the Divisional Court they have been proved actually to result in greater availability of part-time work than would be the case without them. In my opinion that question must be answered in the negative. The evidence for the Secretary of State consisted principally of an affidavit by an official in the Department of Employment which set out the views of the Department but did not contain anything capable of being regarded as factual evidence demonstrating the correctness of these views.[32]

In other words, the Secretary of State had simply failed to satisfy the test of proportionality. There seems little doubt that, had the decision of the House of Lords been left to "right-thinking people", the outcome would have been very different.

However, notwithstanding the potential of the principle of proportionality to subject alleged indirect discrimination to rigorous and sensitive scrutiny, there

[31] In particular, Art. 119 of the EC Treaty, Dir. 75/117, [1975] OJ L45/19, and Dir. 76/207 [1976] OJ L39/40.

[32] [1994] 2 WLR 409, at 421.

has been a marked transition in the attitude of the ECJ to its role in this area. An early example of the use to which the ECJ seemed prepared to put the principle came in the *Danfoss* case,[33] where an employer made supplementary payments to its employees pursuant to a collective agreement and these had the effect of raising average male wages significantly above those of average female wages. There was thus a *prima facie* case of indirect discrimination, and one of the issues raised was whether or not it was justifiable. The ECJ examined the situation in considerable detail, given that this was an Article 177 reference in which the facts were of course for the national court to find.[34] The first criterion for the grant of a supplement was described as "mobility", as to which the ECJ had this to say:

> In applying the criterion of mobility the employer makes a global assessment of the quality of work done by his employees. For that purpose he takes account, in particular, of their enthusiasm for their work, their sense of initiative and the amount of work done.
>
> In those circumstances a distinction must be made according to whether the criterion of mobility is employed to reward the quality of work done by the employee or is used to reward the employee's adaptability to variable hours and varying places of work.
>
> In the first case the criterion of mobility is undoubtedly wholly neutral from the point of view of sex. Where it systematically works to the disadvantage of women that can only be because the employer has misapplied it. It is inconceivable that the quality of work done by women should generally be less good. The employer cannot therefore justify applying the criterion of mobility, so understood, where its application proves to work systematically to the disadvantage of women.
>
> The position is different in the second case. If it is understood as covering the employee's adaptability to variable hours and varying places of work, the criterion of mobility may also work to the disadvantage of female employees, who, because of household and family duties for which they are frequently responsible, are not as able as men to organise their working time flexibly.[35]

It went on to reiterate its holding in *Bilka* that a wage practice which impacted adversely on women might nevertheless be justified by recourse to objective factors unrelated to sex and concluded that:

> Those considerations also apply in the case of a wages practice which specially remunerates the employee's adaptability to variable hours and varying places of work. The employer may therefore justify the remuneration of such adaptability by showing that it is of importance for the performance of specific tasks entrusted to the employee.[36]

[33] Case 109/88 *Handels- og Kontorfunktionærernes Forbund i Danmark* v. *Dansk Arbejdsgiverforening, acting on behalf of Danfoss* [1989] ECR 3199.

[34] On this issue of the division of jurisdiction between the ECJ and the national courts as regards the application of the principle of proportionality see F.G. Jacobs, "Recent Developments in the Principle of Proportionality in European Community Law", this vol.

[35] [1989] ECR 3199, at 3227.

[36] *Ibid.*, at 3228.

Adaptability was thus held to be capable of being shown to be a "real need" of the employer, which could be addressed by "appropriate" and "necessary" measures within the meaning of the *Bilka* proportionality test. Likewise, the Court held that the asserted criterion of training could be used to justify a higher rate of pay provided that it was of importance for the performance of the employee's job. On the other hand, when it came to the third criterion for the payment of a wage supplement, namely long service, despite its potentially adverse impact for women, the Court took a different line. It held that:

> [S]ince length of service goes hand in hand with experience and since experience generally enables the employee to perform his duties better, the employer is free to reward it without having to establish the importance it has in the performance of specific tasks entrusted to the employee.[37]

In other words, rewarding long service was assumed here both to serve a real need of an employer and, importantly, to be appropriate and necessary to serving that need. The ECJ was thus not merely requiring a test of proportionality but also itself applying it. However, it subsequently changed its mind about the relevance of long service.

Nimz v. *Freie und Hansestadt Hamburg*[38] concerned a collective agreement which favoured persons working at least three-quarters of normal working time over part-timers. The alleged justification for this practice was that full-timers acquired job-related skills more quickly than part-timers, but the Court rejected this reasoning as too crude to be acceptable:

> Such considerations, in so far as they are no more than generalisations about certain categories of workers, do not make it possible to identify criteria which are both objective and unrelated to any discrimination on grounds of sex. . . . Although experience goes hand in hand with length of service, and experience enables the worker in principle to improve performance of the tasks allotted to him, the objectivity of such a criterion depends on all the circumstances in a particular case, and in particular on the relationship between the nature of the work performed and the experience gained from the performance of that work upon completion of a certain number of working hours.[39]

An important development in the application of the doctrine of proportionality to indirect discrimination occurred in *Rinner-Kuhn* v. *FWW Spezial-Gebaudereinigung GmbH*.[40] The ECJ's judgment here made it clear that it is not just an employer's practices which must conform with the duty to ensure sex equality but also, essentially in consequence of the supremacy of EC law, the Member States' domestic employment legislation. German legislation restricted

[37] *Ibid.*, at 3228.

[38] Case C–184/89 [1991] ECR I–297.

[39] *Ibid.*, at 319. Cf. Case C–33/89 *Kowalska* v. *Freie und Hansestadt Hamburg* [1990] ECR I–2591.

[40] Case 171/88 [1989] ECR 2743.

the payment of sick pay to employees working for longer than ten hours per week or 45 hours per month. The purported justification for this rule, which again detrimentally affected women more than men because of their prevalence in the part-time workforce, was that these workers were not integrated into their employer's undertaking in a way comparable to full-timers and that therefore the conditions for the recognition of a duty of care from the employer towards them, including the obligation to continue to pay wages in the event of sickness, did not exist. As in *Nimz*, the ECJ rejected this argument:

> [T]hose considerations, in so far as they are only generalisations about certain categories of workers, do not enable criteria which are both objective and unrelated to any discrimination on ground of sex to be identified.[41]

It nevertheless went on to say:

> However, if the Member State can show that the means chosen meet a necessary aim of its social policy and that they are suitable and requisite for attaining that aim, the mere fact that the provision affects a much greater number of female workers than male workers cannot be regarded as constituting an infringement of Article 119.[42]

The way thus seemed to be open for the doctrine of proportionality to play a highly proactive role in relation to the justification of both employer and Member State action. Unfortunately, events subsequently took a somewhat different course, with a markedly more deferential attitude developing on the part of the ECJ towards the legislative discretion of the Member States. This is particularly evident in two lines of cases.

The first group of cases concern the German system of employment staff committees. In *Arbeiterwohlfahrt der Stadt Berlin eV* v. *Bötel*,[43] a woman part-time worker who chaired a staff committee exercised her statutory right to paid time off work in order to attend some training courses related to the staff committee which lasted for longer than her normal working hours. However, she found that she was paid only for her normal working hours. If she had been a full-timer, she would have been reimbursed for all the hours she had spent attending the courses and this, she argued, constituted indirect discrimination against her. The ECJ noted that, whatever the explanation for the disparity in treatment, the fact remained that part-timers were treated less favourably than full-timers, in relation to their attendance at courses which promoted the general welfare of their employers. This was likely to deter part-timers from serving on staff committees or from training to do so, thus making it more difficult for them to achieve representation on such committees. The Court therefore concluded that the unfavourable treatment experienced here by part-timers was not justified by objective factors unrelated to sex discrimination.

[41] *Ibid.*, at 2761.
[42] *Ibid.*, at 2761.
[43] Case C–360/90 [1992] ECR I–3589.

However, this decision prompted considerable controversy in Germany, and the Federal Labour Court therefore asked the ECJ to reconsider its position in *Kuratorium für Dialyse und Nierentransplantation eV* v. *Lewark*.[44] Both the German court and the German government argued that it was important to the staff committee system that those workers serving did so on an unpaid and independent basis; all that ought therefore to be required should be that they be reimbursed for those hours which they would have been at work had they not been serving on a staff committee. The main issue before the ECJ became whether or not the different treatment of part-timers and full-timers could be justified, and the ECJ ultimately accepted this as a possibility, albeit one constrained as usual by the principle of proportionality:

> It is . . . apparent . . . that the Bundesarbeitsgericht considers that the German legislature's wish to place the independence of staff councils above financial inducements for performing staff council functions . . . is an aim of social policy. Such a social policy aim appears in itself to be unrelated to any discrimination on grounds of sex. It cannot be disputed that the work of staff councils does indeed play a part in German social policy, in that the councils have the task of promoting harmonious labour relations within undertakings and in their interest. The concern to ensure the independence of the members of those councils thus likewise reflects a legitimate aim of social policy.
>
> If a Member State is able to show that the measures chosen reflect a legitimate aim of its social policy, are appropriate to achieve that aim and are necessary in order to do so, the mere fact that the legislative provision affects far more women workers than men cannot be regarded as a breach of Article 119. . . .[45]

The ECJ thus apparently permitted itself to be strongly influenced in its application of the principle of equality by the political desires of a Member State, the only consolation being that the dictates of the resulting national legislation had as usual, at least in theory, to be tempered by the doctrine of proportionality.

The second area in which the legislative discretion of the Member States appears to be being allowed a very free rein today is discrimination in relation to social security.[46] Here, as will be seen below, it is not merely that the ECJ is easily satisfied as to the existence of a legitimate aim of social policy lying behind apparently indirectly discriminatory legislation, but also that the scope of the Member States' discretion is being dangerously widened.

The relative ease with which the Member States can justify social security legislation which impacts adversely on one sex was first demonstrated in the *Teuling* case.[47] A woman who had been receiving invalidity benefit under the Netherlands social security system at a rate equal to the statutory minimum

[44] Case C–457/93 [1996] ECR I–243. See also Case C–278/93 *Freers* v. *Deutsche Bundespost* [1996] ECR I–1165.

[45] *Ibid.*, at 269–70.

[46] Contrary to Dir. 79/7 [1979] OJ L6/24.

[47] Case 30/85 *Teuling* v. *Bedrijfsvereniging voor de Chemische Industrie* [1987] ECR 2497. Cf. Case C–328/91 *Secretary of State for Social Security* v. *Thomas* [1993] ECR I–1247, discussed briefly above.

wage found her benefit substantially reduced in consequence of new legislation; this legislation paid supplements to certain people but not to those, like Ms Teuling, who had a spouse with an income above a prescribed level. The government argued that the purpose of the invalidity benefit was to provide a minimum substance income for persons with no other means, and the ECJ agreed that this was an acceptable social policy aim. It concluded that:

> [I]f supplements to a minimum social security benefit are intended, where beneficiaries have no income from work, to prevent the benefit from falling below the minimum subsistence level for persons who, by virtue of the fact that they have a dependent spouse or children, bear heavier burdens than single persons, such supplements may be justified. . . .[48]

Since most social security benefits and the rules surrounding them exist at the very least ostensibly in order to save people from destitution, it followed from this ruling that it would not usually prove very difficult to justify indirect discrimination in this area. However, proportionality then stepped in to restrain the worst excesses of the national legislation:

> If a national court, which has sole jurisdiction to assess the facts and interpret the national legislation, finds that supplements such as those in this case correspond to the greater burdens which beneficiaries having a dependent spouse or children must bear in comparison with persons living alone, serve to ensure an adequate minimum subsistence income for those beneficiaries and are necessary for that purpose, the fact that the supplements are paid to a significantly higher number of married men than married women is not sufficient to support the conclusion that the grant of such supplements is contrary to [EC law].[49]

Subsequent cases in this area, however, show serious slippage over the actual demands made here by the requirement of proportionality. This trend began with *Commission* v. *Belgium*[50] in which the ECJ held that a system of benefits was justified where it was more generous to those (predominantly males) who cohabited with a person having no income than to those living alone or with an earning partner. The Court accepted that the Belgian legislation aimed to take into consideration the existence of different needs and concluded that such an objective was a matter of social policy which was for the Member States to decide for themselves and as to which they enjoyed "a reasonable margin of discretion".[51]

The true measure of this margin of discretion was revealed in *Molenbroek* v. *Bestuur van de Sociale Verzekeringsbank*.[52] The Court was asked whether EC law prohibited national legislation on old-age pensions from making the grant and amount of a supplement payable to a pensioner whose spouse had not

[48] *Ibid.*, at 2521.
[49] *Ibid.*, at 2522.
[50] Case C–229/89 [1991] ECR I–2205.
[51] *Ibid.*, at 2229.
[52] Case C–226/91 [1992] ECR I–5943.

reached retirement age depend on that spouse's earned income, excluding any other income of the pensioner; this was to be understood in the light of the fact that far more men than women qualified for the supplement and that the supplement was payable even where it was not essential to guarantee the couple a minimum income. On this occasion, the ECJ took it upon itself to apply the proportionality test, even though this was an Article 177 reference,[53] and moreover to apply it in a substantially weakened version:

> [T]he allowance granted . . . is in the nature of a basic allowance, in that it is intended to guarantee those concerned an income equal to the social minimum, irrespective of any income which they receive from other sources.
>
> Furthermore, the Court has already held that the allocation of an income equal to the social minimum formed an integral part of the social policy of the Member States. . . .
>
> Finally, in leaving out of account any other income received by an old-age pensioner when determining the supplement payable to him in respect of a younger dependent spouse, the national legislation . . . ultimately allocates to the couple an aggregate income equal to that to which both spouses will be entitled when they are both in receipt of a pension and the supplement has consequently been discontinued.
>
> The supplements scheme is therefore essential in order to preserve the nature of the allowance . . . as a basic allowance and in order to guarantee the couple, where one of the spouses has not yet reached pensionable age, an income equal to the social minimum which they will receive when they are both pensioners.
>
> *In those circumstances, the fact that at times the supplement is granted to persons who, having regard to the income which they receive from other sources, do not need it in order to guarantee a minimum level of subsistence cannot affect the fact that the means chosen are necessary having regard to the aim pursued.*[54]

The logic of this reasoning is defective in particular because the Court concluded that the discriminatory rule was necessary even though it had not investigated whether the legitimate aim pursued could have been achieved by alternative means.

The eventual effective abandonment by the ECJ of its jurisdiction to supervise the justification of alleged indirect discrimination in the field of social security (where the discrimination necessarily arises from national legislation) came with its decisions in the *Nolte* and *Megner and Scheffel* cases.[55] Both concerned the adverse impact on women of national legislation excluding part-time workers from compulsory old-age insurance. The Court further expanded the discretion permitted to the Member States here, saying:

> [S]ocial policy is a matter for the Member States . . . Consequently, it is for the Member States to choose the measures capable of achieving the aim of their social and

[53] See also Case C–8/94 *Laperre* v. *Bestuurscommissie* [1996] ECR I–273.

[54] [1992] ECR I–5943, at 5968–9 (emphasis supplied).

[55] Case C–317/93 *Nolte* v. *Landesversicherungsanstalt Hannover* [1995] ECR I–4625 and Case C–444/93 *Megner and Scheffel* v. *Innungskrankenkasse Verderplatz* [1995] ECR I–4741.

> employment policy. *In exercising that competence, the Member States have a broad margin of discretion.*[56]

The German government maintained that the exclusion of part-timers from compulsory insurance was basic to the structure of the national social security scheme, in which equivalence had to be maintained between the contributions paid in and the benefits paid out. Like the British government in the *EOC* case,[57] it also argued that the system favoured the creation of part-time employment, for which there was a social demand, and that in the absence of the existing system this demand would be satisfied on the black market. The Court concluded that:

> [T]he social and employment policy aim relied on by the German government is objectively unrelated to any discrimination on grounds of sex and . . ., in exercising its competence, the national legislature was reasonably entitled to consider that the legislation in question was necessary in order to achieve that aim.[58]

This is, of course, to take the further and disastrous step of saying that, in order to justify apparent indirect discrimination, a Member State need only show that it reasonably believes the measure to be necessary to achieve a social policy aim, not that it actually and demonstrably is necessary in order to achieve that aim.

CONCLUSIONS

This brief discussion of the application of the principle of proportionality in discrimination law prompts a number of conclusions. The first is that proportionality provides a rational means of patrolling the boundary between the employer or Member State's discretion to act and the right of the individual not to be discriminated against. Because of its coherent and structured nature, and in particular because of its emphasis on the necessity for discriminatory action, proportionality is a much more satisfactory and effective test for this purpose than reasonableness. The contrast between *Ojutiku* and the *EOC* case highlights this distinction and demonstrates how the principle of proportionality, faithfully applied, permits a court to investigate properly the allegations made by each side and to demand objective corroboration for what is claimed.

Secondly, it has been seen that, whilst the ECJ investigates whether the principle of proportionality is actually satisfied in cases involving its plenary jurisdiction, in Article 177 references it has frequently stressed that this role is one for the national court since that court alone has jurisdiction to establish the facts in the case. Although the ECJ has not always managed to resist the temptation

[56] *Ibid.*, at 4660 and 4755 respectively (emphasis supplied). It is noteworthy that the adjective used has now metamorphosed from "reasonable" into "broad".

[57] N. 30 above, discussed above.

[58] [1995] ECR I–4625, at 4660, and [1995] ECR I–4741, at 4755.

to intervene and has on occasion arrived at a conclusion as to whether the principle of proportionality was satisfied in particular circumstances, it would no doubt explain such instances as examples of its giving very detailed legal guidance, made the more helpful to the referring court by reason of a close correlation with the facts of the case. In any event, the ECJ's formulation of the theoretical position would seem to contain the important implicit assumption that the application of the principle of proportionality involves some element of excursus into the facts of the case. This has an important bearing on the traditional distinction between legality and merits in public law. In insisting on using the principle of proportionality to control the legality of the employer's or Member State's action, but requiring the national court to carry out the necessary analysis of the facts, it would seem to be maintaining that a proper review for legality does indeed require some investigation of the facts; in other words, the claim that legality and merits are strictly separable is once again shown to be inaccurate.[59]

A third conclusion to which the discrimination cases point is the tenaciousness of the notion of a state's "margin of appreciation".[60] Although this is not the actual term employed by the ECJ, the German staff committee cases and the social security cases all show a disturbingly large and growing discretion in the hands of the Member States in determining social policy and in enacting implementing legislation. As the most recent cases show, even when the doctrine of proportionality is applied in these areas, its content is seriously watered down.

That such a development might well be applied in future in other legislative arenas appears from the ECJ's decision in *Kirsammer-Hack* v. *Sidal*.[61] This concerned an allegation of indirect discrimination contrary to the Equal Treatment Directive[62] in respect of German legislation, which excluded part-time workers from the count when calculating whether an employer's work-force numbered five or more, the threshold above which such a workforce was entitled to complain of unfair dismissal. The ECJ held that the detriment in these circumstances flowed not to part-time employees but to those employed by small businesses, and it had not been shown that women were especially prevalent in small businesses. There was therefore no *prima facie* case of indirect discrimination requiring justification. However, even if there had been, the Court was prepared to hold that it was justified. In marked contrast to its statements in *Commission* v. *UK*,[63] it accepted that such justification would be constituted by the need to "alleviate the constraints burdening small businesses which play an essential role in economic development and the creation of employment in the Community".[64] Once again, one sees here a marked indulgence towards the

[59] See also N. Green, "Proportionality and the Supremacy of Parliament in the UK", this vol.
[60] See also D.J. Feldman, "Proportionality and the Human Rights Act", this vol.
[61] Case C–189/91 [1993] ECR I–6185.
[62] Dir. 76/207 [1976] OJ L39/40.
[63] Case 165/82 [1983] ECR 3431, discussed above.
[64] [1993] ECR I–6185, at 6223.

legislative discretion of the Member States and a corresponding reluctance on the part of the ECJ to become involved in the sort of political wrangling which would probably ensue from a more critical application of the principle of proportionality.

Unfortunately, the ultimate conclusion to be drawn is a rather bleak one from the point of view of those who would argue for strong judicial review in public law. The lesson seems to be that the principle of proportionality is indeed reasoned, effective and invasive. However, when its full potential impact in a given area becomes clear to a court, it will take a strong-minded court not to shrink away from flexing its judicial muscles in the face of political or executive might.

Index

academic writers, 112, 142, 152
Lord Ackner, 88, 112, 122
Adamovich, 65
Alen, 53–4
Andenas, 89
arbitrariness, 56, 59
  repudiation of, 155
Arndt, 46

Bakker, 56
Barnard, 67
basic freedoms—*see* fundamental freedoms
basic rights—*see* fundamental rights
Belgium, 58–9
  administrative law, 52–5
  Court of Arbitration, 52–5
  Council of State, 52
Bell, 49
Beloff, 91
bilan, 49–50
Binder, 8
Bingham MR, 86–7, 92, 98
Bosnia-Herzegovina, 14–16
Boyron, 48, 50–2, 60, 69
Braibant, 48–50
Lord Bridge, 88, 92, 98, 110, 121, 149
Brown, 49

common agricultural policy, 3, 39, 70, 110
common law, 121, 138
  following EC law, 147–8
  fundamental value of, 93
compensation, 57, 147–9, 155–7
Constantinesco, 80–1
constitutional rights (*see also* fundamental rights), 51, 53
Lord Cooke, 96, 98, 104–6
Costa, 48–9
Cotterell, 118
Council of Ministers
  attitude to proportionality, 81–2
  discretion of, 72
Craenen, 53
Craig, 44, 69, 87, 96, 100, 106, 122, 127, 130, 165

Dadamo, 50
Damen, 57
Dashwood, 81
de Búrca, 2, 44, 59–60, 65, 68, 89, 100
Delpéree, 52
democracy, 45, 51, 60, 110, 121, 143, 146–9, 156, 163
de Moor-van Vugt, 44–6, 48, 55–8
de Munck, 63
Lord Denning, 92
de Ridder, 55
de Smith, 69, 142, 152
Dine, 167
Lord Diplock, 61, 88, 94–6, 98, 104, 108–9, 112, 121, 132, 158
discovery, 106, 160–2
  as means to governmental disclosure, 160–1
discretionary power, 3–4, 6–7, 46–8, 65, 72–3, 130, 149–50
discrimination, 9–11, 19, 24, 28, 53–4, 70, 111, 135, 153
  and margin of appreciation, 33
  EC sex discrimination law, 165–81
  defences to discrimination, 167–170
  indirect discrimination, 166–7, 170–9
  objective justification for, 167, 171–3, 175, 179
Dutheillet de Lamothe AG, 1
Dyzenhaus, 137

ECHR (*see also* European Court of Human Rights), 23–35, 59, 65, 93, 107, 117–24, 130, 134, 149, 164
  categories of rights, 24
  Commission—*see* European Court of Human Rights
  Committee of Ministers, 23
  differing interpretations of convention rights, 119–21
  incorporation in UK (*see also* Human Rights Act), 93
  variable scope of rights, 28–33, 35
EC law (*see also* Council of Ministers, European Court of Justice), 1–21, 62–3, 65–84, 99, 103
  agricultural law, 70–1
  directives preferred to regulations, 82
  general principles of, 2
  import restrictions, 5–8, 72–6
  sex discrimination law, 165–81
  supremacy of, 145–6, 163
  uniformity and effectiveness of, 79–82, 152
  unlawful repudiation of review, 152
economic policy, 76, 96, 98, 109, 111, 162

Edinburgh, 81
Egger, 77
Eisenmann, 48
Eissen, 23, 123
Ellis, 3, 44, 80, 111, 154, 167–8
Emiliou, 2, 44–51, 65, 80
England (*see also* Human Rights Act, Wednesbury test)
  administrative law, 2, 20, 69, 88–93, 108–9, 117, 121–2
equality, 53–4, 111, 154
  as aspect of rationality, 111
European Court of Human Rights, 60, 138, 143
  moral conservatism of, 120
  perceived arbitrary preferences of, 35
  supranational character, 23, 29
European Court of Justice, 60, 70–2, 76–80, 84, 107, 110–13, 153–4, 156–7
  deferential attitude of, 172–81
  hostility towards inflexibility, 19
  leaving issues to national courts, 19–20
  relation with national courts, 8–9
EU Law—*see* EC law
Evans LJ, 130
Eveleigh LJ, 170–1
evidence, 106
expertise
  lack of by courts, 102–3, 136–7, 162–3
  due deference to, 136–8

Farran, 50
Feldman, 58, 119, 124, 126, 131, 136, 141, 180
Forbes J, 150
Forsyth, 96, 128, 130–1, 165
France, 58, 60
  administrative law, 2, 48–52
  Conseil Constitutionnel, 50–1
  Conseil d'Etat, 49–51
freedom of expression, 30–2, 42, 92, 108, 125, 130
  trumped by religious sensitivities of others, 31
freedom of movement, 10–12, 67, 93
free movement of goods, 40–2, 152
Friedman, 118
Fromont, 48–51
fundamental freedoms (*see also* fundamental rights), 12, 51, 67, 69, 78–9
fundamental rights (*see also* constitutional rights, fundamental freedoms, human rights, rights), 1–2, 14–15, 39, 46, 49, 50, 54, 59–62, 91–2, 96–101, 110, 133, 142, 166

Germany, 58–60
  administrative law, 1, 44–88, 51–2, 60, 101, 107, 109, 142, 146
  balancing exercise, 45–6
  Basic Law, 45–6, 51, 65
  basic rights, 46
  constitutional court, 46, 51
  employment legislation, 174–6
  German theorists, 2
Gibson LJ, 130
Gilbert, 136
government
  accountability of, 106, 160–1
Greeks, 65, 108
Lord Greene MR, 94–6, 98, 104–5
Greene, N, 106, 165, 180
Greig, 138
Grundnorm
  shift of, 149
Guibal, 48
Gulmann AG, 78

Hare, 67, 96, 128, 130
Harris, 29, 123–6, 131
Hartley, 80
Heringa, 56
Higgins, 124
Lord Hoffmann, 79, 103, 122, 127, 129, 136, 151, 165
human dignity, 45
human rights (*see also* fundamental rights), 15–16, 23, 31, 45, 67, 92, 104, 110–11, 117–44, 121, 129, 136, 139, 166
  European conception of, 28, 33–4
  objective standards of, 125
Human Rights Act, 99, 103, 117–44
  declaration of incompatibility, 139–40
  potential divergence from Strasbourg, 119–21
Hunt, 142
Lord Hutton, 133

Imholz, 29
international law, 15–16, 129
irrationality (*see also* unreasonableness test), 24, 108–15, 118
  as higher level concept, 109
  who decides, 109–10, 112, 114
Lord Irvine, 141, 165

Jacobs AG, 40, 66, 75, 107, 121, 127, 130, 139, 146, 167, 173
Jones, 124
Jowell, 69, 91, 142, 152
judges—*see* judiciary
judicial review (*see also* proportionality), 3, 4, 8, 20, 47, 51, 55–7, 59–61, 67, 69, 71, 88–9, 109–11, 127, 129, 135, 161, 181
  and chill factor, 148–9
  and Human Rights Act, 140–1
  and level of security, 149–55
  and political sensitivity, 109–10

and substitution of judgement, 58, 85–7, 94, 96, 98, 100, 102, 104, 109
French style, 142
function of, 149
German style, 142
intensity of (*see also* proportionality), 3–4, 8, 20–1, 76, 84, 96–9, 104, 110–11
of legislative measures, 20
of the facts, 159
procedures for, 157–8
related to background values, 45, 141–3, 150
judiciary
judicial discretion, 141
judicial function, 20
judicial restraint, 143
relationship to Parliament, 147–9, 163–4
justiciability, 103, 106, 113, 118, 129–36, 138, 143

Kay J, 163
Lord Keith, 172
Kennedy LJ, 67
Kentridge, 117, 126, 144
Kerr LJ, 171
Koopmans, 56
Kovar, 80

Lavender, 124
Laws J, 84, 87, 96, 98, 100, 126, 128, 153–4, 165
Lawson, 43
legal culture, 118, 132, 136, 143
legal reasoning, 122
Léger AG, 81
legislation
problems in identifying objectives of, 162
legitimate expectations
contrast between English and EC principles, 153
Leigh, 131–2
Lemasurier, 49
Lenaerts, 39, 80–2
Lenoble, 63
less restrictive alternative test—*see* proportionality
Lord Lester, 31, 69, 91, 112, 124, 142
L'Heureux-Dubé J, 137
Lord Lowry, 88, 102, 112, 122
Lustgarten, 131–2

Macdonald, 23, 29, 123–5, 143
Mahoney, 31, 124
manifestly inappropriate test—*see* proportionality
margin of appreciation, 29–35, 47, 110, 112, 117–18, 120, 124–7, 131–2, 138, 143, 154–5, 177, 179–80
criticised, 29–30
different forms of, 124–5
different uses of, 126–7
inapplicability within domestic jurisdiction, 125–7
margin of discretion—*see* margin of appreciation
Matscher, 23, 29, 123, 125
McBride, 26, 29, 35, 43, 120, 123, 138
merits/law distinction, 68–9, 87–8, 128, 180
Merrills, 124
metaphysical problems, 109
Micho AG, 68
Molière, 115
mushroom imports, 5–8, 73–6

national courts, 111
discretion of, 79
role of, 77–80
national security, 13, 78, 84, 112, 130–6, 138
and abdication of judicial role, 131–2
and impact of proportionality, 132–6
Neill LJ, 130
Netherlands, 59
administrative law, 55–8, 62–3
arbitrariness test, 56, 59
compensation, 57–8
Council of State, 57
judicial review, 55–7
principle of substantive carefulness, 57
substituted decision, 58
Nicolaï, 57
Nolte, 46–7
non-discrimination—*see* discrimination
nuclear missile
use of to kill fly, 75

objective justification (*see also* discrimination)
as matter for the court, 111
test of, 155
O'Boyle, 29, 123
Olinga, 65
Oliver, 91, 142, 165

Pannick, 92, 112, 126
Peeters, 53–4
penalties, 78, 91
Petzold, 23, 123–4
Philippe, 48
Picheral, 65
planning, 113–14
political might, 181
political theory, 85
Popplewell J, 90
populism/judicial activism extremes, 110
press freedom, 26, 41
pressing social need, 93
principe de légalité 48
property interests, 31–3
proportionality (*see also* judicial review)

proportionality (*cont.*):
  and Community competence, 80–4
  and Community measures, 2–8, 20–1
  and ECHR, 23–35, 43–4, 121, 123–4
  and Human Rights Act, 117–44
  and less restrictive alternative test, 66, 72, 74, 77
  and manifestly inappropriate test, 66–7, 71–2, 77
  and margin of appreciation, 29, 33–5, 124–7
  and national measures, 2, 8–21
  and procedural points, 157–63
  and relevance of fault, 155–7
  and role of the courts, 59–60
  and weighing of evidence, 33–4
  applied by national courts, 66–7
  as basis for reviewing legislation, 146–64
  as general principle, 107–8
  as ground of review in English law, 99–106
  as market integration mechanism, 66–7
  as species of irrationality, 108–9
  as tool of judicial review, 3, 20–1
  balancing exercise, 24–8, 35, 41, 58, 63, 79, 100–1, 103, 108, 123–4, 134, 139, 143
  Belgian conception of, 52–5
  contrast between German and French conceptions, 51–2
  contrast with Wednesbury/unreasonableness test, 2, 20, 59–60, 62, 69, 88–91, 96–106, 114–15, 127–9, 151–5, 165, 170–2, 179
  criticism of, 48
  different elements of, 37–42, 44–5, 47, 55–8, 60–1, 68–9, 71, 99–101, 107–112, 146, 167
  different forms of, 59–60, 62
  definition of, 37–44, 48, 146
  Dutch conception of, 55–8
  Dutch model commended, 62–3
  EC conception of, 37–42, 59–60, 65–7, 81, 101, 165–81
  effect on member states, 37–63
  English conception of, 69, 88–93, 117, 121–2
  English conception of contrasted with Strasbourg, 142–4
  extent of interests considered, 61
  flexibility of, 20–1, 69, 76, 84, 101–2
  French conception of, 48–52
  future of, 105–6, 114–15, 137–44, 163–4
  German conception of, 1, 44–8, 51–2, 101, 107, 146
  history of, 1–2, 65–6, 69–70
  in EC sex discrimination law, 165–81
  intensity of review (*see also* judicial review), 61–2, 66, 76, 83, 100–1
  proceduralisation of, 63
  related to background values, 45, 141–3
  relationship with irrationality, 127–9
  relationship with subsidiarity, 81
  relevant factors, 76–7, 137–9
  successor to Wednesbury test, 105–6
  underlying interests protected by, 66
  vague concept of, 60–1
public decision makers
  deference to, 118
public interest immunity, 130, 133, 135–6
public law, 158, 181
public lawyers, 144

Rädler, 46–7
rationality—*see* irrationality
Rechtsstaat, 48, 51, 60
reasonableness test—*see* unreasonableness test
Reischl AG, 74
remedies, 148
reservations, 138
rights (*see also* fundamental rights, freedom of expresssion, etc), 80
  greater judicial deference to, 98, 143
right-thinking people, 171–2
Lord Roskill, 88, 121
rule of law, 46, 65, 67

Schermers, 43
Schiemann LJ, 147
Schwarze, 1, 37, 45–9, 52, 65, 146
Sedley J, 91, 93, 95, 133
  herecy over legitimative expectations, 153
  heretical balancing test, 91
separation of powers, 20, 52, 60, 96, 102, 140
Simon, 80
Slynn AG, 38, 73, 152
social policy, 83–4, 109, 111
Social Security Appeal Tribunals, 141
social security legislation, 176–9
sovereignty of Parliament, 20, 60, 98, 118–19, 139, 145–164
  within EC, 145, 147, 163–4
sovereignty of state, 82, 84, 138, 162
Stephenson LJ, 171
Stevens, 126, 136
Lord Steyn, 142
strict liability, 16
Stroink, 56–8
Strozzi, 81
subsidiarity, 21, 81
Suetens, 52
Sunday trading cases, 19

Taggart, 137
Taylor J, 150
Lord Templeman, 92, 121
Ten Berge, 56–7
Tesauro AG, 156
third parties, 61
Tomuschat, 68
Tridimas, 44, 65, 72, 121, 144

UK—*see* England
UN Security Council, 14
ultra vires, 52–3
unreasonableness test (*see also* irrationality, Wednesbury test), 2, 20, 56–7, 72, 87, 108–9, 122, 179
utilité publique 49–50

value judgement, 105
Vanderveeren, 54
van Dijk, 29
van Gerven AG, 19, 37, 68, 107, 130, 139, 142, 146, 151–2, 167
van Hoof, 29
van Wijk en Konijnebelt, 58, 60
van Ypersele, 39, 80–2
VAT, 16–19
voluntary codes of conduct, 82

Wade, 153
Walker LJ, 147
Warbrick, 29, 123
Warner AG, 2
Watt, 167
Wednesbury test (*see also* unreasonableness test), 56, 59, 61, 63, 122, 127–9, 134, 149–55
  different formulations of, 96–9, 103–5
  ineffective in reviewing breach of EC law, 150–5
  nature of unreasonableness, 96–6
  predicted withering of, 164
Lord Woolf, 69, 98, 142, 147, 152, 165
working time, 4–5